The Oldie

Annual 2019
Introduction

By *Harry Mount*, Editor, The Oldie

Editing *The Oldie* is the best job in Fleet Street – thanks to two things. First, the sheer variety of the articles that cross my desk. As I write, I've just received Sister Teresa, our God columnist, writing about Jesus's reprimand to Judas. Nasty Judas had complained about Mary anointing Jesus's feet with a pound of far too expensive ointment (John 12:7). Just before that, I was reading our Bird of the Month columnist, John McEwen, on the oystercatcher's bill, which acts as crowbar, scissors and hammer, all in one. His piece in this annual, on the golden plover, is a modern classic.

The second thing about *Oldie* articles is that you know they will be interesting: the single criterion for inclusion in the magazine, as laid down by *The Oldie*'s founding father, Richard Ingrams, and his much-missed successor, the late Alexander Chancellor. Variety and interest. That's what you get in this annual, brilliantly edited by *The Oldie*'s Supplements Editor, Liz Anderson.

The selection goes right the way back to *The Oldie*'s hallowed origins in 1992, when it was founded by Richard Ingrams and a merry band of conspirators, including Alexander Chancellor, Stephen Glover, John McEwen, Naim Attallah (who financed the magazine during the 1990s) and the late Auberon Waugh – whose 'Rage' column here is as fresh as the day it was written.

Ingrams and Chancellor always gave their writers a full measure of freedom to say what they want. Rude, funny, sad, clever, irritable, outrageous, outspoken... All characteristics are thoroughly encouraged at Oldie Towers. Appearing in these pages is the king of the rude columnists, our very own gentleman of the road, Wilfred De'Ath.

Not that common abuse appears in this annual. Subtlety, combined with irony, wit and sarcasm, has always been the watchword of *The Oldie*. Thus the appearance here of some of

the best writers in the English language in the last half-century, from Beryl Bainbridge to William Trevor.

The Oldie's enemies are bores and pseuds; the most lethal weapon against them is being funny. Two of the funniest living writers – Roger Lewis and Giles Wood, of *Gogglebox* fame – are *Oldie* columnists. The pick of their columns are here.

But that doesn't mean *The Oldie* shies away from seriousness. When other media refused to touch Miles Goslett's brave exposé of Jimmy Savile's disgusting antics, only Richard Ingrams was plucky enough to publish the piece, which appears here. Miriam Gross's interview with Philip Larkin, too, transcends the throwaway nature of most journalism to become an important contribution to literary history.

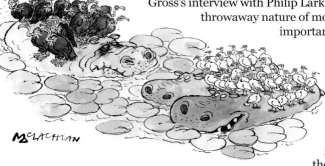

'Harriet doesn't look very well these days'

Like elephants, oldies never forget. While other magazines sacrifice everything to the here-today-gone-tomorrow god of Modernity, *The Oldie*'s gods stretch back way beyond the end of last week. Among the heroes – and villains – of yesteryear who star here are WH Auden, Dr John Bodkin Adams, André Previn, Somerset Maugham and Lady Docker.

Many of *The Oldie*'s great cartoonists are featured here and, for the first time ever, the pick of *The Oldie*'s blogs, written for our website, are in the annual. These are often commissioned to respond to daily events but – as blogs by writers from Valerie Grove to Gyles Brandreth show – they remain ever-fresh.

All human minds – particularly oldies' expanded minds – are like attics, where you've been squeezing stuff up against the rafters for decades. In our brains, old books, childhood toys and adored film stars compete for headroom with fondly remembered meals, snatches of music and favourite camellias. No other magazine crams in so much attic space between its covers. And no other annual has crammed in more than 25 years of greatest hits into 128 laugh-filled, elegiac pages.

Published by The Oldie magazine, Moray House, 23/31 Great Titchfield Street, London W1W 7PA www.theoldie.co.uk
Copyright © 2018 Oldie Publications Ltd. Printed by Wyndeham Roche Ltd
The Oldie would like to thank all the writers, illustrators and cartoonists whose work is reproduced in these pages
Editor: Liz Anderson **Design:** Lawrence Bogle **Cover:** Bob Wilson

Contents

118

124

Mr Fuge's Dream House

By *William Trevor*

Greyly suited, moustached, quite small, quite old, Mr Fuge wore a jewelled tie-pin in the knot of his tie. A watch-chain trailed across his waistcoat, his shirt cuffs were starched, his shirt collar was of shiny white celluloid. Accompanying all this, there was a grey homburg, a raincoat over one arm – the left, as I remember. Mr Fuge came every summer of the 1930s to visit his dream house, to look it over, to satisfy himself that all was well. The first thing he did was to walk to the edge of the

cliff, and what he saw then was always the same: that since last year the sea had claimed another yard of his land.

No door opened to welcome Mr Fuge. No piano ceased to play, no servants were excited by his advent. Businesslike, he made the journey around his property, tapping the boarded windows with his knuckles, pausing to get a better view of his chimneys and his slates. Then he turned the key in his hall-door and stepped into the silence of his dream house, lighting the way from room to

room with matches. So it was guessed: no one ever accompanied him.

Remote on the cliffs of County Waterford, with a view of the empty sea and an empty strand, with the woods of glen behind it and the high grass of a meadow between it and the cliff edge, there can be few sites anywhere in the world as perfectly chosen as Mr Fuge's. Miles from anywhere was what he wanted and miles from anywhere was what he got.

I have imagined him discovering this

'For reasons of his own he turned his back on beauty and on peace, his secret a survivor among fallen ceilings and decay'

inlet on the coast, pacing out the land, approving plans, seeing the foundations laid, talking to carpenters and masons who travelled long distances each day. Glencorn the place is called, or Glencairn; and there are other variations. There being no local people round about, a name has never become established. I have never found one on a map.

It's a single-storey house with a gently inclined roof and deep, panelled eaves. Its concrete rendering was washed with unobtrusive yellow once, its window-frames and hall-door were a shade of grey. But now the yellow and the grey have gone, and the window-frames have gone themselves in places.

The glass of the fanlight is smashed, the timber that covered the windows has rotted away. Initials have been scratched, with dates, and hearts and arrows. A panel of the hall-door was kicked in some time in the 1950s, the beginning of the vandals' fun. For people do, occasionally, come here now; it's not as far away as it was, nor as hard to find. There's even a concrete path, far below the house at the edge of the shingle, where cars can turn: in the past you had to reverse for a quarter of a mile, back to the clearing at the gates.

The only time I met him, Mr Fuge addressed me as 'little boy', as old men who are unused to the company of children sometimes do in stories or in films. I was trespassing on his property, caught red-handed in his wild backyard, where a rock-face had been hewn away to make space for his outbuildings. He looked at me, bewildered and surprised, but he wasn't cross. He asked me who I was, then said a little more before setting off down the avenue he had created, leaving me where he found me. Beyond the white, locked gates, I had seen the car he came in, its driver sunning himself, the *Irish Press* spread out on the bonnet. I heard it drive away, and then the place was quiet again.

In the 1930s, Paddy Lyndon was the only person who knew anything very much about the house. He was a ragged man with rheumy eyes who lived in a cottage in the woods and was retained by Mr Fuge to keep an eye on things. Paddy Lyndon said Mr Fuge was an Englishman who made the journey to County Waterford every July just for the few minutes he spent inspecting his property. One July he would not go back to England: all that was arranged. He would open up his house and live there, as he had always wanted to. That stood to reason, since he had gone to so much trouble to find a place no one knew about, since he talked about a garden, since he had built at the back a modest two-storey dwelling for the servants he intended to employ.

In Ireland, where stories of any kind are particularly valued, they are often decorated, bits and pieces added to make them worthy of a hearing. Paddy Lyndon's insistence that a night's sleep had never been taken by anyone beneath Mr Fuge's roof may or may not be a fact. But certainly it can be said that people never lived beneath it for any length of time. You sense that about a place: you feel no ghosts. When, as a child, I first knew this deserted house, I imagined a past for it because that is what houses have. I heard the chatter of voices, doors banging, the splutter of oil lamps and their homely smell. There was dancing in the rooms I could not see, and furniture polished every day, fires lit in winter.

'You're getting older now. We need to discuss the Pterodactyls and the bees'

Tennis was played before the lawns became a meadow, traps and carts went up and down the avenue. There were picnics on the banks of the stream that made the glen, and people bathed from the house. Shrimps were netted in the rock pools. Now and again a postman called.

But my vision did not hold. My imagery shrivelled and fell away to nothing. Exaggerating or not, Paddy Lyndon was right: the melancholy that possesses the place was born of an emptiness that has never been otherwise. Was there some sorrow, some passing regret, in an old man's eyes when he found me on a July afternoon in his overgrown backyard, all the cobbles of its surface long ago lost? Did he think of other children, those who might have been? Had someone died? The wife he built a house for? Or had he hurried away from Ireland, as many English people did, when the Troubles came in 1916? Had history – cruel again in a distressful country – disposed of a blissful dream?

I have imagined Mr Fuge in a English suburb, going about his city business, drawn in each day to the formalities of office life, returning in the evening to neat laurel hedges and rows of similar facades. The Englishman built his Irish house and left it there: that's all there is to know, all he has allowed. For reasons of his own, he turned his back on beauty and on peace, his secret a survivor among fallen ceilings and decay.

The entrance gates have been immovable for half a century. The smell is of must in one room, of sodden plaster in another. The marble of a mantelpiece has split. Gorse grows in the fissures of the rock-face, the servants' quarters are roofless. The cobbled yard's as soft as velvet, the sea comes steadily.

Mystery is this ruin's character if you happen to know something of the heyday that never was. One lonely ghost is there at last if you happen to have watched a disappointed Englishman tapping his window boards on a July afternoon. Stoically still, he makes his rounds, at one in death with his dream house.

As a few older readers may remember (natural soya lecithin capsules are said to be good for the memory), there were two original inspirations for this column. The first, which afflicted all my generation simultaneously, was a realisation that the Prime Minister was younger than we were. It went without saying that he was an incompetent, a nonentity, a pipsqueak. The point was we had been passed over, we were on the shelf, we were no longer teetering elegantly on the brink of middle age; we were old.

The second inspiration, taken from Dylan Thomas's famous lines 'Do not go gentle into that good night,' was an acceptance that rage is a more attractive posture in old age than its alternative, smugness. Benevolence was out of the question. We can either be furious at the way things are going or smug that our own circumstances are noticeably better than most other people's – our houses and gardens are nicer, our food and wine are superior, the company we keep is preferable... I don't think you can really earn a living writing articles about how pleased you are with yourself, even if Polly Toynbee has been having a tremendous crack at it these last 35 years or so.

I had other intimations that old age was not far away. Not only did policemen start looking absurdly young, but a High Court Judge presiding at a libel trial I decided to attend seemed scarcely out of his teens. On one occasion I sat next to a young man at dinner who told me he was in the army.

'Well done,' I said. 'What a sensible career choice! How are you getting on? Would you be a captain, yet?' I did not actually pinch his bottom, but my manner was distinctly avuncular.

'No, actually, sir, I am a major-general,' he replied.

Such episodes are enough to throw the most equable of temperaments into a rage, and I have been raging ever since at the incompetence and inadequacy of people younger than I am who are inexplicably put into positions of great authority.

Suddenly something rather unpleasant has happened. Rage has become the dominant emotion in Britain – not just from oldies, as we watch our country disintegrate into a sort of kindergarten run by vapid young women with Midlands accents. Teenagers and small

Auberon Waugh
Rage

children are in a rage as they realise they will never be employed, their only escape from a life on the welfare is in stealing cars and burgling houses; horrible young men with beer bellies from Essex are in a rage when they find other motorists on the motorway unprepared to make way for them; New Britons who have been conned into shopping at Sainsbury's by their lazy wives fall into a trolley rage, and batter their fellow shoppers...

All these rages are undignified and vile, a product of the bad manners which convince the New Britons they have a right to shout 'No way!', insult and assault each other at will. Stupidity and bad manners are the chief characteristics of the new Britain; they are what make me yearn for Direct Rule from the Elysée Palace. The current rage as I write is against child murderers, that is to say the murderers of children.

No doubt it will be forgotten by the time these words appear, but at the moment of writing the *Sun* is shouting its head off that these murderers should be

> 'Something rather unpleasant has happened. Rage has become the dominant emotion in Britain'

hanged or at the very least be kept in prison for life in specially disagreeable circumstance. I think this rage is a bogus one. The English are not, by nature, sentimental about children. In fact we much prefer dogs, and tend to dislike other people's children – usually with good reason. Other people's children tend to be noisy, unattractive and bad-mannered. This is no excuse for murdering them, of course.

I had an interesting illustration of the Englishman's preference for dogs last week when I happened to find myself sitting in Paddington Station waiting for a train and in charge of a spaniel. A completely unknown young man came up to me and asked if he could buy me a drink while his nice girlfriend called Chrissie talked to the dog. This never happened to me in twenty years of travelling around with young children.

My wife slightly spoiled it all, when I returned home and told her the story, by suggesting that the young man might have been one of my grown-up sons whom I had failed to recognise.

This bogus rage against the murderers of other people's unknown children comes from the simple desire of the nation's punishment freaks to have someone on whom they can focus their sadistic fantasies and appetite for judicial execution. There are many people of our age, and no doubt many readers of *The Oldie*, who are very keen indeed on capital punishment, and I do not wish to say anything to upset them, but I would urge that they are backing a loser if they think that indignation on behalf of children (many of whom are teenagers) will carry the day. Do they not realise that three out of four burglaries and muggings are done by teenagers?

I feel that punishment freaks and fanciers of the death penalty should concentrate on the murderers of oldies. In many ways, it is much worse to murder an oldie. Today's children have for the most part a dreadful life ahead of them, sponging off an ever-stingier welfare state, terrified of sex for fear of Aids, of food, drink and cigarettes for fear of ill-health. We old people have lived through the troubles and are now taking our reward. Our children are grown up, our houses and gardens are arranged to our liking, we have money to indulge ourselves. I understand why young people wish to murder us, but I feel they should be heavily discouraged.

Miles Kington

Country pursuits

March 1st, the day of the Countryside March, was obviously a good day to be in the country as everyone else was in London marching, so my wife and I decided to stay in the wilds of Wiltshire and enjoy the peace and quiet. I had actually toyed with the idea of going to London for the walk, but I couldn't settle on a good slogan for my placard. One message I had experimented with was: 'ALTHOUGH I AM WORRIED BY SOME ASPECTS OF FOX-HUNTING, I DO FEEL THAT THE COUNTRYSIDE IS GETTING A RAW DEAL ON THE WHOLE', but my wife felt it was too wishy-washy, so instead I tried 'I HATE LONDON' and 'VEGETARIANS FOR FOX-HUNTING' and 'LOOKING FOR A REALLY NICE COUNTRY B&B? JUST STOP ME AND ASK FOR DETAILS!' but still none of them really seemed snappy enough.

So instead we went for a walk in the country, just the two of us, no, the three of us, because we have recently acquired a spaniel, the idea being that it will give our ten-year-old son something to look after and be responsible for. Madness, of course: we now have a dog and a son to look after, both of whom conspire against us. But the son doesn't like walking nearly as much as the dog does, so we left him behind and took the dog.

At this time of year you can leave him off the lead quite a lot, because most of the cows and sheep are elsewhere (please note how much like a countryman I am trying to sound) and the fields are empty, except for other people with half-trained dogs, but you learn to keep your eyes open for sheep in case your dog has to be put on the lead at a moment's notice.

Well, we had a good walk, from Iford Manor to Farleigh Hungerford Castle across the fields and back along the bridle path, with the banks beginning to be full of primroses and the last of the snowdrops drooping and dying (still

trying to sound like a countryman, you notice).

We finally got back to the car and were driving home along the A36 when we noticed a farmer rounding up sheep in a field with the aid of a single dog. You don't get much free entertainment in the country, so we stopped to watch, and indeed it was very impressive the way the single dog rounded up all the sixty-odd sheep and herded them up the ramp into the big lorry backing on to the field...

All except one. One sheep, bigger or braver or brasher than the rest, squeezed past the van and out into the lane, where it ran away, down towards us.

'Better stop it,' I said to my wife, and we stood threateningly with arms stretched wide to drive it back. It took absolutely no notice and ran straight past us on to the main road, where it started running down the A36 towards Bath.

'Better get after it,' I said to the wife, and jumped into the car, leaving her behind, to follow it.

The sheep had clearly never been on a main road before because it trotted straight down the white line in the middle, which might have been fatal, had

'Today you'll learn how to handle an all too common problem. What to do when your leg of man is over fatty'

not all the cars in both directions clearly been driven by country dwellers who respectfully slowed down to about 5mph. Within a minute there was a mighty tail-back in both directions, as nobody seemed willing to overtake the sheep.

This might have grown into a snarl-up big enough to make the local radio bulletins had not the sheep decided to dive into a hedge on the left just before the turn off to Hinton Charterhouse. It seemed quite happy behind the hedge, so I turned round to report back to the farmer, but he was already running up the road behind me, followed by my wife.

Reader, have you ever helped a farmer catch a sheep which is attempting to make a new life for itself between a hedge and a fence? Here are some tips. Use a little gentleness, and a lot of force. Wear gloves, otherwise your hands will be lacerated on the hedge, as mine were. Bring a belt to put round the sheep's neck, otherwise it won't come with you. When you find it between your knees, put your arms round its neck and hang on for dear life. When the farmer says, 'I don't know how I'm going to get it back to the field,' say, 'You can put it into the back of my car if you like,' and when he accepts your kind offer, do remember to get your frisky new spaniel out of the back of your car first, and ask your wife to look after it. And when you try to get the sheep in the back of the car, make sure the farmer lifts the other end, because they're bloody heavy things, and they don't half struggle.

So, if you were driving down the A36 between Bath and Warminster on Sunday March 1st, and you saw a slow-moving five-door Saab with the back door open, and a farmer sitting in the boot with a sheep in his lap, looking like a country version of the Duke and Queen going down the Mall in their coach, that was me in the front, chauffeuring, hands scratched to pieces but feeling strangely satisfied.

Yes, I reckon I did my bit for the countryside on March 1st.

Ad lib - ad infinitum

On the opening night of *Oblomov*, Spike Milligan walked on stage, forgot all his lines, and turned a serious drama into an unprecedented comic triumph. *Ian Flintoff* was in the cast

The curtain came down for the interval, and Spike Milligan walked off stage while the standing-room-only house clapped, laughed and roared. He got into his Mini – parked near the stage door – drove home to Finchley and did not return. Spike Milligan's 80th birthday brought back to mind a couple of years I spent as a very young actor in a West End play of which he was the star.

Oblomov had been adapted by the Italian writer Riccardo Aragno from the 19th-century Russian novel by Goncharov. Spike's firm had bought the script to launch him as a straight and sensitive actor, playing the part of a Russian aristocrat who couldn't be bothered to get out of bed. Joan Greenwood took the female lead, and other major parts were played by Bill Owen and Valentine Dyall. It was a major production for a young impresario, Michael White. The director was Frank Dunlop, who went on to do magnificent work at the Edinburgh Festival.

On the morning of the read-through, Frank spoke of the delicate and sensitive Chekhovian nature of the piece and, for the six or seven weeks of rehearsal, that was the kind of production we were all aiming for.

We opened at the Lyric Hammersmith. On the first night Spike, overwhelmed by stage fright, forgot every line. The rest of us were thrown, but he kept going, making up the missing lines as he went along. Spotting the *Evening Standard*'s critic, Milton Shulman, in the audience, and in gratitude for previous rave notices, he declared: 'Thank God, Milton Shulman's in!'

The notices were generally unkind, but since the show was booked for several weeks, Michael White and Frank Dunlop proposed to save it by allowing Spike complete *carte blanche* on stage. Spike ad-libbed his way through every performance. *Oblomov*, changed beyond recognition, ran for five weeks and broke all the Lyric's box-office records, before being transferred to the West End as *Son of Oblomov*. It could still be running to this day had the exhausting job that Spike took upon himself not made this humanly impossible. No two performances were the same.

Audiences – including the Prince of Wales – could return time and again and see a different show. As a result, there was never a feeling of audiences falling off. *Son of Oblomov* epitomised Spike at his best: inventive, unpredictable and indefatigable.

My first scene was alone with him on stage, and any stage fright I might have had was banished after a couple of weeks in the West End. I'd dutifully learned my lines in response to fixed cues, but, since Spike couldn't be bothered with anything like cues, you got what you were given – which was invariably followed by drowning laughter from the audience. If you were tempted to come in a millisecond too soon and kill the laugh,

'*You never actually own a Patek Philippe – you merely look after it for the next generation*'

he'd gently mumble from the side of his mouth: 'Wait for it, wait for it.'

Once I entered stage right to find that Spike was sitting in the stalls, in his nightgown costume, calling up to me, 'Come on then, Ian, give us a show!'

Another time I did the routine business – came on, sat down, extended my hand without looking to shake his as I'd done a hundred times – and his hand came off in mine.

The Queen and family came on her birthday, with Peter Sellers and Britt Ekland. Spike set up a double-act routine with Sellers across the heads in the front stalls – 'Why does the Duke of Edinburgh wear red, white and blue braces?' 'I don't know. Why does the Duke of Edinburgh wear red, white and blue braces?' 'To keep his trousers up!' The show overran by 45 minutes.

Spike was kind and generous to younger members of the cast, myself included. My first impression of him was of a painfully shy, quiet, gentle, almost diffident man – though an old mate of his, the Australian Bill Kerr who was later co-opted into the cast, once said to me, 'We have to put up with all the shit, mate, because it pays the rent.'

I suspect that Spike was then searching for a full expression of another side of himself: the man who personally repainted the children's Elfin Oak in Kensington Gardens, at his own expense and with an anonymous plaque claiming that the work was 'done by the fairies'; who sat down on pavements in protest against the threats of extinction to wildlife; who never forgot his friends when they needed work and he could help.

All this happened a quarter of a century ago. I've forgotten none of it, and I never will. Next time I'm on stage Spike's 'Wait for it, wait for it' will whisper to me still.

Sitting target

Christopher Howse has been having his portrait painted – warts and all

What could be more pretentious? Here I am, a middle-aged journalist of no public standing, being put in oil on canvas like Doge Loredan. Just the sort of thing that Jeffrey Bernard used to castigate as 'taking yourself seriously'.

Except it isn't like that at all. To sit for a portrait entails seeing yourself as someone else sees you, with Cromwellian warts or Burns's unsuspected louse as appropriate. If humility is truth, this is it. I also hoped it might be a bit like psychotherapy – without the side effect of making me drone on like some divorced royal on telly.

So one morning a week it has been tramp, tramp up the 59 stairs to the artist's studio in a garret in Soho that might have been used as a set for *The Birds*. When we began, my nose would grow bluer with the cold. When the painting was ripe, the suit that had seemed no cosier than a sieve now clung like boiler-cladding round my steaming limbs.

I sat on a high stool, a position I had in past years assumed with comfort for an hour or two each evening. Here there was no bar to lean on, and my lower back creaked. To keep still I chose a chimney pot to line up with a notch in the window frame, as a smuggler's launch steers between the Cornish rocks. The painter never did say: 'Can't you keep still?' but he sometimes looked disappointed – having, I suppose, mixed the right red patch on his palette, only to find the corresponding patch of cheek had vanished.

I had known the painter, Rupert Shrive, for years. He has always seemed to me pretty good, and he has got better. He thinks there is no more demanding challenge for an artist than to paint people. He has attracted some exalted commissions, but he hasn't gone in for those awful smiling dinner-party scenes and billiard-table chiaroscuros that sometimes adorn fashionable gallery advertisements in the *Spectator*.

Because I thought Rupert good, I didn't

> **'I sat on a high stool, a position I had in past years assumed with comfort for an hour or two each evening'**

mind paying. After all, in the time it took, I could have saved up by doing a paper round or something. But it also meant that I intended not to interfere, even by hinting at reservations. The resolution took some keeping. What is that greenish lumpy protuberance on my forehead, I wondered in April. I knew I was fat, I thought in June, but did I sit like an uneasy suet pudding? The expression of anxious doubt I knew was right, a welcome alternative to porcine jollity, which Rupert was too perceptive to allow.

Actually, I might sometimes have wondered aloud, when looking at the morning's work, whether my chin really did look like a cottage loaf. Thank heavens I did not make more such remarks, for I could not see the artist's later intentions. He was always right. A dark suit, for example, does not in truth look like a plain sample of cloth in a shop; patchy grey surfaces are indeed there. The brain, though, usually makes the passive eye play tricks when it looks in the mirror. As for the camera, that always lies.

When Sargent painted the Sitwell children, to keep their attention he would chant: 'There was a young lady of Spain who was terribly sick on a train, not once, but again, and again and again, and again and again and again.' Rupert did not resort to that. The deal was that I should do the conversation, and he should do the painting, joining in the dialogue whenever he was free. In the event his responses were no less connected than most people I talk to. Makes you think.

Anyway, the whole process was even more fascinating than I'd expected. The magazine-reading classes of the 19th century would have seen nothing odd in it. So, if you don't get your portrait painted, you will miss a lot, and your great-grandchildren will too. Sell the car.

The picture is now at the framers, and I feel like the Duke of Devonshire with an early Freud. I don't live in Chatsworth, though. It won't be so hard to choose where to hang it.

Christopher Howse is Letters Editor of the Daily Telegraph

I once met...

WH Auden

By *Simon Hoggart*

WH Auden came to stay at our house in Birmingham in summer 1967. My father, Richard Hoggart, had proposed him for an honorary degree, and offered to put him up. Auden had been raised in Birmingham and said he was happy to see the place again. In fact, he spent a large part of his time in a deckchair in the garden, chain-smoking Lucky Strikes.

I had read little of his work, and was afraid of being grilled about it. In fact he didn't want to talk about poetry much at all; instead his mealtime conversation was more mundane. One dinner time he devoted in part to persuading my mother that she should buy a Kenwood food mixer because it was much better than rival mixers. What did command attention was that famous face, just as astounding a topographical marvel of ravines, canyons and dry gullies as the photographs showed. And his voice was a strange mixture of English and American, with an admixture of German, since he lived half the year in Austria.

On the evening Auden arrived, my parents had invited friends and colleagues round to meet him. I was put in charge of drinks. Auden bustled into the kitchen and asked if I knew how to mix a dry martini the way he liked them. He would show me. He took a three-pint stainless steel jug, tipped in an entire bottle of gin, added a whole tray of ice cubes, a sliced lemon and a single capful of dry vermouth. Satisfied, he returned to the sitting-room, plonked it in front of him, and began to smoke. At the end of

the evening the ash tray was full and the jug empty.

Like many people who spend a lot of time living in other people's houses, he was adept at ensuring his own comfort.

At the end of a small dinner party, for example, he saw that his own glass was

empty and so was the wine bottle. With one gracious gesture, he swept up my father's full glass, bade a cheery goodnight to all, and disappeared upstairs.

Another mealtime, he told us this story. The fashionable drug of the day was LSD, and he and his partner Chester Kallman felt they should try the experience. They invited a doctor friend round one morning to administer it in their New York apartment. After an hour or so, nothing had happened, so they decided to go out for a meal at the diner round the corner. Suddenly Auden saw through the window his mailman, apparently performing an elaborate dance on the sidewalk. This was clearly the expected hallucination, so they rushed back home, where again nothing happened. Next day, the mailman knocked on their door. 'Hey, Mr Auden, I had this parcel for you yesterday. I saw you in the diner, and I waved at you a long time, but you looked right through me.'

His last day was a Sunday. I was the first member of our family up, and discovered him in the sitting-room, with a piece of greaseproof paper he'd found in the kitchen, carefully tracing the grid from the *Observer* crossword, so he could solve it without spoiling the puzzle for anyone else. It was a terrifically thoughtful gesture, though rather poignant too – here was a man who knew that his hospitality depended on his not leaving real or metaphorical footprints on the carpet or visiting minor inconveniences on his hosts, someone who was, for much of his life, dependent on the kindness of strangers.

'At the end of a small dinner party, he saw that his own glass was empty and so was the wine bottle. With one gracious gesture, he swept up my father's full glass, bade a cheery goodnight to all, and disappeared upstairs'

It's the pits

Paul Pickering fell foul of the warring brotherhood of professional ex-miners

It is hard to be upstaged at your own funeral. Especially in Yorkshire. At my stepfather's, the family had been working for days to get the prawn vol-au-vents organised and the right amount of John Smith's pale ale in the garage. The neat man from the bungalow next door, an uncle of David Seaman, the goalkeeper with a ponytail, kept popping in with 'hand-raised pansies' to make sure my mother was not tearful.

But then the doorway darkened to eclipse. It was my stepfather's brother, Wayne, a novocaine-faced man in his seventies who had not spoken to my stepfather for about ten years due to some chance remark my mother had made about his wife's vanilla slices. Next came Wayne's Viking sons, one of whom had his hand bound up in a football of bandages. They eyeballed each other over the floral tributes. Their glacial presence was all that was needed for the man in the coffin to be totally forgotten.

The two brothers, both called Gary (Wayne liked the name), had been miners. So had Wayne; a faceman. In the last miner's strike he and one of the sons had backed Arthur Scargill. The other Gary had gone in to work. They had not spoken since.

Nowadays every pundit, politician and hospital DJ in certain parts of the North trades on being an ex-miner. 'I've seen life, I worked down pit,' is their somewhat contradictory message. Millions of hours of documentary have been made about this voluble, ageing and miraculously ever-growing population. But they can descend on an unsuspecting family gathering like a plague of self-justifying locusts.

I found myself sandwiched between the two Garys, who had no choice but to get into the same funeral car together. The strike-breaker is currently employed as a bouncer at a local working men's club. Whatever had happened to his hand, one look told me not to ask. When I smiled at the other brother, now an electrician, he said, through a mouthful of teeth like broken Sugar Puffs: 'I've never liked it down South …where you comes from…'

The elderly Austin Princess laboured as it climbed towards Rotherham crematorium, and I pondered, as the Garys took snarling glances at each other, not about my stepfather's life, but quite why it was that miners had always been heroes.

> ## 'I were on t' television, I were! Streamin' wi' blood! I were one of those that got run over with the horses'

A miner, for example, never used the pavement to come and go from work. They always walked down the middle of the road, as if they were lords of the manor. Every day one urinated on the polio charity box outside the Conservative candidate's shop. Here were men who, obsessively, would make their own 'snap' – sandwiches – and fill their mashing can with cold tea, getting the ritual exactly right or bad luck would follow. They then went out with the cheerful Orwellian knowledge that they might, if they were unlucky, be squashed paper-flat after a sudden tectonic shrug two miles under Doncaster race course. Or worse, they could find themselves trapped underground as the gas or the water rose, arguing about the dictatorship of the proletariat.

The vicar at the service was nervous at the presence of these demi-gods. The ex-miners are a self-sufficient church. My brother and I were the only ones managing the responses or the 23rd Psalm. The expression on Wayne's face said: 'I am not a bloody sheep.' When we finally got my stepfather 'lit up', Wayne went back to my mother's to talk, not about his brother, but the heady days of the strike.

'I were on t' television, I were! Streamin' wi' blood! Mine and others! I were one of those that got run over with the horses. They just did not care about tramplin' over people. It's twenty years since t' battle of Orgreave and nothin's altered. They didn't win. But do we get an apology?' Everyone else just looked powerlessly on, like the chorus in a Greek tragedy.

By the table the two Garys were tucking into the black pudding and Tex-Mex chilli dip. Their eyes met and I thought there might be trouble. But the electrician Gary said, 'All right?' and the doorman Gary just nodded, propping his plate on his bandaged hand. In an insane way even the brother who had broken the strike bathed in the reflected, redemptive glory of having been a miner. The heretic in the family was my poor stepfather and his blameless career in merchant shipping.

Wayne nodded to himself, taking another sip of his dead brother's malt whisky. 'Sixty-five is no age to die. No bloody age', as if my stepfather had been lazy. Then the only smile I had ever seen flashed across his face: 'He'd a been better off down bloody pit!'

Pooh pooh!

Where sewage was concerned, it seemed that *Donald Carroll*'s neighbours were going to ensure that they all came up smelling of roses...

At last the day of decision for our village had arrived. We had known it was coming for some time – more than a year in fact, ever since the French government had decreed that every house in every small town and village in France would be required to replace its ageing, personal septic tanks with a big new communal one. In truth, however, my wife and I hadn't given much thought to it, as ours is the highest house in a village that meanders picturesquely downhill to a beautiful river, so we could take a more, well... elevated approach to the whole issue.

This doesn't mean that our house had not played a distinguished part in the cloacal history of the village. Indeed, in the 19th century it had the first indoor loo for miles around. In those days it was a Dominican convent, and the facilities for which it was locally famous were situated in a barn (maximum capacity: three, in a row).

Our own septic tank had also entered village folklore. Not knowing how many years' worth of contributions it had received before our arrival, we decided early on that it would be a good idea to have it pumped out. Thus on a bright spring morning several years ago two men arrived in a large tanker to drain away the accumulated excreta of our predecessors. Unnoticed, meanwhile, a workman perched high up on a ladder was replacing roof tiles when the men removed the lid from the septic tank.

There are no words to describe the pong they released on to an innocent world. It was, quite literally, staggering. This was particularly unfortunate for the workman on the ladder. Suddenly his face became contorted, his knees buckled, and he slid awkwardly down the ladder until he managed to cling on to a rung, where he remained motionless while he decided whether he still wanted to live.

But back to Decision Day in the village. The matter would be thrashed out, as are

all important matters in the French countryside, at a meeting of villagers in the *mairie* (town hall). A few days before the meeting the mayor himself delivered a handwritten invitation, bearing his official seal of office, to every house in the village. My wife and I were especially enthusiastic about attending, not wanting to miss the opening shots in what might turn out to be one of the all-time classic Nimby wars. After all, in the list of things you don't want in your back yard, there is nothing, absolutely nothing, that outranks the collected faeces of your neighbours.

Thus it was that on a sweltering summer afternoon *tout le village* gathered in the little *mairie*. Anyone who has seen *Manon des Sources* can imagine the scene precisely: thirty or forty people, many of them already agitated, crammed

into one room with open windows along one wall that let in more noise than air. At the front of the room was a table covered in maps and papers. Behind it sat the mayor and two 'technicians' from the regional public works department (DDE), who were there to explain to us the finer points of waste disposal.

The meeting began inauspiciously. After thanking the mayor for his introduction, the senior DDE 'technician' quickly revealed himself to be afflicted with an almost impenetrable stammer. Then, to make matters worse, a tractor started up outside the window. This led Madame Fleurot to shout 'It's not my husband!' immediately confirming the unanimous suspicion that the culprit was indeed the annoying Monsieur Fleurot.

Seated in the front row were those doomed by gravity to have the most at stake: the people who lived at the bottom of the hill. Among them were Maurice Duchesne the mill owner, a good friend, who also owns both banks of the river and therefore decides who can and cannot swim in 'his' river; Maurice's brother-in-law Jean, a harmless old lecher who retired in order to devote more time to sending obscene emails to my wife; François de Brun, a man of immense charm and sophistication, with two gorgeous daughters, who owns most of the land nearest the bridge; Max Lamiel, a scholar of the Occitan language who in his spare time writes erotic novels – in Occitan; and Jean-Paul Condat, who looks like he might be the nice twin of Mr Burns in *The Simpsons* and who lives directly below us.

Surprisingly, the first and most emotional outburst of the meeting came from the normally gentle Monsieur Condat. He worked himself up into a frenzied rant against the plan before we even knew what the plan was. This was doubly surprising, for not only was Jean-Paul almost certain to be among those least affected, as his house is among the highest in the village, but also because he had a colostomy a couple of years ago. 'What's Jean-Paul going on about? He carries his own *merde* around with him!' someone whispered.

With the help of Madame Lamiel, who

> ## 'The overall noise level rose with the thermometer and only subsided when the words "cost" or "smell" figured in the presentation'

held up a geological map of the area, the man from the DDE stammered his way through an explanation of our unique situation in relation to the river. Hardly anyone paid attention until a raised voice from one of the middle rows informed him that he was pointing to the wrong river. Laughter. Bedlam. Another map was produced.

The overall noise level rose with the thermometer and only subsided when the words 'cost' or 'smell' figured in the presentation. Otherwise the villagers for the most part argued amongst themselves or peppered the hapless official with loopy questions ('Why does the new tank have to be seven metres long?' 'Won't someone have to be specially trained to guard it?'). Throughout all this the people in the front row, especially Maurice and François, remained strangely silent.

Finally, as if performing a conjuring trick, the man from the DDE suddenly produced Plan B, which coincidentally came with its own map. Details of the new plan got lost in the general confusion, but the map clearly showed a pipeline leading downstream towards the next village. Then, with this revised proposal still shimmering like a mirage in the stifling heat, the mayor rose and pronounced Plan B approved. '*Nous sommes d'accord!*' The meeting was over.

Afterwards, in the little square by the church, I found Maurice and François in furtively triumphant mood. I asked them if I was right in thinking that we had just agreed to pass on our dirty little secrets to the next village, underground, without warning. Not quite, they said. The new septic mega-tank would go just this side of the next village. And how did this miracle come to pass with so little discussion? It didn't, they said. They had been discussing it most urgently with the mayor for weeks.

So the long-awaited meeting had just been a bit of theatre to ratify in public what had already been decided in private? They seemed puzzled by the suggestion.

'We prefer to think of it as the perfect example of democracy at work: everyone has a say, and the right conclusion is reached.' But of course. *Vive la démocratie! Vive la France!*

In praise of the people no one has ever heard of

BLOG ANDREW M BROWN, 2017

As the *Daily Telegraph*'s obituaries editor, I am constantly trying to discern systems and patterns in the universe. In fact, I realise this is a fruitless exercise, and people will die at any moment, often when least convenient for journalists.

Even so, there is a degree of seasonality to obituaries, as there is in other sorts of journalism. Generally speaking, in the winter months the queue of obits waiting to get on to the page gets longer. More people pop their clogs in the crisp, cold early mornings of winter – the sudden heart attack when moving from the centrally heated house into the chilly garage, that sort of thing.

In the summer, by contrast, the obituaries department tends to get quieter. Partly the reason may simply be that readers and loyal friends of the desk who tip us off about deaths are on holiday.

But quieter times are welcome because they mean we have a bit more space for the sort of obits I like best anyway – the fascinating people no one has heard of.

Among recent examples are Sarah Holman, the redoubtable West Highland lady and fanatical deer stalker who did the gralloching in her Marigolds.

Or Andy Cunningham, known to viewers of children's telly as the creator of *Bodger and Badger*. Of equal interest to me was the fact that he had been given a place at Caius College, Cambridge, to read English, but had had serious problems putting his thoughts down on paper. After a whole night in the college library trying to write an essay on the romantic movement, he managed to produce only two words: 'Shelley's poems'.

And one of my all-time favourites is Eileen 'Foxy' Fox, self-styled queen of Soho, bohemian, occasional nude model and film extra, who, among other things, took British Airways to the Court of Appeal, alleging she had been bitten on the bum by a flea while travelling on a BA 747 to the Seychelles. She lost the case.

If we occasionally get a few days' relative peace in the warmer months, it is an opportunity to highlight the hitherto under-appreciated lives, those who have contributed their own splash of colour to the rich variety of human existence.

The Times we had

Even in the 1950s the *Times* newspaper was still alive with the spirit of quill pens and dress swords, remembers *Irving Wardle*

The young Irving Wardle and Printing House Square in the 1930s

In the autumn of 1955 I was all set for a future in dishwashing when, thanks to a wire-pulling relative, I got an interview with the arts page editor of the *Times* and made my awed first visit to Printing House Square – an address in Queen Victoria Street opposite Blackfriars Underground station, the facade of which still advertised direct connections to St Petersburg and other Grand Tour destinations. The paper's offices likewise evoked a bygone time. They comprised a huge drum resembling a mouldering Stilton cheese and an elegant building known as the Private House. The drum was for the workers; the house was an on-site club for senior staff.

I went into the drum and took the stairs to the third floor, passing dim Dickensian recesses and a disused lift shaft, and finally found my way to a small glass box where the arts editor lived. I came out with tickets to review a play the same night. A week later he invited my comments on an exhibition of hand-painted eggs, followed by a hypnotist who specialised in snipping off the tips of people's tongues. Shortly after that I found myself on the *Times* payroll and gave up dishwashing.

My benefactor was John Lawrence, a man of saintly appearance known to his colleagues as the Friar even though he had worked as an assistant to Bomber Harris in the war. He can only have been in his fifties at the time, but he looked venerable to me; and his brand of silken courtesy was extreme even in an office where it was the rule for top brass to hold the door open for copy boys and tea ladies.

When Lawrence offered you a job, it was as if you'd given him a Christmas present when you accepted it. His kindness to aspiring nobodies was a legend in the building – which was not short of legends.

The empty lift shaft, for instance, was rumoured to house the ashes of expired leader-writers, like the once unassailable Canon Mortlock, who, an hour after his deadline, was found slumped over a desk alongside an empty bottle of port with the word 'Moreover...' written at the top of page two.

It was not all legend. There were characters at large who, a few years later, could have been earning good money in

> '**He invited my comments on an exhibition of hand-painted eggs, followed by a hypnotist who specialised in snipping off the tips of people's tongues**'

an English heritage theme park. One was Dermot Morragh, the Arundel Herald Extraordinary, an adviser on heraldry who patrolled the building like a Sergeant-at-Arms, and memorably exploded at one Private House function when the major-domo introduced him as 'Mr 'Arry 'Erald'. Further up the hierarchy was the foreign editor, Gerald Norman, who got a recording of Beethoven's 9th Symphony as a retirement gift and responded with a thank-you speech in which he went through the symphony likening each movement to a different sublime aspect of the *Times*.

The offices were shabby, the product was a loss-maker, the wages were meagre, nobody except the editor, William Haley, got a byline (and even he wrote under a pseudonym), but for some of its staff, working for the *Times* meant belonging to the world's most exclusive club. Was John Lawrence one of them? He certainly had the social manners of the house, pushed to a degree just short of parody. He was also full of PHS folklore and stories of former arts page stars, like the Edwardian critic A B Walkley who concluded one notice by saying he was unable to make a definitive judgement on the play as the theatre had burned down during the last act. When a sub suggested that it might be helpful if he mentioned any future occurrence to the night editor, Walker growled, 'I am your dramatic critic, not your newshawk!'

Lawrence had personal memories of

I once met...

Walkley's successor, the novelist Charles Morgan, who was in the habit of attending openings attired in cloak and dress sword, and then returning to the office, where he would sit like the bust of Keats until five minutes before his deadline and then consign the night's offering to the flames in a single flourish of unbroken penmanship.

Pens were still going strong when I joined the paper, and I suffered a pained reproach from Lawrence for battering out a late-night piece on a typewriter to the distress of the then theatre critic, Victor Cookman, who was wielding his quill in the same room. 'Real writing', it was held, could only be done with a pen, but it was also evident to Lawrence that, done with a pen or not, much of the stuff that got into the paper was asphyxiatingly dull. The late 1950s was a lively time on the English arts scene, but you would hardly have known it from the *Times* arts page. Lawrence responded by recruiting a pack of freelance juveniles – including the future art critic John Russell Taylor and the future *Sunday Times* theatre critic John Peter – who might be better attuned than his ageing staff reviewers to the plays of John Osborne and the paintings of Peter Blake.

At the same time he began a purge of the tradition-sanctioned features which had rooted themselves like verrucas in the arts page. One of these was the coverage of an amateur drama club called the Old Stagers; another was the coverage of the annual Sloane School play. For both events a contributor known as 'the loony baronet' was wheeled into position to say the club and the school had excelled themselves yet again. Lawrence quietly buried the Old Stagers and sent me to the school play which, as always, was directed by the headmaster, an adipose firebrand called Guy Boas.

I'd been seeing a lot of school plays for another publication, and most of them struck me as better than Boas's woodenly grouped *Romeo and Juliet*. I said so, and the office telephone promptly went mad with Boas's calls for the head of his anonymous assassin. Lawrence rose to the occasion with a perfumed smokescreen of polite denial and expressions of everlasting regard. Then the calls stopped as Boas had suffered a heart attack. To this day I'm torn between personal guilt and modest professional satisfaction; either way it's good to have got it off my chest after all this time.

(and drew)...
Ernő Goldfinger
by *Philip Thompson*

Looking at Trellick Tower from my window the other day, I was reminded of my one and only meeting, in 1964, with the architect of this iconic and still controversial tower block; one Ernő Goldfinger.

An architect friend of mine who knew him well thought that I might benefit in some unprescribed way from a meeting with the GOM. (I had been working for the Architectural Press for some time so there was a scintilla of common ground.) He was rather a forbidding figure who would have probably made a good fist of Gert Frobe's role as the eponymous villain of the then current James Bond film.

I remember him being terribly unforthcoming, rather like one of his own tower blocks. I couldn't take my eyes off a large drawing of a truncated female nude on the wall behind him and I was reminded of an incident in a half-forgotten novel where the hero looks down at his girlfriend's shoes and instantly falls out of love with her. I was suddenly engulfed in a 'What the hell am I doing here?' Stygian gloom. It was the truncated nude that started the rot. I think our relationship foundered on that particular rock.

Of course this mini-encounter was forty years ago and both Goldfinger's presence and the offending drawing are only the fragments of my fading memory, but this is the abiding image and feeling and for better or worse it's my personal reality, and I'm stuck with it.

Fortunately I'm supported and consoled by Matisse's famous dictum: 'Exactitude is not Truth'.

> 'I remember him being terribly unforthcoming, rather like one of his own tower blocks'

God...

I am in a muddle. Worse. I am sliding towards that secular blasphemy than which nothing is regarded as more reprehensible. I am harbouring Doubts. I am not absolutely certain that freedom of speech is all it is cracked up to be. After all, in our civilised society (as it is described by the bien-pensants when they want to make a point and have their own way), there is little you cannot get away with as long as you take care of the syntax, speak quietly and slowly, use some long words and remember to quote someone else, preferably an obscure but not yet discredited philosopher, whom no one can be sure he understands. As long as you refrain from four-letter words and endeavour not to foam at the mouth, most people won't take any notice, unless you are clearly suggesting that murdering the neighbours is a good idea, when, quite rightly, the forces of law and order will come and get you.

So – here is where I get muddled – we must not incite people to racial hatred, but artistic expression must be free and unfettered. Take the Sikhs and the Birmingham controversy. The artistic establishment insists, with wounded astonishment, that the play in question is a Work of Art, a fiction and as such should be left alone to express itself. The assumption is that the audience will be thoughtful and cultivated and capable of taking a measured view of the entertainment, whereas it is entirely possible that at least part of the audience will be gullible, drunk and easily swayed.

We should never forget the proportion of the population that sent wreaths following the death of Grace Archer. Since then the popular press daily offers analyses and exposés of characters in soaps as though they were real. The fact that they pay equal attention to the 'private' lives of actors, pop stars, footballers etc has a converse effect, leading many to suppose that these are not in fact real at all, which, when you think about it is not unreasonable.

Even the mentally stable, given the complexity of daily life, can find it difficult to discern between fiction, propaganda and downright tosh. There are, for instance, those (I believe there are millions of them) who, having read *The Da Vinci Code,* say 'well maybe it's got a point', thus endangering their immortal souls. Someone has left a copy of this work in a bedroom and when I run short of logs I shall burn it together with a number of other paperbacks. Most of these are objectionable not because of their content but because they are so appallingly badly written. Actually the same goes for *The Da Vinci Code.*

There is an element in human kind that is stubbornly determined to revere *something*. If not the Deity because that is so *vieux jeu*, then Art, the untrammelled human spirit and freedom of speech. We will die for these rights, cry the dedicated. And failing that, of course, there's always the Beckhams.

ALICE THOMAS ELLIS

...and Mammon

For most of the current cohort of *Oldie* readers, I imagine, age discrimination is not the most burning of issues. We may object to being marginalised by our juniors, elbowed aside in supermarkets or forbidden access to expensive NHS-administered drugs, but unless we are actually suffering physical abuse in our old people's twilight homes there is not much chance of finding someone to sue. The more usual complaints, like being forcibly retired, or refused promotion in favour of some inexperienced whipper-snapper further down the executive corridor, no longer apply once we are safely drawing our pensions.

However, that is likely to change drastically for those unfortunates now snapping at our heels. Governments everywhere are pondering changes in the date of allowable retirement and acceptable ways of encouraging the still active elderly to remain at the tax-paying, productivity-enhancing grindstone. But given the ingrained reluctance of most employers to tolerate grey hairs in their workforces, it is almost inevitable that there will be more friction, more unfairness and more temptations to seek compensation. So far ageism has come a poor fourth against racism, sexism and ethnicity in the reparation stakes, but with 12 million-odd over-65-year-olds no longer confident that someone else – the state, the pensions industry, the housing market or their investment managers – will keep them in superannuated comfort till the end of their days, there will be ever-growing pressure for the courts to take a hand.

Two big questions then arise: whom do you blame and, even more crucial, how do you get them to open their purses on your behalf? Until now, in virtually all jurisdictions, success has depended on something lawyers like to call 'disparate intent'. This means that you have to prove your opponent not only harmed you, but positively intended to harm you because of your excessive years. But a fascinating case is due to be heard in the course of this year by the US Supreme Court (all but one of whose nine members are well past the 65-year-old cut-off date).

This will attempt to extend the principle of 'disparate intent' to embrace the much broader concept of 'disparate impact', where damages can be claimed not only when the discrimination was deliberately designed to disadvantage those with too many years on their CV, but when, however innocently and unintentionally a policy was embarked on, its implementation turned out to have that effect.

The case in point concerns a group of senior American policemen. The municipality of Jackson, Mississippi, sought to raise the pay of more junior members of the local force, to stop them being poached by more affluent cities. But by not extending the offer to their more grizzled superiors, it is claimed that a clear and compensatable act of discrimination had occurred.

That's America, of course, and the angst that the case is generating among US employers has not yet crossed the Atlantic. But don't think it won't if the decision goes the top cops' way. And if your law-student grandchildren are looking for a promising specialist niche, they could probably do worse than start mugging up on the anti-ageism rules.

PETER WILSHER

Tales from the crem

Which button to press? Where will the coffin go? Clergyman *John Wren* lifts the velvet curtain on the ups and downs of performing a funeral in a crematorium

Funerals, contrary to popular belief, can be very funny. Priests often swap anecdotes along the lines of 'Guess what happened at the crem today?' Even death can provide its lighter moments for the professionals who deal with it day in and day out.

Working as a curate in the early days of Milton Keynes, the nearest crematorium was 40 minutes' drive away. I was always placed in the front passenger seat of the hearse and took a book to pass the time. Sometimes the purr of the limousine and the sunshine sent me to sleep. Fortunately the driver always leaned over and gave me a nudge as we approached Towcester. It was generally agreed that it wouldn't look good if the vicar was seen to be fast asleep, with his biretta tilted over at a less than decorous angle.

Part of the steep learning curve involved mastering, often at short notice, the mechanics of different crematoria: which button to push; whether the departed slid through curtains or a grille or dropped elegantly downwards; whether curtains would drift across; if music had to be switched on. Sometimes things are operated by clergymen, sometimes by hidden operatives who await your cue – the cough, the tap on the lectern, the over-emphasis on a particular key word.

My colleague, Steven, thought he had it all mastered when visiting a new crematorium. There were two chapels, but only one of them connected directly to the furnaces. In the other chapel, an attendant would come along after the service, raise the coffin (green button) and wheel it through to the furnace-adjacent chapel. Steven was in the dummy chapel, and all he had to do was press the red button when he got to the commital, and the dear departed would glide reverently earthwards. However, Steven had a cold, and when the moment came he sneezed, and couldn't then remember whether he'd pushed the red or the green button. Nothing happened for several seconds, so he pressed the red button again. The coffin did indeed start to descend, but some locking mechanism must have come into operation, because straightaway it began to rise again, then down again, then up again. The situation was saved by the attendant who rushed in and pressed some emergency button, muttering the meanwhile about damn machinery.

Occasionally I got the giggles, but was a master at disguising them with coughs and one of a range of large and colourful snuff handkerchiefs. As when the dear departed had been in the Irish Guards but his widow was very English and a close friend of mine. She arranged it 'properly', as he and his side of the family would have wanted. This included the bagpiper. Bagpipes I regard as an acquired taste, and one I've never acquired. Most of the time, albeit when massed, they are in the open air, but one in a confined space can be unbelievably awful.

We assembled for Jim's service, and the piper was there in full fig, his bag limp, and giving no hint of its latent power. He strode in after the coffin and placed himself on the opposite side of the dais from me. Unbeknown to him he was right inside the area that would later be veiled by acres of red velvet curtain – and, I reflected, well and truly muffled.

At the commital he started to work his elbow up and down to get the instrument going, and much indecorous wheezing and squeaking ensued. Rather earlier than was my habit I pushed the curtain button and it drifted across, but too ponderously to catch our piper on the hop. He marched forward, down the steps and off to the end of the chapel – maintaining a funereal step and appalling din. He positioned himself in the chapel foyer, a veritable boom box, and lamented away. Further prayers were rendered impossible so I nodded to an usher and he closed the doors on the chap. Thus we were able to finish proceedings with the melancholy but mercifully distant sound of the pipes. The widow had spent a certain amount of time throughout catching my eye, raising her eyes heavenward and barely suppressing a grin. When she heard the doors click shut she nodded approvingly.

After the service, as was usual, I was asked to join them for something to eat. I declined, since I had another appointment. At least I didn't phrase my apology in the words of my old friend, Henry, on one occasion: 'Sorry, I've got other fish to fry.'

'How did that get in there?'

I like reading obituaries though I don't like writing them. If the subject is alive and is someone I know, it can change relationships. You start trying to frame their life in an opening anecdote, secretly hoping they'll utter a bon mot before they go, or at least have the grace to have a newsworthy or colourful death.

Some people adore having the last word on their acquaintances. An old chum, L Marsland Gander, who was the *Daily Telegraph*'s first radio critic, got hooked on obituary writing when he retired. He compiled scores of obits on people he'd met, or even just shaken hands with, like Diana Dors. He once asked me for a few notes about myself when he heard I ran marathons; 'nothing too long old boy, just a few jottings.' Who knows, he may still have the last word on me in the *Torygraph* though he's been dead for twenty years. Eventually he ran out of subjects and submitted his own obit to the *Telegraph* together with an invoice. It caused the accounts department to crack their only known joke: they returned his invoice stamped 'Pay On Publication'.

No, I'm a birthday man myself and for the last couple of years I've written the birthday column every weekday for the *Times*. I've spoken to well over 200 birthday folk and nearly all of them are delighted to open up about what they're doing, how they're celebrating, and their plans. Like Will Rogers, I have never met a man (or woman) I didn't like. I choose people I know, people I'd like to know and people who have a story to tell. Many of them appear in *Who's Who* and, having achieved something in life, tend to be in the target age group of *The Oldie*. They ooze wisdom. Sally Greengross, who has made something of a career out of old age through Age Concern and now sits in the House of Lords, put it like this: 'You must have a reason to get up everyday otherwise you rot. We have a much healthier, happier life if we are needed.'

Certainly nearly all the people I speak to have plans; the future may be an unknown country but they have their passports ready. I have only spoken to one person who said he was quite happy to start reading a book at the breakfast table and still be there at suppertime. And he was a former chairman of W H Smith.

Sir Gerald Kaufman, who is now getting so used to his knighthood that he resents it when people forget, says that he

Birthday boy

Russell Twisk has been writing the 'birthdays' column in the *Times* for the last two years. Here he gives us all the inside information...

has no intention of spending the second half of his Parliamentary career arguing about fox-hunting. An avid opponent of the chase, he's already been at the House for 35 years making waspish soundbites honed as a headline writer on the backbenches of the *Daily Mirror*. Sir Julian Critchley once memorably described Sir Gerald as being one part oil, three parts vinegar.

Norman St John-Stevas (aka Lord St John) has no intention of retiring: 'I don't believe in it. I think it's a contemporary superstition. I shall continue to work until I drop. People tell me everyone has to die; but my answer to that

is "Not necessarily".' He adds 'I respect the old, but we young people must stick together.' He is 75. Bruce Kent, without whom no peace march in the last 40 years would be complete, says that his urge to protest grows stronger with age: 'When I think of the stupidity and waste of war I'm indignant, angry and stubborn. I get more determined than ever. The Iraq business has made me even worse.' He retired from active ministry in the Catholic Church in 1987 and married the following year. He is also 75.

Bryan Forbes, actor and scriptwriter of the original – and infinitely superior – *The Stepford Wives* has written 78 screenplays, one for every year of his life. 'Not all of them reached the screen, but I finished every one,' he says. 'I've had an eclectic career, I've never come out of the same box twice.' He claims he can't afford to take life too easy 'with taxes being so high'.

Women are occasionally sensitive about their age though not broadcasters Sue MacGregor, Jenni Murray and Sue Lawley. But Nina Bawden asked 'Do you have to print my exact age?' When told, alas, I did because it was in the public domain, she replied 'Well I'm sorry I shall be 77 personally and socially till the day I die.' She is actually 79. *The Oldie*'s sparky travel editor Rosie Boycott would not return my numerous calls. Can't think why. Still, I'll be after her again this year.

Julian Critchley died in 2000, Lord St John and Nina Bawden in 2012, Bryan Forbes in 2013 and Sir Gerald Kaufman in 2017

'You say your boyfriend did this and it was non consensual'

Brief encounter

Freddy Mullally was sworn to secrecy about
Churchill's platform alteration…

Most former news-papermen can, on retirement, look back wistfully on a story they had once been obliged to suppress for one good reason or another. When it happens to involve a particularly famous person, a time must come when the story has to be shared.

Back in the late 1940s when I was Political Editor of the *Sunday Pictorial* under Hugh Cudlipp, a close and very useful contact was Gerald O'Brien, press officer of the Conservative Party. We had started together in Fleet Street as subeditors on the *Financial News*, and although our political views had diverged, our personal friendship ensured trust in the exchange of 'inside' information.

The Tories, under Winston Churchill, had lost the 1945 general election but their leader's newsworthiness remained. The tip-off from O'Brien was that Churchill would be going unof-ficially to Waterloo Station later that night to greet an American friend off the boat train from Southampton. The friend was Bernard ('Barney') Baruch, the legendary financial wizard, one of the few to have foreseen and profited from the Wall Street Crash and an advisor to every US president from Wilson to Roosevelt.

Churchill would be accompanied by his son-in-law Duncan Sandys and a few party colleagues. The press had not been informed of this private rendezvous, so for what it was worth I had an exclusive. O'Brien would meet me at the station and be with me to observe the meeting from a spot near to the Churchill party.

All was in place five minutes before the boat train's arrival. The stationmaster, clad for the occasion in his formal top

'From the look of him, leaning unsteadily, it was clear that Churchill had indulged in his usual postprandial intake of brandy'

hat and tails, was standing by. A red carpet crossed the platform from where Churchill and his entourage waited to where Baruch's first-class carriage would stop. Our wartime prime minister had

long since dined and from the look of him, leaning unsteadily on his walking-stick while ignoring his colleagues, it was clear he had indulged in his usual postprandial intake of brandy.

If it hadn't actually hap-pened, the scene that now unfolded could only have been dreamed up by a French *farceur*, or by Groucho Marx. The train started to pull into the station. As the first-class section moved slowly towards the red-carpeted platform, Duncan Sandys, at a nod from the stationmaster, murmured in his father-in-law's ear. I watched Churchill pull himself together, champ on his cigar and start purposefully along the carpet towards the now stationary first-class coach.

The door was flung open. A figure wearing the Barney Ba-ruch trademark Texan stetson stepped down onto the carpet and stood rooted in disbelief at the stout party advancing on him with outstretched hand. Only a swift intervention by Duncan Sandys spared the rest of us, including a sheepish stationmaster, the spectacle of this total stranger – probably on his first visit to Britain – being folded in the embrace of the nation's most illustrious personality.

A minute later as Barney Baruch, two doors down from the misplaced strip of red carpet, was greeted by his old friend, Gerald O'Brien drew me aside. 'Promise you didn't see that, Freddy,' he pleaded. 'We both know it didn't happen, right?' And so it has gone unrecorded until now, half a century later. But I like to believe that one elderly Texan, or at least one of his offspring, still dines out on the story of a totally unexpected encounter in London town.

The riddle of the King's Girth

John Michell

Golden Age: Athelstan, King of all the English, presents a book to St Cuthbert

The Anglo-Saxons, according to our old historians, were excellent folk, industrious and law-abiding, the founders of our national character. Originally they were unwanted immigrants from Europe, pagan and barbaric, but soon they became thoroughly English and Christian, and settled down to forming the pattern of country life that lingered on into modern times. Their village communities were self- governing and democratic, and their lands were fairly apportioned among all.

For land surveying and other purposes the Saxons adopted the native system of measures, the ancient British Metrology rooted in the Bronze Age or earlier, with its inches, feet, cubits, rods, poles, perches, acres, furlongs, miles, leagues and many other units, each appropriate to a particular craft or function – but all linked together by a comprehensive code of number which not only applied to measure but also provided a canon of music and standards of proportion in the arts and crafts. This numerical science was the basis of the Saxon culture, constitution and code of law.

A Saxon golden age began in 935, when 'glorious Athelstan' of Mercia, a grandson of King Alfred, was elected 'King of all the English'. Like the philosopher-prince of Platonic idealism, he studied the ancient, traditional laws of the country, codified them and upheld them with justice. One of the old laws he revived was called the King's Girth. It specified the distance from the King's court or presence, within which his aura prevailed, making it a sanctuary where any offence was regarded as an injury to the king in person. The length or radius of the King's Girth was proclaimed as '3 miles, 3 furlongs, 9 acres, 9 feet, 9 palms, 9 barleycorns'.

That is a funny sort of law, you might think – it is like a Druid riddle or an item of law expressed in bardic chant. Certainly it was archaic in Athelstan's time. If it is a riddle, no one seems to have solved it, neatly and with reasons, so I offer it for *Oldie* geniuses to puzzle out. What exactly is the length of the King's Girth? It is not too difficult; three of the six units are still in use today and three are obsolete. The main problem is with the nine acres, evidently a linear measure, so you have to identify the linear acre,

'Be careful, darling – it contains salt'

naming it if you can, and give the name and length of the mile it relates to – bearing in mind that there were different acres for different types of land, and that 640 acres constitute one square mile.

'The King's Girth is not just a jumble of measures, but a cryptic blueprint of an ideal community'

The puzzle gets more intriguing when you realise that the King's Girth is not just a quaint jumble of measures but a cryptic blueprint of an ideal community, similar to that of Plato's Laws but on a smaller scale – a village- rather than a city-state. Each of the six measures applies to a different dimension in the foundation plan of an early pagan settlement – the symbolic, upright pole at its centre, the hearth or altar and the shrine around it, the village with its allotments, the common lands for pasturage and, surrounding all, the circle of wild woodlands. You cannot show all these on the same scale in one diagram, so another problem to add to the King's Girth is what is the least number of drawings in which you can easily depict its several parts?

Actually, this is something more than an amusing puzzle. If you study the figures of geometry indicated by the King's Girth, you soon become aware of the harmonies between the different parts of the scheme and the interplay of numbers and measures within it. The picture of the old English village fades into the background, and you see ever more clearly the cosmological pattern in the foundations of it. You can then see why good King Athelstan included the King's Girth in his law-code. It reminded him of the good old days.

Theatre

Beryl Bainbridge

The Birthday Party, Harold Pinter's first major full-length play performed in 1958, is powerful stuff. It's no wonder that it originally baffled both critics and audiences, causing it to be taken off after only one week, although possibly it was the response of the former so-called experts that influenced the reaction of the latter.

That is not to say that I myself could voice exactly what it was about after visiting the Duchess Theatre to see the latest revival, directed by Lindsay Posner. While it was happening, such was the intense drama of the piece, its ability to draw one in, that I can't say it mattered that I didn't altogether understand the content. Some things can't be spelt out; one is either taken in or left high and dry. Though I kept turning to my grandson, Bertie, and asking him what he thought it meant, I was still strongly affected. He was too, and kept hissing at me to shut up.

The major parts, that of the flaky landlady Meg, her lodger Stanley, the mysterious visitors, Goldberg and McCann, were played superbly by Eileen Atkins, Paul Ritter, Henry Goodman and Finbar Lynch.

Meg and her non-communicative husband Petey, who sells deckchair tickets, run a boarding house by the seaside. Stanley, their only lodger, unwashed, depressive, scared of leaving the house,

once tinkled the ivories at the theatre on the Pier. Meg, forever mouthing platitudes, shoulders bowed, self-engrossed, desperate to be admired, attempts to mother him, and more. The atmosphere is odd, pretty sad, in that life seems to have placed the characters in solitary confinement... but it's not yet menacing.

> 'Though I kept turning to my grandson, Bertie, and asking him what he thought it meant, I was still strongly affected. He was too, and kept hissing at me to shut up'

Then two men arrive, the Irishman McCann and Jewish Mr Goldberg, both dressed in smart black suits. Are they undertakers or insurance salesmen? Goldberg does most of the talking; he puts on the charm with a vengeance. Having been told by Meg that it's the lodger's birthday – Stanley denies it – he arranges a party. Husband Petey remembers another appointment and goes out. Meg puts on her ball-gown and invites a young woman

called Lulu to join them. Lulu, played by Sinead Matthews, has a lovely voice; willingly she goes to bed with Goldberg, though the next day she will accuse him of taking advantage. Obviously, she too is looking for a reason for being alive. The play ends with Stanley being brought downstairs, suited, washed, shaven and wordless. Then he's taken away. We hear the car drive off.

Having made enquiries, I've been told that Pinter himself held it wasn't necessary to know exactly what was going on between the visitors and Stanley. All over the world people have been taken hostage, have vanished without trace or explanation. Life, Pinter seems to be saying, contains no certitude, no guarantee of predictability. One has only to think of those millions rounded up and transported to the death camps, or for that matter, those incarcerated by Americans after the war in Iraq.

If I have made The Birthday Party sound unutterably gloomy, I do it a disservice. It's funny as well as furious, and it does stay in the mind. The theatre critic, Harold Hobson, identified Pinter as a playwright who magnificently uses inconsequential everyday talk to provoke an atmosphere of dread. Meg, even after the lodger has so abruptly disappeared, can only ask her husband the mundane question, 'Is your tea nice?' All the same, we in the audience knew she was terrified.

George Carman, who got Jeremy Thorpe off

BLOG HARRY MOUNT, 2018

In my very brief career as a barrister, the most surprising acts of kindness came from George Carman, QC, the man whose brilliant advocacy got Jeremy Thorpe off the hook in 1979.

Towards the end of my pupillage in 1999, I got the chance to work with him. He was representing Mohamed Fayed against the MP Neil Hamilton. Hamilton was suing Fayed over his allegation that he made cash payments to Hamilton in return for placing parliamentary questions.

Ever since he first made his mark defending Thorpe, Carman's fine oratory meant he was reserved by chambers expressly for court appearances. Other barristers did most of the dreary paperwork while he was brought in for the dénouement.

Like F E Smith and Rumpole of the Bailey, he stood for a type that is rare in real life — the master of the beautifully weighted, erudite phrase; but he has stuck tenaciously in people's minds as the exemplar of the barrister.

By the time of Hamilton vs Fayed, Carman was almost 70, and had only a little over a year left to live (he died in 2001), but he was still at the height of his powers. With an extremely relaxed manner, Carman dealt with the new

arguments that were thrown up by his opponent with exactly the right answer, combining lightning-quick thinking and a large amount of facts trawled from the months of research. With his quiverful of forensic skills – and Neil Hamilton's pattern of admitting only the sins that had been proved against him and denying anything else — victory looked secure as soon as the jury left the room.

Carman won the case for Fayed.

Guarding the big three

Patrick Reyntiens was in the Scots Guards in 1945, protecting Churchill, Roosevelt and Stalin at Potsdam. But when they turned up, they weren't quite what he'd expected...

Two little command cars, a jeep, three three-tonners with a company of Scots Guardsmen in them, and we got to Potsdam at last. It had taken us three whole days from the Rhine valley town where we were stationed. We were not actually in the town of Potsdam but in Babelsberg, quite close by. We found ourselves in a large, fortified and guarded compound that had been the site of the UFA film studios before the war. It was about four hundred yards square and had wire walls crowned with barbed wire. It was guarded by Russian troops who looked as though they had been recruited from Outer Mongolia.

We stayed there about a month, looking after Churchill and then, after the election, Clement Attlee and members of his new Cabinet.

It was not very hard work, and in between our duties we managed to enjoy ourselves. The greatest thrill was guarding the Prime Minister, Mr Churchill, when he gave a dinner to Marshal Stalin and Mr Truman, the new President of the United States. We had to be on our toes.

This is what happened. The company of Scots Guards was ordered to go in full uniform and take up positions round the villa which Churchill had taken over as his private residence. This was a decent-looking villa in a garden of about an acre and a half. There was a nice wrought-iron fence all around it and the front gate opened on to the suburban road which ran towards Potsdam. There were a lot of military policemen, but there was not any traffic at all. Absolute silence prevailed, with the Guards on their best behaviour. We were stock still, formed up in front of the Churchill villa along the broad tree-lined road. The summer air hung a little heavy; it was about 6.30 or 7.00 in the evening. Silence.

The first guest was to be Stalin, we were told. He would be coming by car from the left-hand side, up the road that led to Potsdam. He would arrive bang on time. We all looked surreptitiously up the road to see if the car was coming; nothing. Silence. Then, when we had least expected it, there was an aggressively loud noise of powerful engines coming from the opposite direction. Our military police looked puzzled and rather apprehensive. This was something which they had obviously not been warned to expect. In no time three huge ZIS cars charged down the road, compelling us to involuntarily swing our heads round. Shining ZIS limousines, all alike, each with six doors, driving dangerously close together, screeched to a halt. All the cars kept close together. The doors of the first and the third cars opened with military precision. All six doors to each car opened at once, and a dozen and a half OGPU (secret police) figures got out with the utmost speed and made a beeline for the middle car, clustering all round it. They were all armed as far as I could see. I had expected a fairly dignified Stalin to get out of the middle car. Instead there was this buzzing of OGPU busybodies all intent on, seemingly, getting the great man's autograph. A tiny little man got out – Stalin himself – and he was immediately surrounded by 'OGs' far taller than him. Bees round a honey-pot. Then the whole cluster of twenty uniformed guards, with Stalin invisible in the middle, made its way up the garden path towards the front door, a journey of fifty or sixty feet, like a chorus of Japanese Geisha girls – all closely clustered together, taking rapid little mincing steps in time with one another: chop, chop, chop, chop, chop.

They delivered Stalin at the front door, saluted, and resumed the military appearance of normal Russian security guards. Relaxed, they left in their ZIS cars immediately, without looking to right or to left, straight down the road from where we were told that President

'They had both hands in their pockets, clutching, as we immediately guessed, cocked revolvers, the silhouettes of which were just discernible under their raincoats'

Truman was going to be coming.

What next? We waited for quite a long time, bolt upright, and ready to greet the large contingent of American cars that we had expected. No. There was not a car in sight. We waited in silence. And then we saw a modest posse of men in gabardine mackintoshes, sauntering up the road at a slow pace. They were led by three men who were intent on giving everybody a friendly wave of the hand and a smile.

The middle figure of the three was none other than the President of the United States of America, with a broad grin on his face. Intent on being the most friendly man on earth, he was exposed to any damage that could be done to him. But he was not concerned at all – he simply sauntered up the road with, presumably, the Vice-President on one side and the Secretary of State on the other.

But there was something a bit odd about this reassuring display of benign camaraderie. Only a few paces behind the President's entourage were about a dozen security men, all well over six feet tall, and all dressed alike in gabardine mackintoshes, and keeping an eye on potential assassins. They had both hands in their pockets, clutching, as we immediately guessed, cocked revolvers, the silhouettes of which were just discernible under their raincoats. All these heavily built, fat-faced men were seemingly doing a dance together, but quite unlike the security shuffle of the Russian President's men. Each one of them, independent of the others, was twisting around as he walked behind the President – doing a gentle pirouette, in fact. This extraordinary group of men, each one twiddling his figure round and then in reverse, and then round again, all with benign smiles on their faces, did not miss a thing. Everyone was under intense scrutiny. They were professional marksmen. This extraordinary little dance went on, with the President in front taking no notice at all. We had never seen anything like it.

The American President reached the front gate of Churchill's villa, and in a leisurely fashion sauntered up the garden path with his two companions.

No more waving. The security men slowly walked away and smiled at us as they went down the road, out of sight.

I never knew what the great men had for their evening banquet: by the time it was over we had been relieved of our guard duties and had gone back to barracks in Babelsberg. A pity: it would have been fun to see if Stalin came out of the villa plastered.

'Must do Munch'

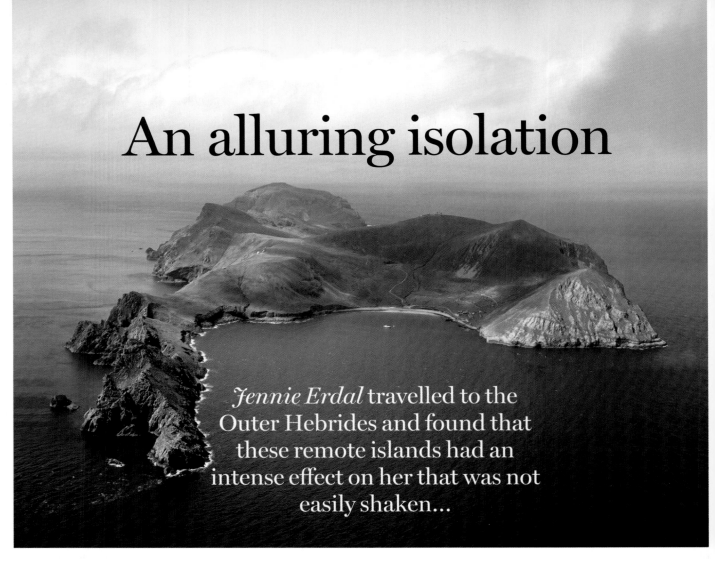

An alluring isolation

Jennie Erdal travelled to the Outer Hebrides and found that these remote islands had an intense effect on her that was not easily shaken…

The Outer Hebrides can easily seduce you. There is something incurably bewitching about these islands, and to know them is to love them. They are different from anything else in the British Isles, with the natives speaking in a strange tongue that sounds songful and emotional. Traditionally regarded as a place apart, the islands lie beyond the barrier of an often treacherous sea, isolated from the mainland since the end of the Ice Age. They form an almost continuous chain – known locally as The Long Island – stretching for about 130 miles from the Butt of Lewis in the north to Vatersay in the south, separated from the Inner Hebrides by a wide and wild channel known as the Minch.

Seen from the mainland, or from a boat, they seem mysteriously to come and go, peeping shyly through the mist or rising dramatically out of the seabed, one minute framed in strong clear light, the next disappearing behind a veil of soft rain, or sometimes quite invisible and out of reach.

'When the wind blows, the sea swells to a prodigious height and rolls with inexpressible violence against the shores, exhibiting a prospect awfully grand beyond description.' So wrote the gloriously named Reverend Clement Crutwell about the Outer Hebrides in 1798.

A couple of centuries later, I had a little taste of this swollen sea, sailing (with five women friends on a 38-ft chartered yacht) across the Minch in 1998, and vainly seeking shelter from an easterly gale in Lochboisdale, the main harbour on South Uist, open to the east. After an uncomfortable night, the boat being spun in the gusting wind, we left in search of calmer waters without ever setting foot on the Uists. We had no sense of the place – it was just somewhere on our chart that was wet and windy and grey and hostile.

In May this year, I decided to go back with my husband and see what we'd missed. At Oban we boarded *The Lord of*

'There is something incurably bewitching about these islands, isolated from the mainland since the Ice Age'

the Isles, the Caledonian MacBrayne ferry bound for Lochboisdale – a six-hour journey. The ferry made its way up the Sound of Mull in the sunshine, then on past Tobermory, leaving Ardnamurchan lighthouse to starboard, past Muck with Eigg beyond it, past the dark hills of Rum and the soft green of Canna, and at last out into the Minch, flat and calm that day, with Skye a distant shade of grey to the north. And eventually into Lochboisdale, which looked wholly benign, unrecognisable from my previous visit. We then travelled the narrow roads up South Uist, where Catholicism has hung on against all the odds, then across Benbecula – from where Bonnie Prince Charlie sailed with Flora MacDonald 'over the sea to Skye' – and on to the Calvinist north where we had rented a cottage.

In the old days it was a hazardous business crossing the tidal sands between these islands. Now, there are causeways, although they were no match for the hurricanes and high seas in January of this year, which claimed the lives of an entire family swept into the sea as they tried to reach safety in Benbecula. There is still evidence of the storm damage everywhere – roofs blown off and boats in the middle of fields. An old islander told us there had been nothing like it since 1920.

Our rented cottage was in Sollas, theatre of one of the most inhumane struggles between the crofters and the clearers. Throughout the 19th century there were recurring famines and shameful clearances, now the stuff of folklore, with whole communities being forced onto emigrant ships bound for the New World.

The cottage was an old restored 'blackhouse', the typical Outer Hebridean dwelling until well into the 20th century. Families lived in blackhouses with their livestock – animals at one end, people at the other – with the floor always tilting so that the dung, liquid and solid, remained at the lower end. They had thick walls filled with clay and peat, which the thatched roof drained into, keeping the walls tight. There were no windows and no chimney, although a peat fire burned constantly in the middle of the room, the smoke rising naturally through the thatch. It strikes us now as intolerable, but the blackhouses were based on sound holistic living, with the urine and the peat acting as a natural antidote to lung disease and other illnesses. When the animals were removed and chimneys installed in the name of civilisation, there were outbreaks of tuberculosis almost immediately.

Even with windows and no animals, our gloriously pretty cottage was dark and cramped inside, but we loved it anyway. And just outside there was a vast expanse of white sand and the ocean stretching out to America beyond. Nearby was the Free Presbyterian Kirk, and the cottage literature warned against noise and the hanging out of washing on Sundays. By 1792, so we read, the North Uist islanders were all of the established religion except for 'four of the Romish persuasion'. (Pity those four.) There was also a book with prayers in English and in Gaelic, still the first language of a good proportion of the islanders, and spoken since before the time of the Romans.

It is difficult for the layman to comprehend the immense geological events that had to take place in order for these beautiful islands to be formed. The landscape consists of white beaches, moorland hills and soft green machair – the local name for the low-lying fertile coastal plains, a mosaic of wild pansies and primroses in May. The machair was common grazing in the past, now increasingly fenced, with rusting vans and tractors, even the odd bus scattered round. And there's water, fresh and salt, everywhere. About half the total area of North Uist is under water, and when you stand on the top of Rueval on Benbecula, the abundance of lochs makes the island look like a great flooded plain. Sometimes the water is blue, other times a luminous green.

This combination of land, sea and lochs, with scarcely any traffic, supports a magnificent variety of birds – every kind of auk, skua, tern and wader. The air is thick and clamorous with curlews and redshanks and oystercatchers, taking up attitudes in the sky. One day we met a man, ecstatic because he had just seen a red-necked phalarope. There's a lot of weather around in the Uists but none of it lasts very long, except perhaps the wind. You learn to keep looking at the vast skies to see what's in store. The clouds will suddenly fold back like curtains, and always there is a mysterious quality to the light, with the lochs and lochans sparkling against the intense browns of the peat bogs.

Some things took us by surprise: a modern lottery-funded internet café and community centre in the middle of nowhere; a Royal Artillery missile range on South Uist not far from a huge granite statue (sculpted by Hew Lorimer) of Our Lady of the Isles; the fact that when you cycle here the wind is always in your face; and that we couldn't quite escape the General Election. There were posters on every gatepost for the Scot Nats and, rather alarmingly, something called Operation Christian Vote (OCV), whose candidate was the Reverend George Hargreaves, a black Christian fundamentalist with a dog collar, a big smile and a gilded bible in hand. He did not win. Perhaps the least expected happening, however, was at Carinish Inn, where we stopped for lunch. The party of six women and one man at the next table got up after their meal and disappeared behind a screen, leaving my husband and me alone in the bar. Suddenly the man's voice rang out from behind the screen: 'This lecture is entitled "Location, Location, Location",' and he proceeded to elaborate on the exact position of the prostate gland relative to the rectum, bladder and urethra. The next part of his talk did not go well with our soup.

The celebrated geologist, John MacCulloch, who visited the outer isles in the early 19th century, wrote in his journal: 'Time is never present, but always past or to come. It is always too soon to do anything, until it is too late; and thus vanishes the period of weariness and labour and anxiety and expectation and disappointment which lies between the cradle and the grave.' Strange perhaps that this should be so in a place where there are reminders of time everywhere: in the huge rock formations, ancient standing stones, Neolithic burial chambers, Iron Age duns and brochs, and in the shallow glens, eerily empty but for a few stones from the old blackhouses, now covered in lichen. Everywhere, so it seems, there are ghosts of the life once lived here.

It is always a mistake to romanticise a place where life is hard and people, in dwindling numbers, have struggled for centuries, and continue to do so. That said, these islands exert a strange pull. The place seems to enter you, rather than the other way round; and when you leave, everything for a while seems less intense.

Left: St Kilda; above: causeway, Outer Hebrides

A life online

To make your way in the world as an artist, you need a little insecurity to sharpen your wits, believes *John Ward*

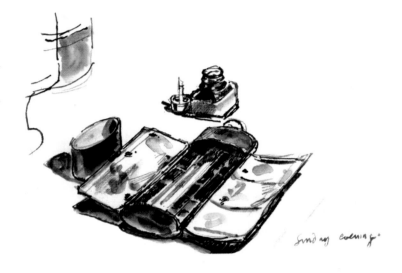

Why do I want to write about learning to draw? Because I so hate the limp horror of the illustration on the folder when I collect my euros, and the sheer badness and poverty of the GPO graphics, and because I realise, on the death of a fellow painter, how poorly his talents had been harvested?

Drawing was deliberately, enthusiastically destroyed in the Sixties. The edict went out: drawing shall no longer be taught. Instead of being numerous, small and lacking in facilities (such as canteens and art historians), art schools were to be concentrated, rationalised and properly equipped. The odd institution of thirty to fifty students was to became – that hideous term – an 'art college'.

Those of us who chose to live by the skills learned in the old art schools had learned to cope with its effects. How well I recall the jeers of an advertising man as he pointed out my inability to draw a pretty girl. He knew as well as I did that pretty girls had been taboo in art schools for years – art was to be found in the drab, the ordinary and ugly – but, if you wanted to earn money, you needed to get your skates

on and shed some of the shibboleths of the art establishment.

My option – to take up fashion drawing – had raised eyebrows amongst my painter friends, but when a modicum of success followed it was greeted with nods of approval. But I came from a family of picture dealers in Hereford. I can remember how, come November, my father, who was a picture restorer, would take up

his paints and produce a set of paintings of kittens with bits of holly etc for the 'Christmas' market.

This gave me a viewpoint not shared by many of my contemporaries, for whom art was a serious matter, a matter of integrity, with the noble example of Cézanne to follow: those who wished to be painters should enter the art-school world, teach as few days as possible – earning just enough

'They failed to realise that being a painter demands a modicum of insecurity – that some talents actually thrive under pressure'

Far left top: Watercolour of John Ward's artist's materials; below: impromptu sketch in Turkey, 1986. This page: left, sketch of Ophelia; below, 'Caprice', an illustration for Vogue, 1948

to get by – and paint free from commercial pressures. Admirable sentiments, but all too often the wherewithal to be a fine painter just wasn't there. It would be nice in due course to marry and settle down, so the two days teaching became a full-time job and 'I will paint in the plentiful holiday time'. These were good people, well-taught and skilful, but they failed to realise that being a painter demands a modicum of insecurity – that some talents actually thrive under pressure.

I blessed the inadequacies of my local art school, which I had entered at the age of fifteen. A staff of two, and three evening teachers, managed the three and a half days it was open. Student numbers must have been around twenty, with a sprinkling of old ladies. The evening teachers included a practising sign-writer who taught lettering. The Roman alphabet was his God, and he was the first man I met who actually earned a living with brush and paint every day. The fact that he dealt with the problems of money and skill on a daily basis added extra salt to his talk. Almost as an aside, he savaged my art-student attitudes. Where would all my talk about Turner, Brangwyn and Wyndham Lewis (the latest craze) get me? How would I earn a living from the training I was receiving in this one-eyed charming art school perched on the banks of the River Wye? Did I ever wonder what happened to my previous students?

Later, in 1936, I had the great good fortune to be taught by Barnett Freedman

– small, dynamic and a first-rate designer and painter. As I was leisurely setting out my palette around 9.30 one morning he paused behind me.

'Gentlman's hours for you, I see. I was up at 6.30am making a lithograph of a child listening to the sea in a seashell against his ear, and neither child nor shell to hand in the primary works...'

My basic greed was stirred – to be wanted, to have someone telephone to say, 'Come and make a drawing'.

There is a Test Match on as I write, and I dimly remember the excitement and fear as that horrid red ball thundered towards the young man with the bat. There's no hard ball in art school education – there

> 'An advertiser jeered at my inability to draw a pretty girl. He knew as well as I did that pretty girls had been taboo in art schools for years'

hasn't been for years – and so few books are illustrated, few book jackets have drawings. Photography has taken over all advertising – not even the dull council literature contains the vestige of a drawing. All those forms of employment for those possessing excellent minor talents wither

away, taking with them both judgements and a sense of fun and interest: hence the limpness, the poverty, as displayed by the Royal Mail.

My county of Kent is amalgamating with another county to produce the ultimate in art colleges, with an ultra-degree in Fine Arts, where students can enjoy a campus and all the facilities that fatuous ignorance can produce. Vigorous art doesn't grow in such scented set-ups, which are suitable only for academics. The plumber-painter-candlestick-maker oddity – like your true painter – is far better off in a small, poverty-stricken setup. It's plain silly, all this wishing Art on to people. As Whistler said long ago, in his ten o'clock lecture: 'Art happens – no hovel is safe from it, no prince may depend upon it, the vastest intelligence cannot bring it about and puny efforts to make it universal end in quaint comedy and coarse farce.'

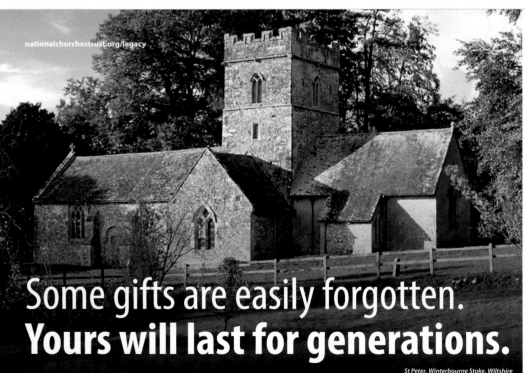

On parade for opera

Philip Purser discovered his passion for opera in the most unlikely way: sixty years ago he was forced to watch the Hamburg State Opera by military order

Panting over the assault course to a live ammunition accompaniment, jogging ten miles in two hours with full equipment and a Bren gun, or manhandling 590lb Bailey Bridge panels into place – none of these military tests of prowess was as daunting as the intensive opera-going Alwyn imposed on his fellow-sergeants sixty years ago.

Our Royal Engineers field company was quartered in the insanely luxurious Hermann Goering Hotel in Salzgitter-Lebenstedt, Brunswick. Built for Nazi bigwigs visiting the Hermann Goering steelworks nearby, it boasted a large ballroom-cum-theatre as well as restaurants and bars, the best of which, naturally, had become the Sergeants' Mess. Normally the Company Sergeant-Major would have presided, but there was an interregnum about this time between the demob of one and the arrival of his replacement. The CQMS, next in line, reached for his first beer of the day at reveille and, consequently, wasn't very active by evening.

So the Chief Clerk, Sergeant Alwyn, ran the show, just as he more or less ran the company. He was not at all clerkly, but young, dashing and Welsh. He had a pretty German girlfriend, and told us shyly of a game they played in which they tossed an orange to each other and every time you dropped a catch you had to take off an item of clothing. Undeterred, Alwyn bullied

five or six of us into setting off to hear *Die Zauberflöte*. The opera house itself had been destroyed in the air raids, but its huge scenery dock and other offices had survived, and been resourcefully converted into a makeshift theatre. It was a simple production, the stage effects mostly achieved with lighting. The only singer whose name I can recall was the Prince Tamino, Joop de Vries, presumably from Holland. Pamina was lovely, the bird-catchers Papageno and Papagena were endearing and funny, the Queen of the Night a right harpy. Sergeant Alwyn was enchanted, and so – grudgingly – were the rest of us.

The second outing, I think, was to *Der Freischütz*, which was also marked well for its spooky qualities. The next was to *Der Rosenkavalier*, which I had to miss because I was Orderly Sergeant that day. When the others got back around midnight, even Alwyn's enthusiasm was a bit muted. 'It was very good,' he explained, 'except that the tenor must have been off sick, and they had to have a girl singing the part.' Well, anyone could have made that misinterpretation, especially when the theatre programme was one small sheet of paper smudgily printed in German. It was some years on before a BBC Third Programme relay put me wise to Richard Strauss's plot.

That was the last opera outing, but meanwhile Alwyn had dreamed up another musical adventure. For a company

dance in the ballroom-cum-theatre he decreed that we sergeants should perform Ravel's *Bolero* during the interval. The music would be amplified from gramophone records, we would mime the orchestra players playing, he would conduct. As we had no evening dress, nor any civilian clothing for that matter, we would wear some weird Prussian hussar uniforms that had been discovered in a store under the stage.

Enough brass and stringed instruments and decrepit woodwinds were similarly rustled up. What should I play? Just to be awkward, how about a harp? The chippies made a brute of a thing, roughly the right shape, about seven feet tall, strung with signal cable. Alwyn equipped himself with a baton and a podium. We had a run-through to get to know the music and devise bits of silly business. Mine was to become progressively enmeshed in the harp's dense strings, until eventually I would reach for a huge pair of wire-cutters to cut myself free.

On the night we all got rather ginned up, I'm afraid, to overcome stage fright. The place was packed with squaddies and their womenfolk, whether German or displaced – Czech, Polish, Hungarian. They sat down in orderly rows when the interval came and looked expectant as we shambled on in our ridiculous uniforms. Golly, were they expecting real art? The music started, Alwyn put on a creditable imitation of Toscanini in full display, and we fumbled into our silly bits. Somehow it all took off, even my fight with the harp. By the end the audience was helpless with laughter, some of the ladies so much so, it was reported, they had wet themselves.

Not an edifying episode, certainly not one I have ever recounted before. But the opera nights – ah, they left me with an appetite for this barmy art-form which I have never lost. Not an all-consuming passion but an unschooled delight in all sorts of opera, from Handel to Berlioz, Britten to Puccini, Mozart to Massenet. And all thanks to Sergeant Alwyn.

But music was his real great interest. When he heard that the Hamburg State Opera was re-opening and British troops would be welcome, he decided that we were in need of cultural refinement and set about organising – or rather, ordering – an expedition.

Looking at the map now, I have to convince myself it really did happen. It was at least a hundred miles to Hamburg. Even via the autobahn, in a white scout car with the MT Sergeant at the wheel, it would have been the best part of a couple of hours each way. And for what? Blokes singing secrets to each other at the tops of their voices.

MOMENTUM TRADING WORKS

Although it has its critics, it is generally accepted that momentum trading works. Today, it is widely used by professional investors, and it has been championed by legendary historic figures.

In the summer of 1891, a 14-year-old farmer's son ran away from home with $5 in his pocket. Thirty-eight years later, having spent his entire adult life as an investor and trader, he was worth over $100million – equivalent to $1.3billion in today's money. His name was Jesse Livermore, and his immense success was largely due to one investment strategy – momentum trading. This remains just as effective today as it was 100 year ago.

The theory of momentum trading, like all the best ideas, is simple – the greater the amount of money that is being invested into a fund, or asset class, the quicker its value will rise. This, in turn, will attract further investment, pushing the price even higher. Obviously, the opposite also applies. As a fund or asset class loses investors, the upward momentum ceases and it will reverse, gaining impetus in the opposite direction. Time to move your money and exit stage left!

Another very successful momentum investor was a man called Richard Dennis. He was born in Chicago in 1949 and in the early 1970s started to trade commodities with a small loan from his family. By 1973 this had risen to $100,000 and by 1975 he was a millionaire. By the early eighties he was said to be worth more than $100million.

It was at this time that he and his long-term friend, the financial genius Bill Eckhardt, made a bet – that any sensible person with training and a supply of relevant financial information could become a successful momentum trader. It goes without saying that Dennis won his bet. He selected 20 or so novices ('turtles'), gave them $1million each, and let them loose. Three years later their combined value was $175million.

Exactly the same momentum principles underpin the Saltydog philosophy and our approach to investing.

At Saltydog Investor we do not believe that people should necessarily work longer, pay more into their pensions, or take out extra insurance in order to cover their living expenses during their twilight years. These are all the things that are currently being advocated by politicians and the financial industry, and which might well be necessary for some, but why oh why doesn't anyone suggest the obvious– make your current savings work harder!

To become a DIY investor with some of your money (while you learn) you will need a source of clear, well-presented fund and asset sector performance data. At Saltydog we analyse thousands of funds and present a summary on a weekly basis in a way designed to help private investors see which sectors are currently performing well, and importantly, which are the best-performing funds within these sectors. The homework has been done and the findings are presented to you on a silver platter.

To make the most of your investments you need to follow a few simple steps:
- Take advantage of the low-cost fund supermarket and discount brokers.
- Use tax-efficient wrappers like ISAs, SIPPs and investment bonds.
- Manage risk. By understanding how different funds are classified it is possible to tailor your portfolio to match your own appetite for adventure.
- Monitor your progress and be prepared to change tack as conditions vary.

We combine the Investment Association asset sectors into our own proprietary Saltydog

Douglas Chadwick, founder and chairman

groups, which are:
- Safe Haven
- Slow Ahead
- Steady as She Goes
- Full Steam Ahead – Developed Markets
- Full Steam Ahead – Emerging Markets.

The nautical names of these groups give an easy recognisable indication of the volatility of the sectors and funds that are allocated to the groups. Using the performance data it is easy to see whether the increased risk associated with the more volatile funds is then being rewarded.

The recent growth in on-line trading has been astonishing. The way we shop, bank, arrange our insurance, book our holidays and choose our utility providers has changed forever. Surely now is the time that our approach to our pensions and savings should follow suit? These are your babies and nobody else should have a stronger desire to see them perform well than yourself.

I am not particularly computer literate, I do not come from the investment industry and I do not have formal financial training – yet my own investments have consistently out-performed the market. The time has come for the DIY investor, and if I can do it, then so can you.

www.saltydoginvestor.com

To receive our **free guide** An introduction to Successful Trend Investing', or to sign up for our **two-month free trial**, please go to our website **www.saltydoginvestor.com**

With our easy-to-use trend investing method you could protect your savings from downturns and still achieve excellent returns when conditions are favourable.

saltydog investor

OLDEN LIFE

What was… knicker elastic?
by *Eleanor Allen*

One minute it's an indispensable household item, the next it's an unlikely historical artefact. I've just learned that a card of knicker elastic has found its way into one of Godalming Museum's Loan Boxes. Labelled GRANNY'S DAY, the box is available to schools as a teaching aid for present-day kids who apparently don't know what to do with such useful items as darning mushrooms, Bakelite thimbles and tins of grate polish.

How do you introduce knicker elastic to a class of mixed Juniors? I suppose you're intended to explain how Granny used it to Make Do and Mend her knickers during and after the War, when new knickers, like everything else, were in short supply. And then let them snigger their socks off.

But you can't ignore the fact that, although Granny's knickers might now look frumpy, back in the sexually repressed Fifties, they were charged with great mystique. No glamour lingerie advertising back then, remember. In drapery shops, knickers were stored out of sight in big wooden drawers behind the counter.

Yet, to the delight of boys of all ages, a strip of ¼" elastic was all that held those mystery-charged objects up. None of the knicker fabrics of the early Fifties had today's light, stretchy, body-hugging qualities. Double cotton interlock, fine knitted wool, even silk – all had to be generously cut then gathered up at the waist by a band of elastic threaded independently through the seam. Unless, fortuitously, hers were also gathered at the legs, that piece of elastic round the waist was all that stood between Granny and public humiliation.

After a while, though, elastic starts to lose its 'go', and that's where the repair stuff comes in. Every household kept a card in the sewing box. A fresh piece was cut off and threaded through with a safety pin, then the ends were painstakingly

Art Frahm: A fare loser, 1953

stitched together – unless you were in a rush, or a bit of a slut, in which case you just tied a knot and left the ends to stick out and fray. Either way, you had to make certain it was secure, because sometimes (rarely, but sometimes) knicker elastic actually did go pop. Potentially, it could happen to any woman, any time anywhere.

*'My husband's great in bed –
he goes right to sleep'*

Popped elastic was the stuff of male fantasies. The American pin-up artist Art Frahm encapsulated the dream – pretty girl with knickers round her ankles; hands full of groceries; gust of wind blowing and a leering working man in a uniform to witness it all. British humour, as expressed in seaside postcards, and *Carry On* and *St Trinian's* films, took a more slapstick approach.

> 'No glamour lingerie advertising back then, remember. In drapery shops, knickers were stored out of sight in big wooden drawers behind the counter'

And still the dream lives on. Male ego has always kidded itself that popped knicker elastic could actually be spontaneously induced by a handsome physique. Or that a few hilarious jokes might do the trick. Even today, the Jeremy Clarksons of this world still sex-up anything from a Ferrari to a mobile phone by claiming it's capable of snapping knicker elastic at twenty paces. And when Daniel Cleaver throatily mutters, 'Well hello Mummy!' at the sight of Bridget Jones's Big Knickers, we all know it's the old 1950s mystique that's twanging his ardour.

You can actually still get ¼" elastic, though now you buy it by the metre and they've dropped the word 'knicker'. My local Sewing Centre sells in excess of 700 metres a year. Much of it, ironically, to schools for masks and costumes. But I like to think it's also being put to its other traditional uses: catapults, repairing household appliances or – in extremis – doubling as a cam belt for an Austin 7.

PJ Kavanagh continues, manfully, to prop up the bar in his local, but it's an increasingly lonely business. Is rural England closing down?

Country matters

I suppose I was brought up in a pub culture. My father wrote radio scripts for the BBC and his shows were rehearsed in the charmingly named Aeolian Hall. Round the corner was a pleasant pub and after rehearsal everyone repaired there; actors, actresses, writers, pretty secretaries, genial hangers-on. The conversation was lively, the jokes good, and I grew to like beer and associate it with amusing company. Not beer in great quantities, it must be said. Later, when I grew to like spirits, it seemed more prudent to drink these at home, privately, and that is the point of this: I now drink beer privately in the pub, alone.

This has only happened round here, in rural Gloucestershire, within the last two or three years. I still go to the local at six, and stay for an hour or less (the beer, Arkell's Kingsdown, is delicious), but whereas the place used to be full of chatting locals and assorted passers-by,

someone to talk to, something happening, now there is no one. Evening after evening I stand alone, feeling increasingly daft.

There are reasons for this sudden absence of company, but none of them quite wash: price (canned beer from the supermarket incomparably cheaper); the smoking ban; the drink-drive laws. But it seems like a more subtle social change.

The occasional people who do venture in seem strangely hesitant, even timid, and they order depressingly soft and expensive drinks. When asked by a male what she would like to drink the female almost invariably replies, 'Um...', as though surprised by the question, as if she had had no time to think about it, driving here, crossing the vast and deserted car park. Then they pore over the menu interminably (because of course there is food) as though it is a difficult text of Scripture. Do they not know that a menu is one of the least informative of

documents, as to quality? That all the items will be the same as elsewhere, and if there is anything exotic, best to give it a miss? (This lone observer, as he quietly sips, is inclined to such irritable questions.) Also (an irritable digression), there are the young couple who come in; the man sits down, the girl goes to the bar with her purse, turns to ask him what he would like, then pays and carries their drinks to the table. This is something so new to this lone tippler that he knows he will never get used to it.

There is a cheerful free magazine called *The Tippler* lying around, published by CAMRA (Campaign for Real Ale). The cover of the Christmas edition was a colour photograph of a pleasant-looking old pub not unlike the one I am in. Round the pub picture in heavy black are printed : '10% Alcohol Tax?', 'Record slump in beer sales', 'Pub closures inevitable', and, at the bottom, gloomily, 'Merry Christmas!'.

Is the rural pub to die? With it would go hundreds of years of history. Coleridge was fond of dropping in to pubs during his long walks in the Lake District; Wordsworth disapproved. When we were young and easy we used to deplore the licensing laws – why could not such places be open all day, as they were in civilised France? How wrong we were.

In northern France, not so long ago, tracing the places the poet Ivor Gurney mentioned in his First World War poems, I stayed at a small hotel in Albert, had dinner there, and went out to sample the town. All the cafés were shut; no customers, so they shut. British pubs at least stayed open during the prescribed hours. I went back to the hotel, ordered a brandy and sat, sadly, to watch television. Then the electricity was switched off by the proprietor, who had decided to go to bed. I sat in the dark with my brandy; it was about half past nine. Now, in Britain, pubs can indeed stay open all day, or not, as they wish. I have heard of a local near here that just shut, as in France, because of lack of custom. (The next morning, in Albert, the proprietor handed me a *fiche* to fill in for the police – passport number, and so on. Under 'occupation' I wrote *Inspecteur d'hôtels* and left, triumphant – only for a moment. Should it have been *Inspecteur des hôtels*'?)

That was some years ago, and France is still blessedly different, but now it seems to represent a topical warning. Will England go the way of France – shut pubs, shut post offices (which are busy clubs as pubs used to be)? Will England soon look like huge swathes of rural France, where whole villages, behind rusted shutters, seem all but abandoned? Or like suburban America, its silent island-houses each with its blue TV?

However, this lonesome, short-time barfly will not abandon his post, whence all but he have fled, and the host of puritans all around. The radio scripts my father wrote were comedies, and Beachcomber (of blessed memory) confided to him that he could no longer write his own absurdist pieces because the newspapers were more absurd than he could ever invent. Recently a doctor at Alder Hey hospital advised that the only safe way to smoke, if children were in the house, was outside, naked, and to wash your hair when you came in. Praise-God Barebones rants on the air-waves ... but that is a (connected) topic for another time.

Whiteboard jungle

Every teacher's worst nightmare – the parents

Parents are, like everything else in this jargonistic word, a resource. Sometimes they are useful – when they are on our side. But you'd be amazed how many parents are not on the school's side.

I was brought up by parents who were totally anarchic about teachers, encouraging me to believe that the chief prerequisite of the job was an ineffable dimness. My mother looks back on those days with some shame now she has a daughter on the other side, but many parents still share the views she had.

The best impression of parents is to be had at parents' evenings, where they can be divided into three types. Firstly, there are the parents of the children you really want to see, but who don't come because they can't be bothered. Then there are the parents who do come and are still terrified of school and teachers.

'It's hot, but it's a dry heat'

These are usually represented by the father, scrubbed up and over-thankful to you for doing your job. They desperately want their children to do well and have an excessive faith in our powers. Sometimes the mother comes, too, dressed up to the nines, nodding, smiling and unsure. The fearful ones make me feel very humble.

The parents who don't make me feel humble belong to the third category. These are the middle-class ones who look down on teachers, who will accept no criticism of their children and offer no help in dealing with them. The mothers usually come alone, confident that they can quell you with a look and put you in your place. (How embarrassingly grand my voice turns, of its own volition, when I feel myself under attack.) A child of such parents once remarked, 'Mummy says you must have come down in the world to be a teacher.' We have to be particularly tactful towards these parents. None of their children is ever less than clever (dyslexic) or lazy (not being stretched) or badly behaved (mixing with the wrong children). Funnily enough, a few years ago when we had a bad drugs problem in the school, the dealers were not the deprived working-class children, but the affluent middle-class ones.

Sometimes parents try to thank us personally. A girl once told me that her stepfather had bought a piercing kit on eBay and had pierced her mother 'down below'. She grinned, pointing at her crotch. 'I'll ask him to do you if you like, Miss. As it's you, I'm sure he won't charge.' She was offended when I declined. 'I was only being nice. I won't bother next time,' she sniffed.

Her parents were quite interesting. The mother had three other children by various men, her father had long abandoned her and her stepfather paid her a fiver a time to do a 'moonie'. 'It's only a laugh,' she said when other girls in the class looked a bit worried about this.

She's a mum now. No GCSEs. Maybe I should have pretended to accept the stepdad's offer. At least I'd have met him.
 KATE SAWYER

I once met...

Dr John Bodkin Adams

Marjorie Groves's appalling obstetric care was not enhanced by the bedside manner and questionable ethics of the doctor who attended her delivery ...

In the winter of 1943 I was expecting my first child. My husband, Shirley, was in the RNVR and we were renting a small cottage on the edge of Eastbourne. Arrangements were made for me to be delivered by the Medical Officer on the base, but he was then posted to sea and we had to find someone else. One day Shirley told me that he had found another doctor. All he knew was that he had a good reputation and looked like Mr Pickwick. Later that evening the front door opened and there he was, filling the doorway. He was not quite the jovial figure I had imagined. He was a big sombre man in a long navy overcoat with long arms and big red hands. He had a round face, rimless glasses and a brown trilby hat set squarely on his head. He had come to examine me and inspect the domestic arrangements. I was not to see him again until I went into labour.

Two weeks before the baby was due the nurse moved in with us. I had never had any sex education or antenatal classes and did not know what to expect. She was not much help. When I asked her exactly how the baby was to get out she laughed and said, 'The less you know about that, the better.'

When I went into labour the nurse gave me a dose of castor oil 'to get you moving', adding, 'you are going to have pain, lots of pain, but at the end of it you will have the baby.' The pains got worse and worse and I was relieved when Dr Adams finally arrived. He took off his coat and jacket, rolled up the sleeves of his shirt, removed his collar and donned a long red rubber apron. I was given a mask to hold over my face and lost consciousness. I awoke to the sound of the doctor looking down at me and saying 'You've got some work to do, my girl.' I remember him inserting obstetric forceps without any explanation: I felt

the most agonising pain I had ever experienced and thought I was about to die. Then, after what seemed ages, I heard the sound of my baby crying and realised it was over. She weighed 9lb 6oz.

During this ordeal my husband had been downstairs listening to my screams and praying for me. Dr Adams stitched me up roughly and left, but no sooner had he gone than the air-raid siren sounded and Shirley had to rush back to the base. The nurse, who had not allowed me to touch my new daughter, took hold

> 'Dr Adams said to me that whatever happened to the mother he was determined he would get the next baby out alive'

of the baby and said, 'We're going to shelter under the stairs. You stay where you are. You are not allowed to move!'

She stayed with us for a fortnight and controlled my every action. She would not allow me to hold my baby and bottle-fed her in front of me even though I was bursting with milk and desperate to feed her myself. Just as she was leaving she confided, 'I'll tell you something I didn't want to say before: Dr Adams lost his last baby and said to me that whatever happened to the mother he was absolutely determined he would get the next baby out alive. I shall never take another case for Dr Bodkin Adams!'

I never saw him again and had almost forgotten about him when, years later, his name and photograph were all over the papers. In 1957 Dr Adams, who was by then a rich and successful society doctor in Eastbourne, stood trial in the Old Bailey accused of the murder of an elderly patient who had left him a generous bequest in her will. He was alleged to have poisoned her with injections of heroin. Police investigations into his time as a GP in Eastbourne revealed he had benefited in the wills of 132 elderly lady patients, inheriting large sums of money, valuable antiques and six Rolls Royces.

After a trial lasting three weeks he was found not guilty of murder, owing to doubts about the reliability of the evidence. He was convicted of prescription fraud and temporarily struck off the medical register. Four years later he was allowed to return to his practice and his adoring old ladies, who thought he had been grievously wronged.

Dr Adams lived to be 84 and a few years before he died a friend of mine came back from a holiday in Madeira saying that she had seen him in the lounge of her hotel sitting with two old ladies sharing a large box of chocolates.

OLDEN LIFE

What was ...'the mechanic's breakfast'?

The majority of us are familiar with what is known as the 'traditional English breakfast', with bacon, eggs, sausage, tomato, mushrooms and beans acknowledged as being the standard ingredients. But hands up those readers who know what the main ingredients of a 'mechanic's breakfast' were. Unbelievable as it might seem, the answer is watercress.

Watercress sandwiches were a favourite breakfast meal for workmen in London in the early 1800s, and their popularity led to the creation of watercress beds along the rivers Bourne, Itchen and other chalk streams. The railways helped develop a thriving trade between Hampshire and London, its main destination being Farringdon wholesale market.

At one time, up to twenty tons per week were sold at Farringdon alone. Much of this was purchased by the itinerant street vendors who were allowed entrance at 3am, one hour before the opening of the general market. As many as a thousand regular street hawkers would make their purchases 'by the hand', that is, by the handful of a wholesaler's own hand.

Each handful would then be prepared into about five halfpenny bundles. As the wholesale price was generally one penny per handful, this gave the vendors a profit of 150 per cent.

The trade was carried out by the very poor, old people and children, who would go about with an armbasket, walking the courts, mews and principal thoroughfares selling their cresses which were generally of the large-leaved, big-stalked variety. These hawkers had to be about their business early as the majority of their customers were the working classes, who would

either breakfast very early before going to work or return for breakfast at about 8am. Sometimes the bunches were eaten on their own, rather like an ice cream cone; alternatively, the cress would be placed between slices of bread and eaten as a sandwich.

London was not the only destination for this peppery delicacy, as the newly built watercress beds and railways made it possible for deliveries to be made to many of the major wholesale markets, including those of Birmingham, Leeds and Manchester.

One watercress seller who made good was Eliza James, who as a child hawked bunches of watercress around factories in Birmingham to sell to the workers. She later earned the nickname the 'Watercress Queen' on account of her near monopoly of the London restaurant and hotel watercress trade.

The watercress hawkers are long gone as are many of the mechanics. But what does remain of that era is the 'Watercress Line', the preserved steam railway which runs between Alton and Alresford.

The year 2008 marks the 200th anniversary of William Bradbury opening the first UK watercress farm near Gravesend. During the intervening years the industry has suffered many ups and downs. However, recent research has discovered that gram for gram, the watercress leaf contains more vitamin C than oranges, more calcium than milk, more iron than spinach and is packed with antioxidants.

Now that these benefits are known, watercress may yet make another comeback, particularly if it is given a favourable mention by one of the TV celebrity chefs!

ALAN THOMAS

RANT

Emails are a barbaric intrusion into our civilisation. Millions are sent every day. It is like a virus.

They are destroying our post offices, creating a neurosis of false urgency and causing illiteracy in the young.

The three great communication inventions – telephone, fax and email – arrived in the wrong order. Telephone first, fax next and email last. Yet email is the most primitive. It needs a keyboard, a screen and you have to be able to type. Fax, you simply write or draw, drop it into a slot and press a button. Phone, and you speak to someone and they reply – live! It's called conversation.

Some people worship email. A bloke phoned me recently after we had missed one another several times.

'How can I contact you, Raymond? Have you got an email address?'

'Yes!' I screamed at him, 'but we're talking now, aren't we?'

Commuters get on the train at dawn and instead of reading the paper or doing the crossword, out come the laptops and work begins at 6.30am. False urgency again.

Emails also destroy conversation. People in open-plan offices email friends they can see across the room: 'c u pub 6?' I refuse to let the virus into the house. My assistant receives the tripe three miles away and every now and again, she cycles over with the latest red-hot emails in the basket on her handlebars. That's the way to do it!

Civilisation.

RAYMOND BRIGGS

Free talk

Superbyways: your guide to digital life, by *Webster*

The internet has made communication almost instant. This has its disadvantages – less time to ponder – but it is a fact, and broadly the effect is benign.

However, whilst emails are all very well, sometimes there is no substitute for a chat, and the internet has much to offer on that score, too. Not least, the possibility of worldwide video calls that cost nothing on top of what you already pay for your broadband. The technology is called VoIP (Voice over Internet Protocol); you don't need to understand how it works – you just have to use a bit of software that does. The best known is Skype, which is owned by eBay.

You'll also need a little extra equipment; you probably already have loudspeakers, but you will need a cheap microphone (less than £5), too. Many laptops come with one built-in.

Then, if you want people to see you, buy a camera. These are typically about the size of a hen's egg, and are usually clipped to the top of your screen. Don't spend more than £30: the quality of the picture will be largely dependent on the speed of your broadband connection, which is out of your control. I paid £10, and it came with a microphone built in, which irritated me as I'd just bought a separate one.

Plug everything in, or get a techie friend to set it up. Then download and install Skype from www.skype.com; it's free. You'll have to pick a unique Skype name. I don't have space to set out in detail how to get it going, and you might like to keep your techie friend handy for the moment. Once it's set up, it will start itself up whenever you switch on the computer.

Now you need the Skype details of the person you want to call. You might have to resort to the old-fashioned telephone at this point. Once that is entered into your 'Contacts', you just click on the green button next to their name and if they are online at the time, and prepared to take your call, they will answer, and away you go.

If you have a camera connected you can press a button that switches it on – you don't have to if you are not looking your best. You have a little version of what others are seeing on your own screen, so if you decide to make a call without trousers on, you can check to be sure the other party can't see your legs.

Of course adding video like this brings its own risks. I am not at all sure that a picture will always enhance the experience. Quite apart from the danger of you being seen reading the paper whilst they drone on, they might also notice that your room is untidy, you are still in your pyjamas and that it's high time you got your hair cut. If video calls really take off, I can see a nice little business opportunity for an entrepreneurial oldie: producing small backdrops that you pull down behind you when making a call. These could give the impression that you are calling from a book-lined study, or in front of the Taj Mahal.

What are the shortcomings? The only real problem is that you are dependent on the internet functioning well, and it sometimes slows up or even falls over; if that is the case you may have to begin a call again. Also, the video pictures may be rather jerky. But there really is no substitute for having a grandchild actually grin at you as they speak to you, however blurred the picture.
webster@theoldie.co.uk

WEBSTER'S WATCH

For Webster's latest top tips, visit his blog at www.theoldie.co.uk

www.hearwho.com
This is not much use to most of us but invaluable to some – type in some text and it will read it out loud to you. It's aimed to help those with trouble reading. Sounds a bit like Stephen Hawking.

www.foodtimeline.org
This presents a fascinating buffet of popular lore and contradictory facts about food through the ages. It's the work of 'a reference librarian with a passion for food history'.

www.searchme.com
A great new search engine – it actually shows you a snapshot of the page it thinks you might want – can save ages looking at the wrong one. Also some highly specialised searches – films, music and so forth. Look out Google.

www.genoom.com
There are many online family tree systems, but this looks easy to use. You can invite family members to add what they know and build a huge tree with photos and videos.

Not so grim up North

Life in the Pennines

I was weeding the backyard when the curlew glided just over my roof, and my heart rose to the bird that has throughout my life meant I am where I have always belonged. I grew up with the curlew on the other side of these hills, and during the years when I lived in the South and even farther afield, what I missed most of all, apart from people who spoke the same tongue as I, who knew the same codes, was the sound of water tumbling and gushing down the Pennine slopes, and the call of the bird that belongs as no other does to the lonely high country of the North. What made yesterday so special is that never before had I seen the curlew so near to the house where I have lived for over a quarter of a century.

The house was built two hundred years ago, its stone walls between 15 and 26 inches thick, depending on which side you measure them. The thicker masonry is on the eastern face, which was an odd 18th-century miscalculation if the worst of the weather invariably came from the west then, as it does now. But the coldest winds blow from Siberia or the North Pole, sometimes with fine powdery snow which will be driven under the great stone slabs that top the building – thirty tons of them in all – unless the roof is kept in good repair: I once shifted 24 fertiliser bags full of snow from the loft during a January blizzard that cut us off for a couple of days.

The weather dictates a great deal of our life, affecting almost everything in this dale to a degree that no urban dweller can quite comprehend. It determines how soon haytime starts after the buttercups have died, whether muckspreaders can get onto land that may be too soggy to take their weight, whether newborn lambs can survive until the callous moment when their throats will be cut.

Most people here are farmers, craftsmen or shopkeepers, and a number of them combine ways of bringing in the

bread. The family that runs the local Spar also raises prizewinning sheep; our taxi is driven by a farmer's wife; and one of the nurses at the health centre in town is as familiar with inoculating ewes as she is with taking blood samples from old gentlemen. 'Town' is an ambitious reference to what is no more than a small isolated settlement, snugged into the head of this dale and separated from anything bigger by the great sweeping expanse of hills that rise to not much more than 2,000 feet, but can be extremely dangerous in a bad winter. Town is down there, closer to the river by a quarter of a mile and a couple of hundred feet, with its sheep and cattle auction mart, its shopping, its tourist trade and traffic congestion, its market day, its four pubs; our village up here has none of these things, and the loudest sound it normally knows is that made by tractors.

This is one of the few places whose population has been virtually unchanged since Victoria came to her throne – 1,500 people and about 25,000 sheep at the last count. We have remained much the same as our forebears hereabouts always were: living marginally off inhospitable land, conscious that we are not quite as other men and women are, willing cautiously to explore the world outside, but mostly still seeing Life parochially; and always, always wanting to come back. This is where we belong.

GEOFFREY MOORHOUSE

The friars' new flock

When the monastery island of San Francesco del Deserto acquired some new residents, *Christopher Hamilton* was there to help settle them in

After a lifetime spent with horses, dogs and farm animals, the only thing missing in my watery existence here on the Venetian lagoon was livestock. So, when three sheep arrived on the nearby Franciscan monastery island of San Francesco del Deserto, I offered to lend a hand.

The donated ewes and lamb are Lamon crosses, a tallish migratory mountain breed farmed for meat and wool, with origins up near Belluno. Little

traditional shepherding occurs there today as many of the old migratory routes are criss-crossed by roads or smothered by new building. Whereas our neighbouring island of La Cura was a working dairy farm just fifty years ago, and lamb is still eaten locally at Easter.

Because it was obvious at first glance that they urgently needed shearing and worming, we decided to keep them in quarantine: though sheep and cattle had grazed these pastures in years gone by, the monastery's ground is now free of intestinal worm and must remain so. We

duly injected them with shots prepared by Luca, an energetic Venetian vet who hadn't done sheep before but who nevertheless proved quick on the uptake. More guidance came by telephone from Alwyn Davies, my old livestock vet near Hay-on-Wye. But what would we shear them with? The Franciscan order has a bewildering array of sympathetic friends and contacts in all walks of life, so when the word went out that we needed shears, it wasn't long before some beautifully hand-forged clippers arrived mysteriously from the hills.

It is hard to round up just three sheep from an open space without the right dog. Since Muttley, the friars' old canine rescue case, is far too laid back to learn new tricks, I put up some pens and coached the friars instead. After much undisciplined dashing back and forth in flapping habits the friars discovered that sheep are easily led once humanised, and that a knotted Franciscan cord can come in handy when leading members of a flock from one green pasture to another. The 'Belluno Three' have learned the ropes now and come easily to hand with a spot of sinful bribery from the orchard and some encouragement in their own dialect: of the half dozen or so Franciscan friars on San Francesco del Deserto today, most come from the mountains of Friuli and speak Ladino.

The hand clipping of sheep is slow to all but the most practised of hands – especially if you're taking real care not to nick and cut the animal. Brother Silvio and I spent a whole day on the job. This is partly because rain stopped play (fleeces are best cut dry) and partly because the ewes, though only two years old, had never been shorn and were 'hidebound', their fleece compacted next to the skin like eggy felt. It normally occurs in older sheep but in this case it could be blamed on some mineral deficiency in their previous grazing. The lamb's wool was softer and denser but gritty where he had basked in sandy soil – fatal to mechanical clippers, which blunt in no time.

Since the Michiel family gave the island to the Franciscans in 1223, their fortune has ebbed and flowed. The name San Francesco del Deserto may derive from its abandonment for more than

'A knotted Franciscan cord can come in handy when leading members of a flock from one pasture to another'

twenty years during the 16th century, when plague and malaria took their toll. Its 15th-century cloister remains, in spite of Napoleon who laid waste to the monastery before handing it over (along with the city of Venice) to the Austrians, who used it as a powder store and magazine before Emperor Franz Joseph II gave it back to the Franciscans, who have been settled here since major restoration works in 1858.

A seamstress visits every couple of weeks and a few others arrive voluntarily to lend a hand about the place. The brothers take it in turns to cross to the island of Burano to buy their daily bread, collect the mail and fetch Diana the cook. Diana's transformation of vegetables, eggs and fruit taken straight from the immaculate walled kitchen garden into sauces,

bakes and salads is matched by no restaurant in Venice. The menu is supplemented by passing local fishermen who frequently drop off buckets full of flapping, squirming bounty from the lagoon, and an abundant surplus is given away to local people in need – as it always has been: Burano endured grinding poverty post-war, when boatloads of islanders subsisted by making their way daily to the Franciscans' refectory. This is remembered by many of the older Buranelli, who come frequently to Mass.

To maintain the island in its pristine condition, and to welcome a steady stream of visitors and guests in retreat, is exhausting. But the friars are tough, with an earthy sense of humour and they have their feet on the ground. Most of them had interesting lives before taking vows and, as members of a sort of spiritual Foreign Legion, several have spent time away on arduous missions around the world.

The islands of Burano and Mazzorbo seem tranquil enough after Venice but San Francesco del Deserto is yet another world. One comes away uplifted and strangely empowered by the forces there: whenever bad weather is forecast, a bell is rung in the tower, and prayers are said to keep the island safe. Last summer a hailstorm devastated the nearby mainland and outlying islands, but the monastery remained unscathed.

Virginia Ironside
on the joys of boring for Britain

Granny Annexe

A great plus to being old is that you can bore for Britain. Indeed, it's almost expected of you. You find some poor young person, then you pin him to a wall with an Ancient Mariner's skinny hand, fix him with your glittering eye, and begin.

'When I was young,' you say, 'we didn't have computers, we had things called typewriters – you put the paper in, rolled it up, and at the end of a line – ting! And we didn't have photocopiers either, oh no. We got these huge bits of waxed paper and typed on them and if we made a mistake we had to correct them with little red spots of liquid ... and when I was a child I had to go to the fishmongers and collect huge slabs of ice to break up and put in our icebox, we didn't have fridges then, and when I was a girl, a man would come round every evening on a bicycle holding a light at the end of a stick to light up the gas street-lamps ... I remember the days when the only fruit for sale were oranges and apples, and you had to buy your olive oil at the chemist. Garlic was unheard of – and there were no microwaves ...

'You won't believe this, but there were things called bus conductors in those days, and they punched little coloured tickets ... and no mobile phones or even answering machines. If we wanted a call we just had to stay in and wait for it.'

If, at this point, the young person starts to look a bit bored, it's quite possible to embroider the truth to keep his attention. 'Oh yes, it was tough flying a Sopwith Camel in the war,' you can continue, doggedly. 'I was in the Women's Corps and the first night I crashed into No Man's Land' (you've got his attention back now) 'and it was there that I ate my first roast rat. Tasted rather of human flesh, but that's another story.'

The young seem to think of the past as a totally other country, and have no concept of the difference between the First and Second World Wars, nor women's role in either. I sometimes feel I could claim to have been at the Battle of Hastings, leading a troop of archers, and boast that I once, when I was a very, very young girl, actually shook Joan of Arc's hand, and the innocent faces of the young would still be gawping up at me, thinking, 'She must be jolly old ... but still, it's amazing ...'

Another topic with which you can bore people to death now you're old is ailments. There is nothing that goes on longer than an 'organ recital'.

Now when I go to a party, I don't say 'And do tell me, what do you do?', I say 'And do tell me – what's wrong with you?'

'You remembered!'

I only have to see an old gent sitting with a walking frame propped up beside him and I'm there, settling in for a good old natter about the state of his health, and what he makes of hospitals and does he think mixed wards are a good idea.

And I only have to hear the word 'pills' whispered across a cocktail party on the other side of the room and, with the speed of a character from a Bugs Bunny cartoon, I've joined the group and started to discuss the merits and demerits of glucosamine sulphate and fish-oils and whatever else is on the agenda.

'It was in No Man's Land that I ate my first roast rat. Tasted rather of human flesh – but that's another story'

Someone started telling me about her bad back the other day and then, half-way through the most fascinating story about discs and bone degeneration, she suddenly broke off apologetically saying she must be boring me. 'Boring me?' I said. 'Not at all. What else would we be talking about? The state of the Middle East? Will the internet mean the end of books as we know them? Those topics aren't for me. Big yawn. You had got, I think, to the fifth vertebrae going north to south down the spine. Please continue. I am all ears. And talking of ears ...'

And if anyone gets bored with your list of ailments, throw in a joke. Like the one about the Australian nurse who told an old lady that she would be 'going home today' and her patient broke into racking sobs. (...Try saying it.)

A Genius Gift...

AQUILA *Children's Magazine* celebrates its 25th birthday!

Established in 1993, AQUILA was originally developed for gifted children, but over the years its unique mix of facts and fun has made it an obvious favourite with thousands of families around the world. Much of AQUILA's founding spirit remains and its ethos hasn't changed a dot: we asked Editor Freya Hardy how it has managed to stay so fresh and relevant? She explains: "The world may have changed quite a lot over the last 25 years but the kind of children who love AQUILA have not! They are a switched-on bunch – well informed and eager to learn, so as long as our content is colourful, interesting, intelligent and fun, it remains relevant and engaging to our discerning audience".

"Humour is essential ..."

Freya has been AQUILA's Editor for 5 years now, and as a mother of 9-year-old twins she is well placed to make sure it keeps up with the times "The magazine has thrived on being an independent publication – rather than following fads or current trends, we set our own agenda with humour as an essential ingredient; we know it helps children retain information, and to feel part of our special gang! That's what AQUILA really is – a club for kids who are creative, curious and up for a challenge".

One of the best parts of Freya's job is the feedback she gets from the readers. "There's the boy who was so inspired by our interview with a coracle maker that he made his own boat and sailed it down a river! Another child was inspired to make our *Dig for Victory* garden with his granddad, and ended up learning all about his experiences during World War II. We get great letters from kids every day, and every one of them makes us feel privileged to be able to come to work and do this job!"

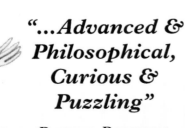

"...Advanced & Philosophical, Curious & Puzzling"

RICHARD ROBINSON
BRIGHTON SCIENCE FESTIVAL

DECEMBER 2018

Big ideas for inquisitive kids

Charles Dickens

Celebrating **25** Years of Facts & Fun!

Charles Dickens

In the December issue, AQUILA looks at the life and times of the world's first literary superstar: writer, actor and anti-poverty campaigner: Mr Charles John Huffam Dickens himself!

AQUILA's monthly topics introduce 8 – 12 year-olds to a thought-provoking mix of Science, Arts and General Knowledge. Diverse topics planned for 2019:

SUPERVOLCANO
REAL-WORLD MATHS
CURIOUS CATS
LEONARDO DA VINCI

TIME TRAVEL
ALEXANDER THE GREAT
SCIENCE OF HAPPINESS
GLORIOUS GEORGIANS

Subscriptions from £30. Welcome pack and gift message with first copy. Subscribe online or call 01323 431313 9-4 weekdays.

www.AQUILA.co.uk

Marcellina's last stand

Should a diva go out with a bang or a whimper? International mezzo *Anne Howells* chose to make a low-key exit. Pity about the clothes, though …

I now know what happens to Carmen when she gets old – she becomes Figaro's mother.

On the last night of my operatic career I sat in my dressing-room in Barcelona's shiny new Liceu Opera House and my reflection looked back at me in the mirror. I had had enough. Marcellina's vile fake fur and rigid hair-do had followed me from Paris to Tel Aviv to Barcelona. I had reached the point where I feared that if I ever heard those scurrying bars that open the overture to *Le Nozze di Figaro* once more, I would bring back my lunch. But it was more than custom that was staling my infinite variety – I was becoming *Disgustada y Furiosa* of Tunbridge Wells over the sheer awfulness of some 'innovative' productions. I was becoming an anachronism in a fake fur.

The conductor that evening was a pleasant Spaniard whose name now escapes me. He had called in to my dressing-room as part of his rounds before curtain-up.

'You?' he asked in surprise, 'tonight? … feeneesh?'

'Yes,' I said. 'Tonight. Feeneesh. Terminado.'

There are those whose retirement comes in well-publicised chunks: 'last operatic performance by …', 'last recital by …', 'last Oratorio performance by …' But one of my heroines was the wonderful English mezzo, Josephine Veasey, who simply invited colleagues back to her dressing-room for a drink after a performance and said, 'I'm retiring tonight.' That impressed me and I followed her example.

How can anything as sublime as Mozart's *Figaro* ever pall, you might ask. Believe me, it can and did. I had performed all the roles my voice was equipped for and Marcellina had been on my tail for many years before she finally caught up with me.

If you are lucky enough to be born with the sort of voice that has the penetration of a Black & Decker drill, the 'old bat' roles await – by composers like Janacek. But if you have a medium-weight voice, there's nowhere to go but Marcellina. And if the venues and the money are good, you'll probably say yes. My agent was American and practical. 'Somebody's godda pick up the goddam cheque – why not you?'

So you pack your bags and get yourself to Tel Aviv/Brussels/ Los Angeles etc.

'If you have a voice with the penetration of a Black & Decker drill the "old bat" roles await. But if you have a medium-weight voice, there's nowhere to go but Marcellina…'

'Am I too vain to wear frumpy costumes? In a traditional production at the Bastille I wore such a sexy creation that it attracted the attentions of the stage crew'

I am told that you cannot ruin Mozart but I have to tell you that I have worked with directors who have come very close to achieving just that. Peter Hall, the finest director I ever worked with, said that 'theatre should not be about innovation for its own sake – it should be about the obvious – well done.' Well, innovation in opera is certainly alive and well and for some reason poor *Figaro* and *Don Giovanni* seem to invite the worst directorial excesses – usually from directors with French or German names, but not always.

The production in Barcelona was one I had already performed in Tel Aviv and in Paris at the Théâtre des Champs Elysées. It seemed to be set in the Thirties but my costume was Fifties for some reason, and my hated fake-fur coat went with a short, tight tweed skirt and striped silk blouse. I have always been of the opinion that what people wear dictates the way they move and so consequently had something to say about flinging myself onto a mattress on the floor and lounging at Bartolo's feet while he sang his aria.

How, I wanted to know, would a woman of a certain age and wearing a tight skirt then rise to her feet? This was brushed aside and I could feel myself being branded as a Tory Home Counties Reactionary Matron – or the more cosmopolitan equivalent. As is often the case in such a production, people wearing boots and shoes jumped all over the furniture and the beds, and the last scene was festooned with bare light bulbs which hung at intervals of a couple of feet apart and just stopped short of brushing the stage. Long lengths of flex disappeared into the flies. I was mystified but the French declared that the effect was

'*génial...extraordinaire*'. They were equally enthusiastic about the priest, Don Basilio, costumed in ecclesiastical red which opened down the front to reveal stockings, suspenders and a garter belt – but then they were French.

Am I too vain to wear frumpy costumes? In this case, almost certainly. However, as Marcellina in a traditional production at the Bastille in Paris I wore such a beautiful and sexy creation in black lace that it attracted the attentions of the stage crew, and at La Monnaie in Brussels I wore a tight black skirt with satin bustier, black lace 'body' underneath and black stockings with stilettos. A stunning little hat with veil topped it all off. I looked like Joan Crawford on her way to poisoning a rival at a cocktail party. The Figaro in question quietly confessed to me that it was the seamed black stockings that had made him completely re-think his relationship with his mother...

A further feature of the Brussels production was that Marcellina's aria had been included. Most of the role lies well within the mezzo range, but the first Marcellina must have grabbed Mozart in rehearsal and said 'Look – how about writing an aria that no mezzo with her larynx in the right place can possibly sing? A good third higher than the rest of the role? Wouldn't that be good?'

This aria is cut more often than not – it's not a great aria anyway and Mozart probably wrote it on the bus going home – but Antonio Pappano had decided to include it at La Monnaie and as this occurs in the last and fourth act, I had plenty of time during the first three acts in which to look forward to it and to chew my nails down to the elbow with fright.

A lot of my colleagues and friends (and especially my agent, who liked being paid) have told me that I 'got out' too soon and they could be right – but it's so much better than staying on and getting reviews that include the words 'unfortunately, Anne Howells in the role of ...' An older colleague had once told me, 'It's the breath that goes first, Annie,' and when I noticed that my pre-performance warm-up was taking longer, I knew the writing was on the wall.

Do I miss performing? Not in the least. Keeping 'the voice' up to international performance pitch can be a nightmare. But I do miss my colleagues and the gossip in the canteen ... that's another story for another day.

Facing the Moment of Truth

When *Trader Faulkner* was cast as a matador, he took 'the Method' seriously enough to have a go at the real thing …

The well-known director Peter Hall once rang me. 'I'm considering a play called *Bullfight*,' he said, 'and you'd be right for the lead matador.' Peter then went to Stratford and the project was shelved, but not before I'd gone to Granada to research my character.

In Granada I was befriended by an old ex-matador called Rafael Fandila, who had lost his 'nuts' in a one-to-one with a deadly fighting bull many years before, and now gave lessons to young aspiring *toreros*. Morning after morning this poor fellow would limp towards me with a single bicycle wheel, its handlebars surmounted by a pair of viciously sharp bull's horns. Rafael showed me some of the many different passes with the *muleta*, that little piece of red cloth used to enrage the bull, including a very dangerous one where you have to swivel round on both knees as the animal charges you and, as he charges back, your cloth wipes his sweating snout. In no time I was hooked, and determined to give it a go with some tame beast like those with which I'd seen the street kids stylishly making their passes. Rafael eventually invited a crowd of his Granadin amigos to witness the progress of El Inglés. They sent me up rotten, claiming I'd cut a dash as a cabaret *torero* leaping about in a sequinned bullfighter's suit in a nightclub. Off they went into a huddle, which gave me time to nip off to get the box of Havana cigars I'd bought as a gift for Rafael, since he'd refused any payment. But when I presented them, I might have offered him those cheap little cigars called poop sticks. Was there anything I could offer him instead? 'Yes. We are all very impressed. You are a natural. I'll make you an offer. Are you a man true to his word?' 'Of course, try me.' By now the others had gathered round. We shook hands on it. 'You will cape a live bull. I will select. We can see you are ready. Or are you an English coward?'

Trader Faulkner performing in *Lorca*, an evocation of the playwright with music and dance, scripted and staged by Faulkner and first performed in 1970 with Ben Kingsley and Helen Mirren also in the cast

I decided to go for it. For the next week I practised, prayed and sweated drops of funk in case the wretched beast horned off my manhood. When the day came, I was kitted out in the grey outfit worn by novices. A 1930s Packard arrived at my *pensión* to collect me. From its boot protruded the handles of several swords with which I was expected to dispatch the beast. At the bullring Rafael introduced me to Manolo and Xavier, my two assistants. He told me I was to salute the President in his box and ask permission – '*permiso*'. The keys would then be thrown to me, I would throw them to Manolo, and he'd let the minotaur out.

I was so terrified that I barely remember entering the bullring. The trumpet blasted and the *toril* gate jammed a quarter of its way up. All I could see was a wet angry snout underneath and the animal impatient to get out. The trumpet blasted a second time, up shot the gate like a guillotine. I thought I was going to faint, and was overcome by a feeling of nausea. I closed my eyes, just conscious of the soft thud of hooves padding across the sand towards me. Closer and closer they came, and then stopped. I opened my eyes. There, in front of me, was a tiny little

> 'They sent me up rotten, claiming I'd cut a dash as a cabaret torero leaping about in a sequinned suit'

bull calf with two large oranges fixed on his nubby hornlets. He nuzzled me in the belly with his wet snout, blinked in the sun and lay down at my feet. For the first time in the annals of bullfighting, *toro* and *torero* were evenly matched.

Fifty years later I was lunching with friends in Arles at the Hotel Nord-Pinus, a favourite haunt of Picasso, Cocteau and many matador legends. 'Dead on five,' to quote García Lorca, I took my seat on the stone ledge of a vast ampitheatre, very relieved not to be in the ring where, in Caesar's time, thousands had cheered on gladiators, Christians and lions. As I watched, a gargantuan bull unseated the *rejoneador* Pablo Mendoza, who, mounted on horseback, was engaging his adversary with a long thin lance aimed at the bull's withers. Horse and rider were flung to the ground, but both got up unhurt. Pablo remounted, received another lance and placed it, before dismounting and executing his series of passes with the *muleta*. The kill was clean and quick. I've seen the best, and I never want to see another.

Tips for meanies

Garden snobs may recoil, but Meanies should embrace the pot marigold, *Calendula officinalis*. A dead-cheap substitute for expensive saffron in paella and risottos, it provides a similar flavour and colour. Just dry the petals in the microwave and grind up. The flowers can also be rubbed on bee stings and insect bites, having antibiotic properties, and if you grow them next to your tomatoes they deter pests.
JANE THYNNE

Memorial service

James Hughes-Onslow

Paul Scofield (1922-2008)

A host of luvvies swept over Westminster Bridge after Paul Scofield's memorial service. They were on their way to the Lyttelton Theatre where a galaxy of stars, including Ralph Fiennes, Diana Rigg, Robert Hardy, Peter Hall, John Hurt, Claire Bloom, Peter Brook, Nick Hytner, Donald Sinden, Anna Calder-Marshall and Samantha Bond gave a one and a half hour feast of memories of the great Shakespearean actor. Some stories were funny, some moving, some nostalgic but, as you would expect from such a distinguished ensemble, many of them theatrical knights and dames, their timing, however doddery they pretended to be, was immaculate.

The service was held at St Margaret's, Westminster. Eileen Atkins read from T S Eliot's 'Little Gidding', Seamus Heaney, from *Boewulf* and Sir Ian McKellen from St John: 'In the beginning was the Word, and the Word was with God.' Scofield's son, Martin, read from *Henry VI, Part III*, and his widow, Joy Parker, read from Thomas Hardy's 'Afterwards'.

Hymns included 'The Lord's My Shepherd' and 'Now Thank We All Our God'. The choir sang 'Mannin Veen' and 'The Cloud-capped Towers' by Vaughan Williams, and the 'Lacrymosa' from Mozart's *Requiem*, and the organist played Bach's 'Prelude and Fugue in C minor'.

The address was given by Simon Callow who began with Scofield's emergence as an actor: 'Discovering at an early age that his scholastic gifts were meagre, he fell with inexpressible relief on acting for which his gift was instantly apparent,' said Callow. 'Scofield was not a boastful man, and not given to hyperbole, so we may believe him when he says that his thirteen-year-old Juliet was "a sensation".'

Callow spoke about Scofield's 'great artistic partnership' with Peter Brook,

Scofield as Thomas More in *A Man For All Seasons*

who taught him that he must 'connect with the thoughts of the character and ultimately those of the author: how to lay what he called the groundwork of the character'. His life's work was to make the audience 'forget the art of acting – above all, he wanted them to forget about him', he said.

The address also covered Scofield's extraordinary sense of privacy, his love of his family, dogs, horses and gardening, and his avoidance of the culture of celebrity: 'The more the acclaim, the further he withdrew from the social world, immersing himself ever deeper in his private life. He was a countryman by temperament; his horse, his dog, his garden, his reading, his wife, his children: these absorbed him deeply and renewed him. As Eliot says in Scofield's favourite poem, "a condition of complete simplicity/ (costing not less than everything)". On horseback, or riding across the Downs for hours on end alone or with his hounds: it is an unexpected image for an actor. But Scofield was nothing if not his own man.'

Is there a doctor on the bus?

Although *Francis King* never fulfilled his childhood ambition to become a doctor, his interest in medical matters has stood the test of time

Do children still play Doctors and Nurses? Probably not – unless in a computer version. That was my favourite game when I was six, and eighty years later I still continue to play it. When a visitor to my childhood home once asked me 'What do you want to be when you grow up?', I replied, without a moment's hesitation, 'A doctor.' My father – perhaps because he had spent so much money on Swiss sanatoria in a futile attempt to be cured of the TB that eventually killed him at an early age – at once firmly intervened: 'Certainly not.' From this opposition he never deviated; and since paternal authority and filial piety were both far stronger then than now, I abandoned any thought of entering the medical profession but consoled myself by still secretly pretending to myself that I belonged to it.

One of my neighbours is, according to her own accounts, a prey to an astonishing variety of ailments. If another (male) neighbour happens to be chatting to me as she emerges from her house, he at once abandons me – 'Oh, God, there's that ghastly woman! I avoid her like the plague.' But I, in my doctor's role, am delighted to see her. I am fascinated by whatever is her symptom of the day, the more abstruse the better. I am flattered when she asks me 'Do you think it normal that I itch so much?'

I have now convinced myself that I have acquired the almost supernatural diagnostic powers once ascribed to Lord Horder, who within five minutes knew exactly what was wrong with a patient without all the elaborate and expensive tests now available to even the humblest of practitioners.

The way in which so many doctors today lack such diagnostic powers was confirmed for me when I visited a GP about an agonisingly swollen foot. 'I think I've got gout.' There was no thinking about it, I was sure. She examined the foot with evident distaste. 'That's not gout. That's cellulitis.' She then dashed off a prescription for an antibiotic. Eighteen months later I was back with the foot again agonisingly swollen. 'I'm afraid my cellulitis has returned.' 'That's not cellulitis. That's gout.' Her tone was the same withering one on both occasions.

Doctors rarely welcome self-diagnoses.

> '**I am convinced that I have the almost supernatural diagnostic powers once ascribed to Lord Horder, who within five minutes knew exactly what was wrong**'

Four years ago, having suddenly lost much of my peripheral vision, I took myself off to my nearest hospital. 'I have a detached retina,' I told the doctor. After he and a colleague had examined me, he said firmly: 'No, there's no sign of a detached retina. I'm afraid you must have had a stroke.' Then he asked in far from friendly voice: 'Are you by any chance a medical journalist?' To my shame, my diagnostic intuition had for once failed me.

Not long ago I was travelling on a bus when suddenly a female passenger at the rear became violently ill. The bus-driver did not shout 'Is there a doctor on the bus?', but in a foreign accent pleaded, 'Can anyone please help?' I began to struggle to my feet when a young man announced, 'I'm a nurse,' jumped up and scuttled down the bus to the still-vomiting woman. Meanwhile the bus-driver was telephoning for an ambulance and a bus replacement.

I felt a resentment towards this creature who had so brutally usurped my starring role in the drama. I was therefore not best pleased when he came across and stood beside me while we all waited at the bus-stop.

'I think that poor thing must have eaten something,' he said.

I shook my head 'No, I don't think so.' I did not attempt to conceal my scorn for his diagnosis. 'It's this norovirus that's been sweeping London. Projectile vomiting,' I added. 'The distinguishing symptom.'

'Yes, yes. That must be it, doctor. Of course.'

He now gazed at me with a new respect.

What a happy day, a day to be remembered! It was as though an actor known for his playing of the Gravedigger in *Hamlet* had suddenly been mistaken for a real-life gravedigger.

Music

Richard Osborne on the multi-talented André Previn

Not many composers have an opera première in their eightieth year. There was Verdi, of course. And now there's another. In May, André Previn's *Brief Encounter* opened in Houston.

Previn was eighty in April and to mark the occasion BBC Four screened an hour-long documentary on him. It was called *All the Right Notes*, taken from the moment in the immortal TV sketch when Eric Morecambe seizes Mr Preview by the lapels and announces, 'I'm playing all the right notes but not *necessarily* in the right order.'

The documentary began in Berlin with the five-year-old André being taken to a Furtwängler Brahms concert that so excited him he ran up a fever. The influence clearly lingered. One of the greatest performances I ever heard of the Brahms *Requiem* was conducted by Previn.

In 1938 the Previns fled to Paris and thence to LA where André's barrister father had a rough time trying to pass the California Bar Exam whilst his *Wunderkind* jazz-piano-playing son was learning English in the movie houses and Selma Avenue Grammar School. Word gets round in Hollywood. At the age of seventeen he was called in to help heart-throb pianist José Iturbi who'd been signed for the comedy *Holiday in Mexico* with starlet Jane Powell but couldn't improvise a jazzed-up 'Three Blind Mice' for her delectation. Previn not only dashed off the variations, he played and orchestrated them as well. He was a made man.

Previn's memoir about his life in Hollywood, *No Minor Chords*, is the funniest of all musical autobiographies. If you've read it, you'll understand Tom Stoppard's delight in Previn as a man who never misses a jest or a hidden irony.

There's a scene in the book that could come straight from a Stoppard script. Young André is walking to a gig at Pickfair, the palatial home of Mary Pickford and Douglas Fairbanks, when a limo draws up and he's offered a lift. Inside is MGM boss LB Mayer and a lickspittle called Lester. At one point the lickspittle says, 'I sure hope it

'Previn learned the conducting trade writing music and trying it out on the Hollywood studio orchestras. As a conductor-arranger there was no one to touch him'

doesn't rain, LB, and spoil the garden party.' Mayer looks out of the window, then says in a dark voice, 'They wouldn't dare.' As Previn admits, 'I never figured out who "they" were.'

Previn learned the conducting trade writing music and trying it out on the fabled Hollywood studio orchestras. As a conductor-arranger, says composer John Williams, there was no one to touch him. Among his triumphs were the movies of *Gigi* and *My Fair Lady*. And it was *My Fair Lady* that Previn the jazz pianist turned to for a stunning disc of improvisations which he did with Shelly Manne and Leroy Vinnegar, the first jazz LP to sell more than a million copies.

His decision to leave Hollywood in the mid-Sixties shocked a community that never really forgave him. He began his new life as Barbirolli's successor in Houston (on Barbirolli's recommendation, I'm told). In 1968 he came to London to take over the LSO. Which is where the BBC Four documentary briefly fell apart, as the talking heads began pedalling the agenda-driven half-truths about the past that are part-and-parcel of the contemporary media's view of classical music.

'In 1968,' droned the voice-over, 'the LSO was an all-male [unacceptable], conservative [dread word] orchestra looking for a new injection of life.' This was largely untrue but worse followed. Previn was 'young and sexy', raved conductor Charles Hazlewood, the BBC's resident purveyor of claptrap about the profession he purports to represent. Previn may have had 'little real experience' alleged Hazlewood (I wonder what André thought when he heard that) but he turned the culture round at a time when classical music was like 'a maiden aunt sitting in the front parlour who no one wants to talk to'. Poppycock. London in the 1960s was the vibrant hub of the world's classical concert and recording business and the LSO was its sleekest and most dynamic ensemble – thanks in part to its time with the great Pierre Monteux, Previn's own former conducting guru.

It was the perfect orchestra for Previn and he led it in unexpected ways, not least by programming many of the masterworks of English music by Vaughan Williams and others he'd fallen in love with as a teenager in LA in the 1940s.

I remember Previn saying on *Desert Islands Discs* how he knew the shape and feel of the English countryside long before he saw it simply by knowing the Elgar Cello Concerto. That's quite an insight. But as John Williams says, this is some musician and some mind: a truly glistening intellect.

'What do you recommend to go with this model of phone?'

Unwrecked England

Hanham Court Gardens, Gloucestershire
Candida Lycett Green

On the eastern outskirts of Bristol, where villages have been swallowed up by the ever expanding city, there is a magical pocket of timeless pastoral England caught between Keynsham and Kingswood. It has miraculously escaped the hand of the planner and developer and is now a conservation area. Hanham Court lies in its midst.

Approaching from Willsbridge, past the handsome mill and age-old Queen's Head pub where the ghosts of Roman soldiers lurk, the villas begin to fade away into fields as you descend the hill down Court Farm Road. On a shady bend, an unassuming drive leads towards the settled group of tithe barn and church huddled together with the ancient gabled house of layered centuries. All is harmonious and built of the same mauve brown pennant stone. The buildings once belonged to the abbots of Keynsham Abbey, but soon after the Dissolution Hanham became the country estate of the Creswicke family, who were Mayors of Bristol for nearly four hundred years.

A small door set into the great oak gates under the entrance arch leads, as

Left: Hanham Court, below: The garden at Hanham sailing through the fields

though you were Alice in Wonderland, into another world. It is gloriously unexpected. A promontory – like the prow of a gigantic liner carrying the garden with it – sails above ancient fields and tumpy hills, commanding a spectacular view over the Avon valley towards Somerset. Trains bound for the West Country or London occasionally streak like lightning across the middle distance on an embankment beyond the unseen looping river below. Ferry Road

> ### 'Nothing succeeds like excess, and the garden is one of the most extravagantly romantic and imaginative in the land'

skirts the fields to the west, dipping down a steeply-wooded slope to The Old Lock and Weir Inn at Hanham Mill.

The garden designers Julian and Isabel Bannerman came here in 1993 and found a long-abandoned garden whose faded vestiges had almost disappeared. Nothing succeeds like excess, and today the garden has been rendered one of the most

extravagantly romantic and imaginative in the land. From nothing, yew trees cut like giant skittles have sprung up; armies of blood-red lilies mix with deep orange sunflowers, and then, suddenly, the brightest, most electric-blue explosion of giant eight-foot-high delphiniums, like some extraordinary firework display, ephemeral and fantastic. Grand golden ironwork gates lead through to a gigantic spreading walnut tree and mown paths entice you to unknown places. Green oak balustrades top the ancient retaining garden walls, all hovering high above the dipping valley. Paths lead down towards the liner's prow, and, walking between box hedges holding back a voluptuous abundance of old roses, lilies, mock orange, peonies and crambe, you feel as though you are on the ship's deck. A grotto beside the rectangular pool drips water over tufa, giant pots spill with lilies, bulls' heads spew water from their mouths, myriad obelisks foam with clouds of Sander's White roses, a gothic tree-house with wooden fishtail tiles hangs high in the yew. And always there are glimpses of the jumbled mauve stone house with its conical-hatted Tudor tower.

You can walk down from the prow and through an oak-pedimented doorway to follow a winding path through long grass to the top of the far hill. There, on the other side, is the sad and mountainous Fry's chocolate factory stranded beside the spread-eagled industrial landscape of Keynsham. Then you can return to the house up the shady glade past martagon lilies, stepped ponds, giant gunnera and tree ferns. At the top, an amazing cascade tumbles over rocks and tufa, beside a stumpery set with foxgloves and ferns, and into a pool, where a high jet of water holds up a dancing golden crown as though by magic.

Richard and Julia Boissevain moved to Hanham Court in 2015 and are restoring/preserving the gardens; for opening times and events see website: www.hanhamcourtgardens.co.uk

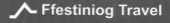

Dame Margot's surprise

In 1955 *Margot Hewitt* and her husband John swapped their sensible and predictable GPO jobs in Skegness for a once-in-a-lifetime opportunity in London

I n 1951, my husband John and I got married in Lincolnshire and spent our honeymoon in London. I had previously written to Margot Fonteyn asking if we could see her for a few moments after the performance of *Swan Lake* which we were seeing during our stay. She replied with a friendly letter inviting us to meet her backstage. I probably shouldn't say this, but her performance and the anticipation of meeting her was the highlight of my honeymoon.

For the next four years I wrote to her from time to time, and whenever she was touring America I sent flowers for opening nights. She always replied and when John and I celebrated wedding anniversaries in London we would meet her for a chat after she performed.

In the summer of '55 we received a letter saying she was getting married to Dr Roberto Arias, who was later to become the Panamanian Ambassador. When they bought a house in Knightsbridge she asked whether we would like to come and work for them as live-in housekeeper, personal maid, chauffeur and butler. I replied straight away: 'When do you want us?' and after Christmas our new life began. Friends and colleagues told us we were mad to give up our safe, pensionable jobs at the GPO, where we had both worked since leaving school.

John could drive and I'd done some part-time waitressing. I could also sew, iron and arrange flowers, and what I lacked in experience I made up for in determination and devotion.

With Dame Margot's help, John soon knew his way around London blindfolded and adored driving the Mercedes. His duties involved taking Margot to and from ballet class every day except Sunday, and then changing uniforms to serve lunch, dinner and supper. He

Left to right: John Hewitt, Margot Hewitt, Roberto Arias and Margot Fonteyn

would also ferry Dr Arias to meetings, functions and the airport.

One of my jobs was to keep all Margot's clothes in order (the first time I had to press one of her Dior creations I was terrified) and make sure each outfit was

> '**Every time she danced there were so many bouquets that John had to hire a taxi just to transport them home**'

ready with matching shoes and bag. I also oversaw the laundry and washed all her silk underwear by hand.

Every time she danced there were so many bouquets that John had to hire a taxi just to transport them home. Arranging them the next morning took hours, and I was grateful for the ones in baskets which needed no attention.

Tito (Roberto) and Margot had to entertain all the other ambassadors and their wives. The wives would come for afternoon tea in groups of three or four whenever they could be slotted in to Margot's busy life. Margot and Tito also gave dinner parties at their home. These were held after the performances, so everyone arrived at about midnight. It was easier to have lots of guests at once and Margot would often invite members of the Royal Ballet, film stars, actors and actresses as well as ambassadors, politicians and their wives. This mixture worked wonderfully and the parties were always very successful. We never got to bed before 3.00am and then were up again at 7.00 to serve breakfast at 8.00. It was hard work but we loved every minute of it.

In 1956 Danny Kaye came to London to appear at the Palladium. I mentioned my admiration for him to Dame Margot and asked if she would be seeing him. She told me that she wasn't sure, and I thought no more about it.

A big party was arranged and to my surprise I was told to 'rest' that afternoon so that I would be nice and fresh for the evening. After collecting Margot from the theatre, John was busy, stationed by the door, taking coats and serving drinks. He was used to doing quick changes from chauffeur's uniform to butler's to waiter's. Being rather shy I always kept well in the background, and so was in the kitchen with the cook and the ladies who came in to do the washing up when John rushed in and asked me to help him with the serving. I panicked. 'No! I'm not going in there! I couldn't.'

'Please, pet,' he begged, 'just bring the ice bucket for me – it's like Paddington Station down there.'

So I followed John down the corridor and right at the end I could see Margot

'So when does the feeling kick in?'

talking to a very tall, red-haired gentleman who had his back to us. As I got closer, Margot said, 'Oh, Danny, there's someone here who's dying to meet you.'

He turned. It was Him. My legs turned to jelly. I dropped the ice bucket, and ice cubes scattered everywhere. I turned and started to run but was restrained by a hand on my shoulder.

'Where do you think you're going?' said the star of the most successful season the London Palladium had ever had.

'B-b-back t-t-to the kitchen.'

'Then I'm coming with you.'

So the two of us returned to the kitchen, him clutching the ice bucket and there we stayed for at least an hour, – myself, John, the cook and the two

'It was a cold night. He pulled open the oven door, spun round and warmed his bottom, saying, "Gee, my ass is cold!"'

washer-up ladies, slack-jawed and sudsy in the midst of washing glasses. He put us all at ease right away. It was a very cold night and, pulling open the oven door, he spun around and warmed his bottom in the oven, saying 'Gee, my ass is cold!'

We were mesmerised. I wish I could remember what he talked about, but he could have read off a sauce bottle and it would have been magic. Eventually, Margot came in to gently remind him that he was the guest of honour and he'd better come right back in and talk to some of her other guests.

A few days later John and I, the cook, the ladies who washed up, and the cleaner, her husband and son were sent the best tickets in the house for Danny's show. We were picked up and brought home by chauffeured car and entertained afterwards in his dressing room. We were on cloud nine for days afterwards.

John of course was 'in' on the whole plan and received a compliment from Danny who said, 'John, you're a quicker costume-change-artist than I am.' What a lovely man. What a star.

I have no idea whether Mr Bercow is any use as Speaker of the House of Commons: what I can't stand about him is that he turns up for work looking like a cross between a bank clerk and an old-fashioned school master. I knew his predecessor would be no good when he refused to wear the full-bottomed wig that goes with the job, but Mr Bercow has gone much further, dispensing with the gaiters, silver-buttoned black jacket and the bit of lace about the neck on the self-indulgent grounds that they 'aren't me', but condescending to wear some kind of academic gown. What a very dull dog he must be – and impractical, too.

I feel passionately about uniforms, whether formal (nuns' habits, judges in full regalia, red-coated Chelsea pensioners) or informal (farmers' tweeds, a literary man's crumpled cords). Part of my enthusiasm is aesthetic, in that they lend colour and variety to an increasingly drab male world in which everyone wears grey business suits or black T-shirts and trainers. But there's more to it than that. Most of our lives are spent at work: all jobs involve a degree of acting and make-believe, and as often as not we find ourselves feigning enthusiasm, indignation, hilarity, rage etc. A uniform not only makes it easier for us to play the parts expected of us, but for others to interact with us in turn (a bank manager who rose from behind his desk wearing sandals, shorts and a string vest would not inspire confidence). Uniforms are useful as well as decorative, and the sooner Mr Bercow mends his ways, the better.

JEREMY LEWIS

Profitable Wonders by *James Le Fanu*

The eloquence of eyes

The most difficult of all scientific propositions to come to terms with is that the three-dimensional world we inhabit is not as it seems 'out there' but is created by the electrical activity inside our brains. Yet it must be so, for our brains, hidden away within the dark recesses of the skull, can have no contact with, no direct knowledge of that objective world other than through the senses – and as we close off each in turn, shut our eyes, block the ears, pinch the nose, so the colours, sounds and smells of the world are extinguished.

Further, and this is yet more difficult to credit, while we have the overwhelming impression that the greenness of the trees and the blueness of the sky are streaming through our eyes as through an open window, yet the particles of light impacting on the retina are colourless, just as the waves of sound impacting on the eardrum are silent and scent molecules have no smell. They are all invisible, weightless subatomic particles of matter travelling through space. It is the brain that impresses the colours, sounds and smells upon them. 'For the light rays, to speak properly, are not coloured,' wrote the great Isaac Newton in his *Treatise on Opticks*; 'in them there is nothing else than a certain Power and Disposition to stir up a Sensation of this or that Colour.'

More than three centuries on we are no more reconciled to this extraordinary proposition, made more extraordinary still by the recent revelations of neuroscience that the image of the world 'out there' is not, as commonly supposed, impressed on the visual cortex as on a photographic plate. Rather the brain fragments it, like an exploding firework, into thirty or more 'maps' of electrical activity without the slightest hint how they might translate into that subjective awareness of colour, movement, position and so on – nor how they might be re-

'We have the overwhelming impression that the greenness of the trees and the blueness of the sky are streaming through our eyes, yet the particles of light are colourless'

integrated back into a unified, coherent perception of the ever-changing external world. This, for obvious reasons, has become known as the Humpty-Dumpty dilemma: 'That image obviously must be reassembled,' writes David Hubel, past winner of the Nobel Prize for his experimental investigation of vision, 'but where and how we have no idea.'

And if there is so much more to seeing than 'meets the eye', so too there is vastly more to the eyes than seeing – in their parallel function as the 'windows of the soul', permitting others to divine our innermost thoughts and intentions.

The eye conveys more eloquently than words ever can (if at times unwittingly) our 'true' feelings, whether smiling or indifferent, bewitched or hostile, fearful or apologetic.

The most eloquent eyes in literature belong to Madame Bovary. Julian Barnes in his book *Flaubert's Parrot* takes issue with Dr Enid Starkie, erstwhile Emeritus Reader in French literature at Oxford, for criticising Flaubert for 'not building up his characters, as did Balzac, by objective external description', rather, she claims, Flaubert is apparently 'so careless' that at different times he gives Emma variously 'brown', 'deep black' and 'blue' eyes.

On the contrary, argues Barnes, Flaubert's kaleidoscope of colour is the mark of his genius in his attention to detail in portraying the eyes of a tragic adulteress – as shown in just one of several passages: 'They were black when she was in shadow and dark blue in full daylight; they seemed to contain layer upon layer of colours which were thicker in hue deep down, and became lighter towards the enamel-like surface.'

'I know it's annoying – but I like to post pictures of my food on Facebook'

words (WERDS) *words. n.*

Drum and base...

A young Viennese friend of mine, who can play the cadenza of Bruch's lovely violin concerto with amazing facility even before she has reached her tenth birthday, surprised me the other day by telling me that she has decided to lay the fiddle aside and to become an orchestral tympanist. God help her parents, is all I can say about that decision; when her set of drums arrive they will probably regret their decision to humour her.

Tympanist is an interesting word. It's from *tympan*, a drum, from Latin *tympanum*, of Greek origin, or directly from Old French *tympan, timpan*. It is a well-travelled word. The Spanish and Italian have *timpano*, the Old High German *timpana*, the Old Icelandic *timpan*. In Old English and early Middle English the word is found only in renderings of Biblical passages. There is a *tiompán* in Medieval Irish, but this a stringed instrument, not a drum.

There was another kind of *tympane*, described by many writers from the Tudors to Blount (of law dictionary fame) in the mid-17th century, to Dunglison, whose specialism was medical words, in the mid-19th. This *tympane* we now call

'wind'. It was considered a serious problem in the old days: Blount described it as an intestinal affliction in which 'the belly swells up, having great store of windy humours...which being smitten with the hand, makes a noise like a tabor.' Thomas Peynell, a 17th-century medical guru, said that the tympane was 'engendered by coldness of the stomake and lyver, not suffering man's meate or

> ## 'Queen Elizabeth was, it was said, a martyr to tympanic ventuosities'

drynke to be converted into good humours, but tourneth them into ventuosities.' Queen Elizabeth I was, it was said, a martyr to tympanic ventuosities, and freed herself from them in company without any sign of embarrassment. And yes, this *tympane* comes from the same Greek and Latin source as does the word for the orchestral kettledrum. I wonder why Oxford has omitted this elegant word.

The other day the postman brought me

a present from a friend: a revised edition of *The Slang Dictionary* published in London by Chatto & Windus in 1874.

The *chaunters* of London provided its author with a rich vein of secret words. They were sellers of broadside ballads, and they worked the streets until quite recently. I remember buying political ballads about Mrs Thatcher from one of them in Regent Street. Our author printed this interesting and, it would seem, genuine letter from a chaunter to a gentleman who took an interest in both his ballads and his welfare. He alludes in his letter to Thomas Drory, and to Sarah Chesham, two notorious murderers. I have given the meaning of the cant words in parenthesis.

'Dear Friend: Excuse the liberty, since I saw you last I have not earned a thick un [sovereign], we have had such a Dowry of Parny [a lot of rain] that it completely Stumped [bankrupt] Drory the Bossman's [farmer's] Patter [trial], therefore I am broke up and not having another friend but you I wish to know if you could lend me the price of a Gross of Tops, Dies, or Croaks [last dying speeches], which is seven shillings, of the above mentioned worthy and Sarah Chesham the Essex Burick [woman] for the poisoning job, they are both to be topped [hanged] at Springfield Sturaban [prison] on Tuesday next. I hope you will oblige me if you can, for it will be the means of putting a James [sovereign] in my Clye [pocket]. I will call at your Curser [house] on Sunday Evening for an answer, for I want a Speel on the Drum [spin on the coach – to be off to the country]. Hoping you and the family are All Square [all right]. I remain your obedient servant...'

The book includes appendices on back slang and rhyming slang, a glossary of gypsy words, short histories of cant and slang, and a fascinating account of the hieroglyphics used by vagabonds. Some of the etymologies are wrong, but no matter: this is a valuable work.

DIARMAID Ó MUIRITHE

ALCOHOL ADVISORY COMMITTEE

K.J.Lamb

'And this is our out-of-focus group'

EUROPE'S MOST LUXURIOUS RIVER CRUISES

SCENIC°
LUXURY CRUISES & TOURS

Save up to
£1,500
per couple

Plus
FREE
City Stay^
*on selected
2019 itineraries*

SUMMER SALE NOW ON – BOOK FROM ONLY £1,545 PER PERSON

Scenic set the precedent for river cruising on Europe's waters. Fine-dining, spacious suites and a butler for every guest promises a service that is second-to-none, and award-winning excursions provide unique insights into culture and tradition.

Choose one of our extraordinary 2019 river cruises, you can **save up to £1,500 per couple**. Plus enjoy a **FREE city stay or extension on selected itineraries** when you book before **30 November 2018**.

Choose from a range of itineraries throughout Europe and experience the ultimate in luxury river cruising from the comfort of our state-of-the-art Space-Ships whilst uncovering each destination in its purest form.

A personal butler service for every guest

2019 RIVER CRUISES

CRUISES	STD SUITE FROM (pp)	BALCONY SUITE FROM (pp)	ROYAL SUITE FROM (pp)
Iconic Danube	£1,545	£2,195	£3,740
Rhine Highlights	£1,695	£2,345	£3,890
Bordeaux Affair	£2,195	£2,595	£4,390
Jewels of Russia	£4,145	£5,040	£6,840

LIMITED AVAILABILITY ON STANDARD SUITES

Truly All-Inclusive

○ Flights from a **choice of up to 16 UK airports**, or a NO FLY option via Eurostar

○ **Unlimited premium branded drinks** and in-suite mini bar* throughout your cruise

○ **Five dining options, from casual to fine-dining** and a **private invitation** to Portobellos or L'Amour – fine-dining with wine pairing

○ **Award-winning** complimentary shore excursions and **Scenic only** events

○ **Largest suites** on Europe's rivers

○ **Exclusive** GPS devices for self-guided touring and use of our e-bikes

○ **Butler and laundry service** for all guests

○ **Complimentary** Wi-Fi

○ **All tipping**, transfers and taxes

Call our expert reservation consultants Mon-Fri 9am-5.30pm, Sat 9am-5pm & Sun 11am-3pm
Order a FREE brochure on 0808 301 7134 or visit scenic.co.uk

My aunt, Elizabeth Coxhead, novelist, biographer and journalist, had many claims to fame. Her novels, written over nearly forty years in the mid-20th century and including the mountaineering novel *One Green Bottle*, were well reviewed and received, and her biography of Lady Gregory – the co-founder with WB Yeats of Dublin's Abbey Theatre – earned a lasting niche in the literature of the Irish renaissance. But it may prove to be for one suggestion to her good friend Stella Gibbons that Elizabeth will be best remembered. In 1932, Elizabeth and Stella shared an office in the tiny editorial department of *The Lady*. Stella had passed the previous few months penning a highly comic, mock Gothic novel and had called it 'Curse God Farm'.

As soon as Elizabeth, just down from Oxford, read the manuscript, she recognised that Stella had written an enduring masterpiece. However the title struck her as off-key and she had the perfect alternative in her mental locker. Her father, my grandfather, was headmaster of the small grammar school at Hinckley, near Leicester, and the school then owned a farm, felicitously named 'Cold Comfort'. Like a tailored jacket, *Cold Comfort Farm* slipped effortlessly over the shoulders of Stella's novel. 'Curse God' was consigned to the literary dustbin.

Elizabeth told Stella: 'Cold Comfort deserves its name because tenant after tenant has gone bankrupt and had to emigrate to Canada.' Stella asked: 'Do you think that the present tenants would mind if I took the name?' Elizabeth replied: 'You may be quite certain they'll never read the book.'

Stella's novel – a parody of melodramatic novels of its time – concerns the doings of Flora Poste, a hyperactive young lady who invites herself to stay with the Starkadders, relations living on a ramshackle farm in a state of primeval dystopia. The family is presided over by Aunt Ada Doom, who seldom leaves her room but rules the tribe with a rod of iron, her life apparently blighted by having seen 'something nasty in the woodshed' at a tender age. Against massive odds, Flora sets herself the task of sorting them out and returning them to civilised normality.

In February last year, Hinckley

Cold Comfort Farm

Robert Chesshyre reveals how Stella Gibbons's comic masterpiece got its name

honoured Elizabeth Coxhead with a blue plaque on the walls of Hinckley Grammar School (now Mount Grace High School). Greg Drozdz, one of Hinckley's movers and shakers, had conceived the idea and contacted the family. On a blustery day, fifteen of Elizabeth's relations gathered at the Grammar School for a touching ceremony which had its own comic aspects that both Elizabeth and Stella would have greatly enjoyed.

A red cloth – bigger than a duster, but smaller than a table cloth – had been hung over the plaque, held in place by a pole perched on a step ladder. Speeches done, it fell to me to hold the

pole while the school 'premises manager' removed the steps. The cloth briefly and obstinately stayed put. Eventually, after some poking, it fell to reveal the plaque and its tribute to Elizabeth.

Cold Comfort Farm still exists and we went to have a look. Down an unmade track, a stone's throw from the site of the battle of Bosworth where the Wars of the Roses ended and Richard III perished for want of a horse, there it stood.

Never can an actor have been more naturally matched to a part than the bricks and mortar of Cold Comfort Farm are to its fictional re-embodiment. Chickens wandered outside the farmhouse, its battered stucco heavily pock-marked, while the red brick farmyard buildings looked as if they might crash to ruin in the next strong wind. Beneath a precarious green corrugated iron lean-to, there was even a woodshed – had anyone, we wondered, ever seen something nasty there?

If Stella Gibbons's novel is refilmed – there was a TV adaptation in 1995 – the producers need look no further. Little can have changed in the 75 years since my aunt knew the farm. One expected Adam Lambsbreath, the nonagenarian farm labourer who tends Cold Comfort's animals, to emerge at any moment from the tumbledown sheds driving Feckless and Aimless – so were the cows named –before him.

We were about to leave when a young woman, Ella McManus – who with her husband Christopher has owned Cold

Mind the age gap

Lizzie Enfield

Left: the yard at Cold Comfort Farm, Hinckley, something nasty in the woodshed? Above: Elizabeth Coxhead

Comfort Farm for the past two years – returned. She proved to be hospitality itself – light years away from the deranged Starkadder family of Stella's farm – and invited us in to the kitchen, where she produced a large bundle of documents she had found mouldering in an outhouse.

They were deeds and mortgages covering the history of the farm for over 300 years. As we carelessly leafed through them – I felt we should have been wearing white gloves – we glimpsed the twists and turns in the story of the real Cold Comfort Farm – loans raised, fields sold, deals done – that might themselves be worthy of a book. Outside, the wind had turned icy – cold comfort indeed.

Who knows how 'Curse God Farm' might have fared? I suspect not as memorably as 'Cold Comfort'. My hope now is that the indefatigable Greg Drozdz might persuade the Hinckley and Bosworth Council and the Hinckley Civic Society to commission another blue plaque: 'This Farm Inspired the Title of One of English Literature's Greatest Twentieth Century Comic Novels – 1932'. All that then is needed is another red cloth, another pole and another set of steps to give its unveiling the charm that enhanced my aunt's posthumous moment of recognition.

My father arrived for lunch the other day wearing a pinstripe shirt, jacket and tie.

'You look smart,' said my son, who was wearing jeans and a tracksuit top.

'Yes,' agreed my daughter (leggings and T-shirt). 'Are you going somewhere?'

'He always looks very dapper,' said I (jeans and T-shirt), introducing them to a word they had never heard before, albeit one they will probably never use.

'Dapper' cannot be readily applied to anyone under the age of fifty. You can't be dapper in a hoodie and jeans, so it won't be long before a dapper old man is a relic of the past, something to be read about in pre-nylon literature.

There is a dapper old man who is often to be found sitting in our local park. His wool trousers are pleated and belted, his felt hat looks as if he brushes it before each outing, even his walking stick looks elegant.

'Why does he always look so smart, just to sit on a bench?' My children find him a source of great mystery. My father would find him a kindred spirit.

When I worked full time in London, Dad would occasionally come up and meet me for lunch, arriving in the foyer of Broadcasting House resplendent in a three-piece suit, his shirt secured by gold cufflinks and his tie held in place with an opal tie-pin.

If I commented on his appearance, suspecting he had a more important engagement to run off to once he'd finished lunching with me, he would invariably reply, 'This is my going-to-London outfit.' A bit of extra effort, he thought, befitted a visit to the capital, whereas for cycling to the pub for lunch with retired friends, a jacket and tie would do.

Dad's gardening clothes are smarter than the clothes I wear to go to London. My mother is the same. Neither of them sees walking the dog as an excuse for tracksuit bottoms and T-shirts and they would no more dream of owning a pair of jeans than of wearing them.

The way we dress is one of the many ways in which we disappoint them.

'Is that your uniform?' This sounds like a question, but the way my mother

asks it makes it a damning indictment. My daughter shrugs; her school's uniform policy is merely 'no logos'.

'Have you had a day off work?' This to my husband, who arrives home from work wearing a shirt with a collar but no tie, and jeans.

My father robustly opposed my plans to apply for a place at Sussex University on the grounds that 'the lecturers wear jeans', as if anyone in such apparel could possibly impart anything worth knowing to anyone.

I now have a friend who is a professor at Sussex and adheres to my father's image of lecturers there. He is usually in jeans and an open-necked, often collarless, shirt. Up until Christmas, when his wife bought him one, he did not own a coat (by mid-January he had lost it). When a friend with the same shoe size offered him a pair of brogues he'd bought but decided he didn't like, the professor said 'But what will you wear?' The idea that someone should own more than one pair of shoes was as alien a concept to him as keeping an eye on his new coat. (He does, however, know a lot about Beckett.)

These days I work mainly from home and wear mainly pyjamas. I do have a wardrobe, which contains things I once wore when I worked at the BBC and the chance of running into Tony Blair and wanting to make a good impression was higher. They remain largely unworn.

Recently, though, I decided to let one particular outfit see the light of day and wore it to lunch with my parents.

'You look smart,' they both said immediately – and suspiciously. 'Are you going somewhere else later?'

'No,' I told them, noting my father's tie and neatly pressed trousers and my mothers tidy tweed skirt. 'I am having lunch with my parents.'

'Mercer once horsewhipped a servant for failing to draw a curtain, so allowing the sun to shine on a picture'

Hitler lookalike: Dornford Yates, 1933

What a bastard!
or 'The Ninety-Eight Steps'

Major C W Mercer, aka Dornford Yates, was a rotter and a reactionary. But, says *Derek Parker*, he wrote some rattling good yarns

I recently managed to find on the internet a copy of *Lower than Vermin*, which completes my set of all 32 books by Dornford Yates. I left it until the last moment before searching for it; after reading his two books of memoirs, *As Berry and I were Saying* and *B-Berry and I Look Back*, I wasn't at all sure I wanted to read it, his hanging and flogging views not really being my thing.

Yates – in real life Major C W Mercer – was one of the most popular authors of the first half of the last century. His first book came out in 1914 and his last novel in 1949. His success was mainly in two genres: he wrote a series of excellent thrillers – the eight 'Chandos' books – and eight 'Berry' books, which relate the adventures of a somewhat incestuous group of intermarried cousins. There is a miscellany of others, including collections of romantic short stories and a full-length fairy tale. Yates was by far the top-earning novelist of the '20s and '30s, even out-selling Somerset Maugham.

Reading and re-reading his books is an equivocal experience for a demi-semi-leftie such as myself. *Lower than Vermin* for instance (the phrase was Aneurin Bevan's, used to describe the idle rich) is really less a novel than a polemic dedicated to showing that the death of the British aristocracy would be the end of life as Mercer knew it. His whole philosophy was founded on a belief in the undeniable decency and faultlessness of the nobly born, and of their right to rule. 'Socialism is unnatural, and, therefore, false,' says one character. 'Except by force, you never can have such a state... The socialist hates the aristocrat and he hates the rich, because he covets their rank and their worldly goods. Give them to him tomorrow and he would abuse them both: but he'd never give either up, and, if anyone tried to share them, he'd stamp him under his feet.' When a neighbour's servant rapes and murders the daughter of an honest miller, the neighbour is condemned – he knew the man was a socialist, and yet he employed him!

Mercer passionately believed all this. He wrote *Lower than Vermin* (he told me in a letter just after its publication) because 'the present generation is growing up in the belief that the nobility and gentry of the old days were no better than so many oppressors of the poor'. Well, yes; but the tirades go well over the top. Added to which Mercer was an extremely unpleasant man, who once horsewhipped a servant for failing to draw a curtain, so allowing the sun to shine on a favourite picture; and when he built a house for his second wife, who had had polio and had difficulty walking, it was halfway up a hill and approached by 98 steps.

The building of that house is described in *The House that Berry Built*, and a very entertaining book it is. That's the trouble: Dornford Yates remains a great entertainer – even his memoirs are worth reading for his anecdotes about his days as a barrister (he appeared for the prosecution in the Crippen case). But the novels are set in some impossible ideal world which never existed: the faithful servants who support their masters in the thrillers end up rich (they share in various spoils) but would never think of retiring

and living like gentlefolk; they wouldn't presume. The masters and mistresses are gentle, romantic, witty, generous, impeccably honest, have good taste (which means they abhor modern art and music), behave beautifully to their inferiors, and spend their lives commending the Good and smiting the Evil.

Both Yates's books of memoirs are full of little tirades which would warm the heart of many *Oldie* correspondents. He was a stout defender of hanging and flogging: 'Arguments for and against the rope,' he writes in *B-Berry and I Look Back*, 'bring us straight to the old, old question – Which of the two do you propose to consider, the community or the convict? Boil it down and skim off the emotional scum, and it's just as simple as that. If you are to consider the community, then, for every reason, the man should be hanged... if murderers were regularly hanged and flogging was awarded for all other brutal crimes, in six months' time the crimes of violence would have fallen by eighty per cent.'

He fumed, too, on lesser topics. In *B-Berry and I* there are several pages about the disintegration of the English tongue. Nothing has been the same at the BBC since Stuart Hibberd: 'I have heard "controversy" pronounced with the accent on the second syllable, and "remonstrate" pronounced with the accent on the first. I have heard "formidable" pronounced with the accent on the second syllable. Only the uneducated made those mistakes when I was young.'

Take all this or leave it alone. My problem is that while I'm absolutely sure I couldn't have spent five minutes in Major Mercer's company without feeling physically ill (not for nothing was he a dead ringer for Hitler) I can't read a page of Dornford Yates – certainly of the thrillers – without turning to the next. It's sickening.

The pubman: a spotter's guide
BLOG FERDIE ROUS, 2018

Last weekend, I found myself enjoying a glass of wine with some friends in one of the many fine pubs around Clapham Common. Among the pub's occupants was an example of one of our finest native species – the Great British pubman.

The pubman manifests in several different forms: the teller of tales, the man of the world, the pontificater and the intellectual.

The common-or-garden pubman is the teller of tales. He has been a pub regular for a decade or more. He knows everyone and will tell anyone who is listening about his life and dreams. There is just such a man in deepest, darkest Cambridgeshire. He tells and retells stories of his experience with an illegal plant readily available in Amsterdam. One of his favourites is about a day spent on a beach in Jamaica, where some of the local produce knocked his bloody socks off.

The pontificater is usually very drunk, has a burning passion about a subject and totally believes in his own infallibility. He prowls the smoking area for unsuspecting victims. There is a keen amateur ecologist in Battersea who spent three hours of a cold December night lecturing some friends of mine about how we have destroyed the sea. Though he will listen to you if you ask a question, his mind is set and the conversation is repeated, never moving on from his chosen topic. All in all, the pontificater is a bit much.

The man of the world is rarer. He isn't necessarily a pub regular, he has a few years on him, and he is not as naturally gregarious as his storytelling cousins. He will approach you with a nugget of wisdom. Although, if this nugget is financial in nature, you do well to avoid following the advice. A couple of years ago, I was at a pub on Newcastle's Osborne Road and, while I was ordering a G&T, a man joined me at the bar and, channelling his inner Jordan Peterson, said: 'Put your shoulders back and smile – good things will come.' Butting into other people's business is not an appealing tendency, but advice from someone who doesn't know you prompts more self-reflection than that from people you do know – as there is no beating around the bush and no unnecessary diplomacy, they get right to the point.

The intellectual – the rarest of pubmen – commands a dizzying array of conversation topics, is always keen to hear an alternative view, but loves a good counter-argument. Back we go to the Clapham pubman. When we crossed paths, he was sitting alone, reading a book – military fiction, the finest thereof. A quick question about the book and we were off. From fantasy fiction to the legitimacy of the House of Lords, the Gosforth Cross and the Icelandic Jökulhlaup – glacial gush – in 1997. The geological background of this particular pubman was terribly helpful in explaining the latter. This is the intellectual. Much as with the man of the world, there was no personal politics, no nervousness about ideas – he spoke openly and we were free to engage on a purely discursive level.

All pubmen wear their hearts on their sleeves and speak without the need to edit their speech – though it might be nice if they did so once in a while. The anonymity of the pubman is what allows him to speak so freely and makes these encounters that much more memorable. To a pubman, you can speak without judgement and without consequence, as in the coffee houses of old. And though it's not always an easy ride, it's never dull.

'Local character with a fund of interesting stories. Buy me a pint and I'll clear off'

ONLY **1 HOUR**
TO INSTALL
WITH NO MESSY PLUMBING

Which?
Trusted trader
Approved
Installation Service

ENJOY **SAFE**, COMFORTABLE, **FULL DEPTH** BATHING

Enjoy safe, comfortable, full depth bathin

Safely lowers & lifts at the touch of a but

Rediscover the relaxing warmth of a deep bath with AquaLift. Getting in and out of the bath **safely and independently** is made easy thanks to its innovative slimline design. **Simple to install with no fuss or mess**, it has been made to be one of the most affordable ways of enjoying your existing bath without compromise for you or other bathroom users. The digital display allows you to set the right temperature too, for your maximum comfort. Rediscover independent bathing with AquaLift.

✓ **Safe, comfortable and reliable**

✓ **Slim and unobtrusive**

✓ **Lowers & raises you comfortably**

✓ **Fits into your existing bath**

✓ **Retractable for conventional use**

✓ **Fully guaranteed for peace of mind**

AquaLift
BATHLIFTS

☐ **YES** I want to enjoy a deep, relaxing bath again with AquaLift - please send me a free brochure.

Name _____

Address _____

Postcode _____

Tel _____

OLDAN04/10/18q

NO STAMP NEEDED **Please send to: Freepost RTUZ–RZKY–EHYE, Mercury House, Kingswood Road, Hampton Lovett, Droitwich, WR9 0QH**

For a brochure or FREE home t

Call **0800 028 280**
or visit **www.aqualift.uk.co**

* VAT-FREE available to eligible customers: for details please call our helpful customer service

OLDAN04/

Shopping

Alice Pitman

'DO you think you could get me some purple hearts off the internet?' announced the Aged P on the way back from the weekly shop at Waitrose. I was momentarily confused, wondering why she wanted to start collecting American military decorations at her time of life, until she added: 'My doctor prescribed them to me in the early Sixties as an appetite suppressant while I was expecting Edward. For nine months I felt on top of the world.'

I know you can purchase most things on the internet, but I was fairly sure that what the Aged P desired was not just a click away. I had a vague memory that purple hearts were somewhat disreputable. Mods and rockers and Vietnam vets took shed-loads, and wasn't Eden supposed to have knocked them back like sweets during the Suez debacle? Like so many drugs doled out by the medical profession in the 1960s, Drinamyl (its medical name) turned out less beneficial than everyone had been told. But the Aged P was having none of this: 'If everyone took a purple heart every day the world would be a happier place.' She paused. 'And it never did your brother any harm either.' Then she rattled off all the other benefits, including the time she had to speak at a literary do after my father's death and needed to settle her nerves: 'I

thought, "I know what I need: a purple heart." So I got one off a friend and it really did the trick.'

I had no intention of supplying dodgy substances to my 85-year-old mother via the internet, or anywhere else, come to that. It was all too risky: supposing she got all amphetamined up, speeding up and down on her stair lift and kicked the bucket? I could end up in prison like Gail in *Coronation Street*. Anyway, it looked as

> ## 'I had no intention of supplying dodgy substances to my 85-year-old mother via the internet, or anywhere else, come to that'

though I'd have a bit of a job scoring on the internet, as a search revealed the drug was banned in 1978. It also yielded up a number of horror stories about Drinamyl addiction. 'The type of patient to whom this drug is given,' wrote the *British Medical Journal* in 1963, 'is usually in the category of the serious social problem group.' When I told the Aged P she had been classified as a menace to society she seemed rather pleased.

In recent years, there has been an explosion of medicines for sale on the internet. It is estimated that two million of us now shop online for our drugs. Many sites are perfectly legitimate, but as with any large market, there are cyberspace cowboys offering counterfeit or substandard medicines, and at crazy prices too. Last year, one in four family doctors treated patients for adverse reactions to online drugs. The message is clear – shopping from illegal sites that don't require a prescription is fraught with risk. An acquaintance recently purchased anti-inflammatory drugs from an overseas company and ended up with a box of fake pills from Spain and no legal recourse.

But how to tell if a website is kosher? Look for The Royal Pharmaceutical Society of Great Britain (RPSGB) logo on the front page of online pharmacy websites. Best of all, avoid the internet altogether and consult your doctor.

And what are the most popular drugs online in the UK? Well, perhaps unsurprisingly Viagra is the top of the list, followed by a scary amount of weight loss medicines, Prozac and drugs for insomnia (mind you, we could do with all of those in our house). It seems we are no longer a nation of shopkeepers, but like our American cousins, a bunch of pill-popping Judy Garland wrecks.

See it, say it... Stop it!

BLOG NIGEL SUMMERLEY, 2018

I thought it was just me – until a colleague said, 'Isn't it simply dreadful?!'

Yes, it is. The 'it' in question is 'See it, say it, sorted' – surely the most execrable (and grammatically questionable) public announcement ever released.

Somebody somewhere must have actually come up with this as a bright idea... and, even more unbelievably, some department must have given it official approval.

Not only are recordings of this puerile pronouncement now ubiquitous on all forms of public transport, but hapless employees appear to be obliged to recite it – all of them doing their best not to sound embarrassed, but few of them succeeding.

The 'say it' bit – which should be 'report it' but which doesn't begin with an alliterative S – is particularly annoying. But then that is surpassed by 'sorted', a phrase that jars with its matey attempt at the vernacular.

It was something of a relief to be on a train from Euston to the Midlands the other day which played a recording of a posh-sounding woman (not a million miles away from the

sublime voice of Charlotte Green) who very obviously refused to say 'sorted' and very clearly made it 'sort it' – still awful but not quite as ugly.

We will presumably have to put up with hearing 'See it etc' every time we get on a bus, tube or train until the murmurings of irritation grow louder.

Until then, I'm tempted to say 'Hear it, hate it, hignore it...' which seems to be a suitably obtuse response.

Just the one

Jaci Stephen remembers writer, journalist, drinking companion, wit and best friend, Keith Waterhouse

Keith Waterhouse was a member of my boules team. And at his memorial service in St Paul's Church in Covent Garden, I was able to share the memories of our team's progress during the annual boules tournament which took place in Queen's Square in Bath, where Keith and I had both moved at roughly the same time in the late Eighties. Not together, I hasten to add.

Boules is the French version of bowls. It requires a great degree of co-ordination, precision, observation, close reading of your opponents' tactics and teamwork with your co-players. None of which Keith had. In fact, I think it is fairly safe to say that not only was he the worst player on my three-member team, he was the worst player in the tournament. Consistently. Every year in the history of the event, if I'm honest.

I blame myself. I was team captain, which meant I was the person to sort out the forms, payment, and the actual arrival of the team at 8.30 on a Saturday morning (no mean feat in itself). My mistake was appointing Keith as Head of Strategy.

It wasn't a complex job as he saw it, and could be summed up in one word: champagne. After losing every single one of our eight games in the first year we entered, Keith reckoned that we were way too sober from the outset and that far from waiting until lunchtime to get tanked up, we needed a champagne breakfast before the competition even began.

So the next year, that's what we did. And we won our first game. So excited were we with Keith's new strategy, which obviously worked, we had two bottles of champagne to celebrate – and lost the next seven games.

Keith wasn't a great thrower, and basically had just two techniques for the

two boules he was required to throw: one involved the boule landing at his foot when he underestimated the distance of the piste; the other, smashing Jolly's shop window when he overestimated it. And I have the footage to prove it, just as, I suspect, Jolly's has the insurance claims to back up my story.

My friendship with Keith during the twelve years I spent in Bath were among the happiest of my life. We regularly met up for lunch or dinner, usually in the theatre pub, the Garrick's Head, where we were both members of what Keith called 'Enemies of the Theatre', patrons who got to meet the stars of the performance after the show on opening night.

I constantly sought advice from him during my difficult first years in Fleet Street, when I hated doing certain pieces but needed the money. On one occasion I was in tears having been asked to do some inane piece about dogs. As I sat with

Keith, sobbing over what was probably our fifth 'just the one', he asked: 'And how much are they paying you for doing this piece?' '£200,' I wailed. He whipped out his cheque-book: 'Then I will pay you £200 NOT to write the piece!' I kept the cheque as a constant reminder of the fact that sometimes you really do have to say no, if only to save your own sanity.

Stories about Keith are legendary. I smile about one of them now, but less so on the day when I believed I had killed him. We used to frequent Gerry's Club, a basement bar in Soho's Dean Street where the fabulous owner, Michael Dillon, encouraged singing and dancing from the many performers who used to go there knowing they could rely on the discretion of the members. I'm an ex-ballroom dancer, and one night I decided to have a jive with Keith and threw up my leg, sure in the knowledge that he would catch it. He didn't see it coming either literally or metaphorically and my limb just whacked him sideways. He went backwards like a skittle, hit his head on a pillar and fell to the floor unconscious. He recovered, thank God, but it was a trying three minutes. I remember him coming to and declaring he would have 'just the one' before going home.

The second occasion I nearly killed him also involved Gerry's Club. This time we were dancing to *Mack and Mabel*. Tap-dancing, to be precise. On the bar. Keith fell off.

He was always a bit disoriented leaving Gerry's. The clock might indicate, say, eight o'clock, but he was never quite sure whether that was eight at night or eight in the morning. One night – or morning – Keith left Gerry's and after gathering himself up from the pavement on which he had lost touch with gravity, leapt into a taxi demanding to be taken to Brock Street. He later told me that the driver had become very irate as Keith's demands to be taken home increased. It took them both an hour to work out that Brock Street was where Keith lived in Bath, and he was in a different city altogether.

I had many special days with Keith and was lunching with him when the Twin Towers came down. Keith's column the next day told of how he learned about the event on TV, and how he kept getting up to change the channel in disbelief at what he was seeing. I rang him. 'No you bloody

didn't,' I said. 'The TV was ten feet in the air and we were in the Groucho Club.' 'Hmph. Artistic licence,' he said.

I learned a lot about artistic licence from him in my early days at the *Mail*, which had sent me to cover the Tory Women's Conference. I had been poring over a jigsaw of Norma and John Major. I suddenly thought how funny it would be if there had been a couple of women talking about how expensive it was, and which half of the couple they would rather buy. So I put the imaginary conversation into the copy.

Peter Wright, now editor of the *Mail on Sunday*, came over to my desk to congratulate me on the piece. 'And that bit about the jigsaw was hilarious,' he said. 'Oh, thanks so much,' I said, really pleased. 'I made that bit up.' It was the closest to seeing an editor's face self-combust I have ever seen.

'Big mistake,' said Keith when I confessed my sin. 'Not that you made it up, but that you told your editor that you had.'

My favourite day out with Keith of all time was when he took me as his guest to Cheltenham races for Clement Freud's seventieth birthday. We were sitting with the delightful Leslie Phillips and his wife, and Leslie was, as always, completely hilarious, charming and exquisite company. On the aisle opposite sat Michael Winner and his then very young companion. She may even have had her Barbie doll with her.

Leslie kept our side of the carriage entertained while Winner spoke non-stop at – and I mean at – his companion, who never uttered a syllable during the two-and-a-half-hour journey. Keith didn't speak a word – he was a great observer of

'I'm an ex-ballroom dancer, and one night I decided to have a jive with Keith and threw up my leg, sure in the knowledge that he would catch it. He didn't see it coming either literally or metaphorically and my limb just whacked him sideways'

people and absorbed everything, always, without necessarily feeling the need to join in. Towards the end of the journey Winner joined in our conversation and related a story about a gorgeous house in which he had filmed, but sadly wrecked in the process. The owner came back early, he said, much to everyone's embarrassment, but was charm personified. 'Mr Winner,' he'd apparently said, 'I know you are a gentleman and I have no doubt that you will return my home to the perfect state in which you found it.'

'Honestly,' said Winner, holding up his thumb a short distance from his forefinger. 'I felt this big.' At which Keith, uttering his only words of the entire journey, turned and said: 'No great distance to travel, then.'

He was a great writer; we all know that. He was clever, funny, sometimes irascible and curmudgeonly (but often hilariously so); he was great company, he had the appetite of a rabbit and the liquid capacity of an empty reservoir.

We all have our memories: friends, families, colleagues, readers, and even the Christmas tree on whose branches he one day had to place a tie to get it into the Garrick Club – having stolen it en route because he'd forgotten to buy one for his children.

He was my friend. One of my best. I miss him every day, but I have so much to thank him for. The laughter, the advice, the food when I couldn't afford it. I am sure that wherever he is, they are already queuing up to be his mate. Just don't, for God's sake, enrol him in your boules team.

Just what makes you tick?

my pacemaker

GED

On being labelled a subversive grandma

Why *Susan Bassnett* got into hot water over the doggy method

I had just given my grandson a biscuit, when my daughter snatched it out of his hand and threw it into the fire. 'Dirty, nasty,' she said, making a face, and gave the bemused toddler a second biscuit out of the packet. Then she turned on me. Paraphrasing roughly what she said, she appears to think that I have barely progressed from the peasant days of my medieval ancestors when we kept pigs and goats in the kitchen for warmth. It is a miracle, she went on, that she and her three siblings had not caught some deadly disease given the hygiene levels in my home.

I tried to protest that they had all made it to twenty and beyond under my care, but she was having none of that. Her trump card was the fact that my son-in-law had had to see his doctor with an allergic reaction to flea bites after spending one Christmas with me. Frankly, I thought him a bit of a wuss, but when you shower twice a day and wear Armani you are probably going to be more particular than your mother-in-law, whose method of rinsing dinner plates is to give them to dogs to lick before putting them in the dishwasher.

Having always had dogs and cats in the house, I am used to picking up a biscuit or a piece of toast that has accidentally fallen into a feeding bowl, dusting it off and carrying on regardless. I once served a large Wensleydale cheese with the top sliced neatly off to disguise the canine teeth marks, and though Geoffrey flatly refused to touch it, everyone else enjoyed it and suffered no ill effects. But though that may work with adults, my daughter belongs to the Mumsnet generation, for whom perfection in child-rearing starts with obsessive cleanliness, and I am consequently regarded as a dirty old woman. No matter that I raised a family of four, wrote a load of books and ran a university – I am just one step above the primitive in my daughter's eyes.

Our biggest crisis came last year with toilet training. She, the perfectionist, was engaged in guerrilla warfare with a child who kept refusing to use the loo. As with all small children, they can spot your weakness a mile off and thereafter know exactly how to torment you. So one day when he was alone with me and we had gone through two pairs of trousers and he was still clutching himself and claiming he didn't need to go, I suggested that we might step outside and do as dogs do – wee up walls or trees. This worked brilliantly, and he even performed on the wheel of his aunt's car, after which we rang her up so he could boast about it. When my daughter collected him he was proud as could be, and even she seemed convinced that for once my poor hygiene had led to a good result.

But a week later she rang me furious, to tell me how my grandson had watered a wall in the café in Kew Gardens and how he was now refusing to pee anywhere except in gutters or up trees. Look what you've done, she cried, it's absolutely disgusting. I protested that what I had done was to make toilet training fun, and reminded her of how her sister had used the garden for weeks before agreeing to sit on a lavatory, but I failed to convince her. Even my son-in-law had a go at me when I went to visit them. Apparently grandmothers are meant to be models of refinement, not subversive old bats.

I am looking forward to my grandson spending a week with me this summer. Then we'll find out what subversion means.

> '**My grandson watered a wall in the café in Kew Gardens and was now refusing to pee anywhere except in gutters or up trees**'

A brief history of shorts

Chaps: ignore *Tamasin Doe*'s advice at your peril...

Hunstanton, on Norfolk's west coast (yes, it does have one), is a quiet place, civilised by its large retiree population. Last summer, though, there was a rare storm on its sunny shores when Mr Edward Wheatley penned a poem, 'Summer Seen', to the *Hunstanton Newsletter* imploring men with legs like his own to cover them up:

*What are these giant parsnips doing
round the town?
Poking out of baggy shorts that are
nearly falling down
Pale as drowned cadavers, varicose
and blotched
Ugly and misshapen as if Frankenstein
had botched...*

Mr Wheatley's colourful appeal went unheeded, of course. The town was no less decorated with a seasonal display of British male leg in all its marvellous varieties.

One of the problems with Brits and their shorts is that we don't seem to be very good at them. Why would we be? In Bermuda the shorts season lasts from May until November. In the UK it is abbreviated to a few days in July and August. Until the North Sea and the Atlantic meet somewhere near Birmingham the weather will never be good enough for us to properly acclimatise to the sight of men's legs in our heavily trousered culture.

But shorts cannot be ignored or discarded. They must be confronted and mastered. If this is beginning to sound a little like a battle plan, we're in the right territory: like so much modern menswear, the best shorts have their roots in British military tailoring.

Back to Bermuda, then, where the classic way to avoid too much exposure is with a pair of tailored shorts worn with long socks. A century ago the style was adapted from army-issue trousers lopped just above the knee for the comfort of the Empire's servants who were wilting beneath the tropical sun. Bermuda shorts have since become the key item of national costume, acceptable for any event other than black- or white-tie.

There are rules: the hems should finish three inches above the knee and they should ideally be worn with navy socks, which apparently convey the right degree of seriousness even if the shorts are sunshine yellow. The jacket should be a different colour to the shorts and for business, a formal shirt and tie must be thrown in.

If this all sounds too buttoned-up and colonial, the modern, military-inspired version is cargo shorts. They are cropped combat trousers, all rugged and baggy and covered in pockets, each designed to carry one of the many accoutrements a man has to carry with him these days (cash, cards, phone, keys, iPod, pomade). They are a sort of wearable man-bag for a man who would never be seen dead wearing a bag.

Other shorts *de nos jours* include 'jorts' (jeans cut-off to make shorts), 'carrot-legs' (tapering to the knee), 'boardies' (surfer shorts, bright and billowing), male hotpants (!) and leather shorts, the sticky marriage of a resolutely winter material with a garment defined by its summer purpose. Approach all with caution. As US Senator Scott Brown discovered, the memory can be long when it comes to shorts. He was recently outed by his teenage daughter for wearing a pair of pale pink leather shorts on his first date with her mother. In mitigation, the Republican politician explained, probably not without reason, that 'It was the 1980s... If I wore these now, I'd get shot.'

Some things are better left to history. Whether or not that extends to a public airing of your legs is a matter for your conscience.

I'll be glad to see the back of the backpack pack

BLOG BY PAUL BAILEY, 2018

I shan't be travelling on the London Underground this summer. The rush hours that occur in other seasons do so at predictable times of day. But from May to September the trains are crammed with people, tourists mostly, every morning and afternoon.

I am happy to walk alongside them in the always-crowded Oxford Street, say — it's only on the tube that they fill me with terror. Not all of them, of course. I am referring, specifically, to that copious global family — the Backpackers. They come in all colours, all sizes, all shapes. They are old, middle-aged and young. They speak languages both familiar and unfamiliar.

What they have in common is robust health. They bring the spirit of the Great Outdoors to the confined space of a railway carriage, and some of them behave as if they are still climbing a mountain or at least crossing a field.

Although I'm old, I look younger than my years, and, thanks to the NHS, I can ignore those who won't give up their precious seats. That means I often have to stand next to Mr or Mrs or Ms Backpacker.

Some Backpackers sport state-of-the art backpacks with gleaming steel frames. They have a habit of turning round quickly, unaware of the contrivance they are carrying, and the poor wretch beside them is the recipient of a sudden stab to the chest. I was that poor wretch not so long ago. And the big lederhosened brute didn't even say sorry.

Ypres and beyond

Rosie Boycott travels to the battlefields
of Flanders with historian
Richard Holmes

I t's the numbers that get you. They're so staggeringly huge. I tried converting them into English towns: Ludlow for example, where I grew up, population around 10,000. Enough British soldiers to populate Ludlow six times over were killed in the first hour of the battle of Loos. Four and a half Ludlows of dead German youths lie in the mass grave in the German cemetery at Langemark. The same again in the French mass graves at Thiepval. And the distances being fought over were so small – opposing trenches just a hundred yards apart. Four years spent pushing to and fro across the now fertile and green fields of Flanders to try to move the Western Front a few yards further north. If it wasn't true, you wouldn't begin to believe it.

Ypres is an entirely rebuilt city: by 1918 the bombardments had completely flattened it. Germany paid for the rebuilding as part of its war reparations. The cathedral, the huge cloth exchange, the grand Dutch-style houses round the main square – every brick replaced in the same position. The Ypres Salient ('salient' means a bulge) pushes the Western Front round the town. Throughout the war, it remained in British hands, even though at

times the Front crept very near.

We began our journey into the battle-fields at Hooge Crater, on the Menin Ridge, the scene of so many fierce battles. Hooge was the first crater created by tunnelling and mining. It's not that big compared with some we were to see in the coming days – one in Verdun had used 66,000 tons of explosives, this one a mere 3,000 tons – but it was still a giant hole in the ground. The owners of the wood had allowed it to fill with water and a couple of ducks floated peacefully on the surface.

Richard Holmes explained that to blow

up a crater-sized area behind enemy lines meant digging a tunnel over 300 yards long, starting way back inside your own lines. It took days: you couldn't throw the earth up behind you as that would reveal tunnelling activity to the enemy, so all the soil had to be carried discreetly away. The tunnels varied according to the soil. In the Somme, where the land is chalky, they didn't need a lot of reinforcement, but round Ypres, where the water table is close to the surface, they had to be propped up by wooden beams. Once dug, the explosives were carried in and packed tightly together at the end of the tunnel which was then closed off so the explosion went upwards, rather than backwards towards you. Then – boom – hundreds of enemy soldiers would fly into the air, body parts sailing skywards, helmets and weapons littering the smashed-up earth.

It's hard to look in any direction without seeing a cemetery: there are over 300 on the Western Front. Some are tiny, like the one Richard showed us for a group of engineers who had been blown up while tunnelling to lay a land mine, and some enormous, like the famous Tyne Cot, where nearly 12,000 are buried and names on the wall honour those whose bodies were never recovered.

Many graves simply have a cross and the words 'Known Unto God'. When a name is known, there is sometimes an inscription below, ordered by loved ones at home through the War Graves Commission, but many are blank: letters cost a penny each and in the years after 1918 a large number of families could not afford this. The graveyards are, in a curious way, very lovely. If a group of bodies was so mangled as to make individual identification impossible, they were buried in a row, their named tomb-stones touching each other.

Richard was a mine of information: the Highland Regiments didn't wear knickers until the gas attacks started in 1916, when the army issued 'drawers: anti-gas'; the Germans were the first to use mustard gas, and before soldiers were routinely issued with gas masks, peeing on a hankerchief and holding it to your nose was the only way to try and ward it off. (No one ever found a way to cure its effects. About ten years ago, two shell hunters came across an unexploded canister of gas which broke open as they were carrying it. They rushed to hospital, but like the soldiers eighty odd years earlier, they died.)

We met Jacques, whose family decided not to reclaim the battered earth as farm land, but to preserve the trenches round his house as a museum. There he sits every day, a huge man with a face like a bloodhound, surrounded by the relics of war: helmets, shells, uniforms, swords, horse bridles. As a means of defending yourself against an advancing army, they seemed woefully inadequate. In glass cupboards, there were examples of 'trench art': copper shells engraved with flowers or cut down into candle holders, made by men waiting endlessly in trenches for their wives and girlfriends back home, but left behind, along with their bodies, in the cold, wet earth.

We visited the Essex Farm cemetery where the poet John McCrae worked as a doctor, just behind the lines. One day, a soldier was stretchered into the dressing station. McCrae came out of the bunker to inspect the casualty. He was delighted to see it was a friend and that he was not badly injured. After making arrangements for him to be collected by the next military transport, he went back inside. Seconds later a shrapnel bomb exploded overhead, killing his friend instantly. McCrae walked

up the canal that runs close by the bunker and wrote the immortal lines 'In Flanders fields the poppies blow / Between the crosses, row on row/ That mark our place; and in the sky / The larks, still bravely singing, fly /Scarce heard amid the guns below.' McCrae was killed in 1918.

At eight every evening at the Menin Gate in Ypres, the local fire brigade play the 'Last Post'. They have done this every night since 1919, breaking only when the Second World War was declared, recommencing the day it was over.

Inside the huge arch, the names of the missing are inscribed according to rank, regiment and nationality. The Indian regiments are especially harrowing: because of their religion, they brought 'untouchables' with them to organise the latrines. They died alongside their masters, thousands of miles from home, in wet, muddy fields, employed just to empty the slop buckets.

'To blow up a crater-sized area behind enemy lines meant digging a tunnel over 300 yards long, starting way back inside your own lines. It took days: all the soil had to be carried discreetly away'

Left: Ypres, Belgium, with the restored cathedral in the background; opposite: the cross in the centre of Tyne Cot Cemetery, near Passchendaele, around which the 3rd Battle of Ypres was fought in 1917. The spires of Ypres can be seen in the distance; opposite left: Rosie Boycott and her husband Charles in a trench in the grounds of Jacques' museum at Hill 62 of the Ypres Salient

We stood in a huge, jostling crowd of Canadian, Australian, American and British visitors. All the different nationalities who fought now have their own memorials. We visited the Irish memorial on a bitter, rainy morning – a huge column visible for miles around, with great slabs of granite brought from Ireland, inscribed with poems, prose and letters written by Irish servicemen, seventy thousand of whom were killed or wounded in the Great War.

We were assailed by facts and stories: the British gave English names to the places whose names they could not pronounce, hence Clapham Junction, Essex Farm and Tower Hamlets; it was not until 1916 that officers were allowed to shave off their moustaches; the men earned one shilling a day, while their girlfriends back home who were working in the munitions factories earned three times as much; once troops had been sent forward, there was no means of communicating with them except by carrier pigeon (as Richard was to point out frequently, a mobile phone would have saved endless lives); the youngest person to die on the front was Private Valentine Joe Struddwick, whose grave is at Essex Farm – he was just fifteen. The French soldiers, for whom the conflict was harrowing in a particular way – it was their land being smashed to pieces – nicknamed the officers who stayed behind the lines but earned copious decorations 'Chinese porcelain' as they were decorated before going under fire; over the four years of the war, the French lost one and half million men with over four million wounded.

The war bent our society, and indeed all of Europe, out of shape. Injured men, bereaved families, ruined lives and so, so many dead. So much bitterness. On the head stone of Kipling's treasured son John (Jack) who died on the second day of Loos, 22nd September 1915, are the words 'If they ask you why you died, tell them that their fathers lied.'

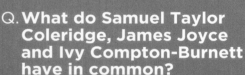

Arrested again!

But this time, *Wilfred De'Ath*, the Houdini of the Highways, manages to escape…

20 METRES TURN YOURSELF IN ….

I set out on a very hot day to walk from Caen to Falaise, birthplace of William the Conquerer, a distance of 36 kilometres, which would have been my personal best for a day's hike…

But 12 kilometres in I got picked up, arrested in fact, by the national gendarmerie who told me it was now an offence to walk on the highway in case you caused an accident. (President Chirac's laudable attempt to reduce road deaths.)

The cops were extremely unpleasant, took away my passport and only returned it with the utmost reluctance. (I overheard one whispering to the other: 'Well, he's obviously *un escroc* – a crook.' But who doesn't look like a crook in his passport photograph? I look like an international pimp and drugs baron.) They tried to check out my passport against the French national police computer to see if I was wanted anywhere. This alarmed me a lot because the fact is I am wanted in about ten different *départements* (for unpaid hotel bills) and visions of spending the next year being transported from police cell to police cell swam before my eyes, However, nothing turned up, which just goes to prove that the French national police computer is a good deal less efficient than the British one.

Good may come out of bad, as it so

> 'Who doesn't look like a crook in his passport photograph? I look like an international pimp and drugs baron'

'Looks like we're eating in again tonight'

often does in my strange, adventurous life, and I was able to persuade the pigs to drive me as far as the straggling hamlet of Potigny, which was only nine kilometres from Falaise, my day's destination. Verily, I am the Harry Houdini of the French highways. (You are still allowed to walk on the minor roads, where there is less traffic.)

The legend goes that William the Conqueror's father, Duke Robert of Normandy, surveying the scene from his battlements, spotted Arlette, a noble young laundress, daughter of a tanner, washing her scanties in a stream by his château. A few months later, she was pregnant with his child Guillaume, future conqueror of England. Arlette was a shrewd woman, proud of her pregnancy which she flaunted in front of Falaise's indignant inhabitants…

I don't have much time for this kind of touristy tittle-tattle, but I thought you might like to know why Falaise is so famous. (I must be the only person who visited nearby Bayeux and decided to skip the Tapestry in favour of the beautiful cathedral.)

Next morning, I stuck circumspectly to the side roads which are relatively free of oncoming rushing traffic but present a far greater hazard: huge, vicious dogs which guard the Normandy farms and can't wait to chew your genitals off. Really, as I write, I feel lucky to be alive.

East of Islington

The Good Samaritan

Never let it be said that the age of heroism is dead, says *Sam Taylor*

As McBoot stepped off the train at Bank station he could tell there was something missing. It might have been the six pints of London Pride or the two whisky chasers, but despite the desperate calls of his fellow passengers, it took a while for him to realise that the thing that was missing was the platform. As public information announcements went, 'Mind the gap' had been wasted on McBoot.

Ten feet down in the murky crevice, his hands waving up at his long-suffering girlfriend, McBoot could tell that it wasn't a good look for a man who only five minutes earlier had been boasting of his future career expansion plans. 'I'm going places,' he had assured her. 'You can rely on me.' Keen not to hold up their forward journeys, four men in pinstripe suits hauled the dishevelled hack back onto the train before hurriedly heading to the next carriage.

McBoot and his girlfriend sat down again and acted as though nothing had happened. The fact that his trouser-legs were covered in axle grease and one sleeve was hanging off his jacket seemed to draw little attention. It was, after all, Friday night. Nobody cared. Nobody, it seemed, except the man who finally looked up from his paper and gasped in horror at McBoot's left calf.

'Your leg is bleeding,' he screamed, charging towards them. 'Stand back, I'm a doctor. You need to get off the train.' Miraculously, they pulled into a station seconds later and the exercised medic was able to rugby tackle his startled patient onto the platform floor. 'I'm a doctor,' he screamed again. Within seconds, McBoot's jacket had been removed and his poly-cotton shirt had been ripped

off. By now quite a crowd had gathered. This was surgery in the raw. One spectator offered her Bic biro, but even McBoot was sober enough to point out that you don't usually need a tracheotomy for a leg wound.

Working fast with the shirt, and all the time imploring McBoot's girlfriend to give him 'room to work', the doctor tied the shredded garment above his knee. 'This tourniquet will get you to A and E,' he said. 'But hurry, you may have no time to lose.' And with that, the next train arrived and he was gone, barely able to

> ### 'Even McBoot was sober enough to point out that you don't usually need a tracheotomy for a leg wound...'

call out his name to the cheering crowd.

After arriving at A and E topless and with one leg dressed for Morris dancing, McBoot slowly came to the realisation that on balance, his life wasn't in immediate peril after all. Seven hours later, during which time his name sank further and further down the waiting list, he was eventually seen by a junior houseman who provided twenty stitches, a shot of penicillin and a suggestion that he look where he was going next time.

As McBoot limped back to the station to make one more attempt to get home, his girlfriend suggested that perhaps they should send a bottle of champagne to their 'have-a-go hero'. True, there had been some confusion at the hospital over the exact purpose of the shirt tied round McBoot's leg – something the triage nurse didn't wholly identify as a tourniquet – but she felt that shouldn't detract from the man's selfless intervention. 'After all,' she said. 'He must have got home late.'

A cursory look on the internet revealed that the MASH-like modus operandi of their saviour sat rather awkwardly with his listed day job in an English faculty. Still, they sent the champagne together with a thank you note: 'I was the injured Scotsman on the tube last night,' McBoot wrote. 'Thanks for all your help and sorry I was so drunk.' An hour later an email arrived. 'No problem,' the man replied. 'Actually, to be honest, I can barely remember last night myself. I didn't pretend to be a doctor again, did I ?'

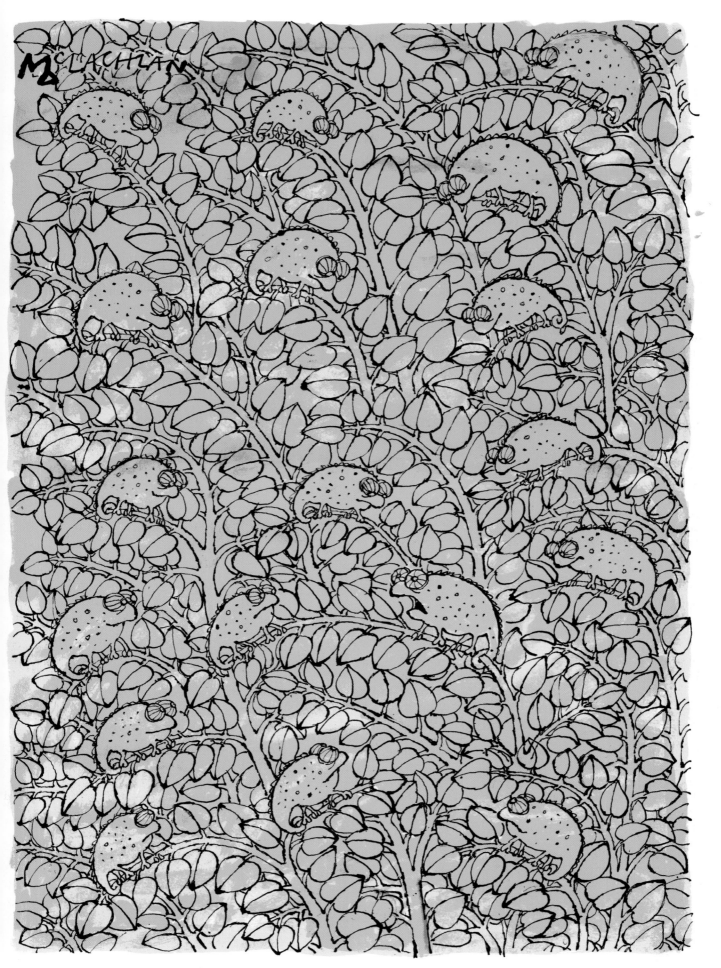

'Couldn't we chameleons play something else other than hide and seek?'

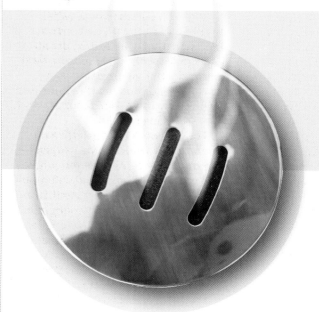

My brilliant career as the office youngster at The Oldie

BLOG BY ANNABEL SAMPSON, 2017

I must be eight months into my tenure at *The Oldie*. I continue to be surprised – and often amazed – as the 'novelty youngster' in what occasionally feels like the lunacy-breeding wilderness of the older generation.

As the office member who answers the phone, there are voices I've grown familiar with – namely, Paul Bailey, John McEwen and the late Jeremy Lewis – as well as mannerisms. I'm no longer baffled when somebody says that they don't have an email account, or frustrated – as a young person who takes herself very seriously – at being called 'love', 'dearie', 'darling', 'poppet' or, the absolute worst, 'pet'.

At our monthly Literary Lunches, I think I might have been accepted into the inner circle. Nowadays when I answer the phone, lunches' ringleader Barry Cryer will say: 'It's your ol' man Baz.' Neil Spence, the photographer, greets me with a hug; David Oldroyd Bolt of the *Times* diary, who, I hope won't mind me saying, is thirty going on sixty, is widely believed to be my 'work crush'. Reader Anne Husk, a Literary Lunch regular, gave me a book by Rory Stewart that she'd given to all her grandchildren as an apology for holding me up on the phone. Elizabeth Poston, who works at Hatchards, has even suggested we spend time together, outside of work – this can only be a good thing.

At 27, I've become a regular on the 'memorial service' circuit, rather than the wedding one I had rather hoped for, following the great round of 21st birthdays.

Despite all this groundwork, however, nothing could have prepared me for ninety-year-old actor Trader Faulkner's visit to the office last Friday (pictured). He came to Oldie Towers to drop off some articles. A vision – 'You've got to look the part' – in head-to-foot scarlet, with a flaming beret and embroidered cowboy boots, about as

'A lot of Oldie readers are fun and batty'

conspicuous as 'Where's Wally' and a battleship on our vigilant office manager's CCTV radar.

All his bravado disguised partial blindness ('I pretend I don't have it, so I'm not treated any differently'). Over coffee and shortbread, Trader told tales of run-ins with Vera Lynn, John Gielgud and being taught flamenco by a legless – literally – instructor. *The Oldie* editorial team – Harry, Deborah and I – were invited for a slap-up Saturday lunch at the Muffin Man off High Street Kensington in return for our hospitality. We've also been invited to his birthday party in June. *Oldie* editor Harry, who has been to Buckingham Palace, The Ned and an ultra-glamorous wedding in Azerbaijan in the past month, thanked him for sorting his social diary for the summer.

It's for reasons like this that I love working at *The Oldie*. People such as Trader are simply not encountered in normal everyday life. Like Trader, a lot – of course, not all – of the *Oldie* readers whom I get to meet, speak to on the phone or receive letters from, are fun and batty and eccentric. They have the very best of stories and deep minds, full to the brim with experience and knowledge. I can only hope to be a shadow of that if I live to see the grand age of ninety.

Trader Faulkner: at home in The Oldie

RANT

I recently had to go to Cambridge. Known to my children as Goodie Godders I therefore bought my return ticket a fortnight ahead and was on King's Cross station 45 minutes before departure. Anxiously I waited at the notice board as a great litany of trains was announced with maddening slowness. At last the Cambridge express came up and a lemming rush of would-be passengers set off at a fair clip across the no-man's land of building works to the far end of the station (a great new station is promised for 2011 – meanwhile chaos reigns). Some actually ran. Limping along gamely on my stick at top whack I finally reached the platform.

But the express was parked at the far end of another deserted train so there were another 200 yards to go. 'We don't hold the express for anyone,' the ticket collector declared lugubriously. Nor did they. It drew out when I was within twenty yards. I could have tried running too, but did not want to drop dead like Dr Zhivago. Most of the passengers were youngish – but some had luggage. It seemed like an obstacle race devised by sadists to make a quick cull in a world with far too many OAPs.

The next week I was going from Paddington to Pewsey and had just the same experience. At Waterloo, where I had a ticket to Alton, a kindly information clerk took pity when I accosted him an hour early. 'Leave it to me, young man,' he said – and came out of his kiosk to leak the platform number to me ten minutes before everybody else. I just made it – but would have failed without the Good Samaritan of South West Trains.

Ian Coucher, the outgoing chief executive of Network Rail – which runs these billboards of despair – has just been paid £1.25 million. Discuss…

GODFREY SMITH

TOM PLANT

I once met...

Somerset Maugham

Aged twenty, *Jonathan Cecil* journeyed to the French Riviera. He recalls meeting a bitter and elegant host surrounded by luxury

In 1959, when I was just twenty, my father (David Cecil), who was writing the official biography of Max Beerbohm, took me with him to the South of France to stay a night at Somerset Maugham's house and later to meet the artist and designer Gordon Craig. My father knew Maugham only slightly and Craig not at all, but he was anxious to talk to two of Max's remaining contemporaries.

Arriving at Nice airport in blazing sunshine, we were hailed across the tarmac by Alan Searle, Maugham's long-standing secretary-companion. With his immaculate white suit, deep tan and discreetly 'aided' black curly hair, he looked the image of the well-kept ageing gigolo. A limousine took us to the Villa Mauresque at Cap Ferrat – Maugham's residence.

I remember the villa's luxuriant garden with its heavily scented plants; I also remember the drawing room: a Renoir here, a blue period Picasso there, among many priceless others. My father and I were shown to our rooms by one of several white-jacketed manservants. Our rooms were luxurious and beside my bed I noted a carafe of water, a flask of brandy, a box of biscuits and a miniature Japanese wireless – then still an expensive novelty. There were also three books as yet unobtainable in prudish England: *Lolita*, *The Casement Diaries* and *Lady Chatterley's Lover*.

Our venerable host did not emerge until tea-time. On the stairs I had noticed a picture of an ancient, bejewelled and shrivelled Japanese empress. Maugham looked very like her. He was small, fragile and wizened, with tiny feet and hands; elegantly dressed, unsmiling but courteous, with a pleasant timbre of voice marred by a slight stammer.

He was very deaf and during tea Searle interpreted for him in a high-pitched squawk, like an impatient female companion:

'We're talking about Max, Willie! MAX!'

Somerset Maugham (left) with his companion and secretary, Alan Searle (1955)

After tea my father remained closeted with Maugham who, he later told me, was not excessively pleasant about Max Beerbohm. Meanwhile I was taken for a walk by Searle who pointed out a nearby house rented by Jean Cocteau, of whom he spoke waspishly. Cocteau's ex-lover, Jean Marais, was staying there with an American airman friend.

'The most beautiful human being I've ever seen,' gushed Searle.

> '*I had noticed a picture of an ancient, bejewelled and shrivelled Japanese empress. Maugham looked very like her*'

Dinner back at the Villa was a formal black-tie affair; the guests a sample of elderly Riviera society with a few widows and a rather affected old Bloomsburyite, Clive Bell.

Conversation was urbane; with Maugham, in a brown velvet smoking jacket and a large, loosely tied black silk bow, holding forth in his trademark cynical vein.

After dinner he drew me aside to a sofa and told me about a shipwreck in which he had nearly drowned. It became clear that he thought me much younger than I was and decided such a seafaring tale would appeal more to a boy than the grown-ups' talk. Although I could not make out much of his mumbled saga, I was touched by his thoughtfulness towards someone he took for a child.

The next morning – that of our departure – hospitality seemed to have been, in the words of P G Wodehouse, turned off at the main. We had no wake-up call, no idea of the time and, it seemed, no breakfast. My father vainly pressed a bell and we fluttered furtively along the gallery in our pyjamas hoping to alert one of the manservants below. But apparently none of them lived in.

I don't remember how we got away but I dimly recall coffee finally appearing and I assume Searle, with his usual ingratiating efficiency, saw us off on our way to Vence and Gordon Craig.

For me all the affluence and sophistication had been exciting but it left my father rather thoughtful. There was a depressing aura around Maugham, and his ungenerous words about Max – who had never said a bad word about him – left a rather bitter taste.

Later my father's diagnosis went as follows: Maugham, despite his best-selling millionaire status, was an intelligent enough critic to know that he was not quite a first-rate writer. And this had soured him irrevocably.

Great Bores of Today

'...I missed Wednesday's episode because I had an appointment at the evening surgery but you can always catch up with the Omnibus edition which is on Sunday mornings which is a godsend Helen has been pushing herself too hard and it's getting on Tony's nerves if you ask me there'll be something wrong with the baby and serve her right I mean without a partner it's going to be tough going for her either way to my mind it's never been the same since Phil died and they don't talk about farming any more...'

© Fant and Dick

Gardening

David Wheeler on camellias

Love 'em or hate 'em, camellias at least deserve full marks for braving the February weather. Many years ago I planted a long hedge of them for a client when I worked for a short time as a jobbing gardener in Surrey. But my enthusiasm waned during successive March visits to Cornwall a few years later. The camellias had mostly finished flowering by then and the dead brown vestiges of their brief glory hung on the bushes like so many used tea bags.

Camellias are, of course, members of the tea family, with an ancestry in China and Japan that goes back some 5,000 years according to Jennifer Trehane, our very own *dame aux caméllias*, who has travelled in search of these evergreen plants throughout Europe, the far-flung Orient, Australasia and California. Her book, *Camellias: The Gardener's Encyclopedia* (Timber Press, 2007) represents a lifetime's study, backed up by her family's famous Trehane Nurseries in Dorset (www. trehanenursery.co.uk).

Camellias are named after one George

'I'm sorry I don't have any form of identification. Isn't being your husband enough?'

A living camellia 'house' in Portugal

> 'Their beauty and history is at least as colourful and intriguing as that of two other familiar garden plants, the rose and the tree peony – each with some Far East blood in its veins'

Joseph Kamel (or Camel), a mid 17th-century Moravian Jesuit priest, and it appears (Ms Trehane again) that they were growing in England 'in the late 1730s because the first European coloured print of a camellia is in *A Natural History of Birds*, published… in 1745'. Their beauty and history is at least as colourful and intriguing as that of two other familiar garden plants, the rose and the tree peony – each with some Far East blood in its veins.

Jennifer Trehane says that camellias thrive in gardens that experience 'cool' winters and warm summers without too much humidity, and where there's well-drained acid-to-neutral soil with plenty of water in the growing season. They also appreciate shade and shelter

from strong winds. No wonder they thrive in Cornwall – especially at Caerhays Castle near St Austell where, since the 1920s, they have been lovingly fostered by members of the Williams gardening dynasty.

J C Williams (1861–1939) invested in George Forrest's plant-hunting trips to China in the early years of the 20th century, and work to 'improve' some of the seedlings raised at Caerhays resulted in the creation of *Camellia x williamsii,* wonderfully successful hybrids first propagated and distributed in this country by Jennifer Trehane's father, David. Most are free-flowering with blooms that 'shatter or fall whole when they are spent', thus eliminating my worries about untidy plants. 'Charles Michael' has single flowers of the palest pink. 'Donation' ('possibly the most famous camellia in the world') is described as 'semi-double, orchid-pink with darker veining', while 'Night Rider' (bred in New Zealand from the camellia world's two darkest red varieties) has 'very dark red, velvety textured petals' on a flower that reminds me of exotic water lilies.

Another Caerhays (but not *williamsii*) camellia is 'Cornish Snow', with pink-flushed white flowers that appear prolifically for many weeks, earning it great popularity among camellia growers in several of the world's temperate regions. Ancient trees of the thoroughly reliable Camellia japonica embellish temple courtyards and public parks in Japan, where 'camellia festivals' that can last for several weeks are a lively part of the country's springtime culture.

Not all camellias are grown as specimen plants (I must one day revisit that Surrey hedge I planted more than twenty-five years ago): I've seen them as street trees in Spain and grown as shade-giving 'houses' in Portugal.

Three West Country properties have supreme camellia displays: Antony Woodland Garden at Torpoint, Marwood Hill Gardens near Barnstaple, and Mount Edgcumbe in Cornwall. Wrap up warm.

Sylvia strikes back

Medical Secretary gives something back to research and treatment

Sylvia's friends remembered her for her kind heart, and her strong desire to help others. Even though she suffered lifelong poor health, while also caring for her critically ill mother.

But Sylvia did more than put on a brave face: she struck back against illness by working as a medical secretary, and following medical advances keenly. That's how she found out that with conditions such as stroke, the right treatment and back-up can make all the difference when given promptly.

So it's not surprising Sylvia decided that **one of the best things she could do would be to strike back again, by supporting the work of the Stroke Association – and leave us a generous gift in her Will.**

Today, we take time to remember her. Because Sylvia is still playing an important part in helping us create a future free of stroke, and turn around the lives of thousands of stroke survivors each year.

Together we can conquer stroke.
Call **020 7566 1505** email **legacy@stroke.org.uk** or visit **stroke.org.uk/legacy**

Lester Piggott

Jamie Douglas-Home on racing's favourite son

'He overcame deafness and a minor speech impediment with the single-minded determination that has always been his trademark'

The Golden Boy, the Long Fellow and even Old Stone Face are all epithets that have been used to describe the man who was arguably the greatest jockey of all time. These days, Lester Piggott, now a well-preserved 75, lives quietly in Newmarket in a large bungalow next to the stable yard where he once trained, surrounded by mementos of his glittering career.

Ernie, Piggott's paternal grandfather, rode three Grand National winners in the years around the Great War. Father, Keith, scored more than 500 times as a rider over the sticks before becoming a successful trainer on the Berkshire Downs, and mother, Iris, was a Rickaby from the famous Newmarket racing family.

So, when little Lester Keith Piggott arrived in Wantage Hospital on Guy Fawkes Day in 1935, his proud parents probably expected that the baby would make a living in the racing game. But they would not have predicted that their only child would become the most successful Flat jockey ever, with a CV containing a record nine Derby wins, numerous other big race victories, both here and abroad, and eleven British Flat Jockeys' Championships.

The blood of famous riders pumps through Piggott's veins, but, in some respects, he is an unlikely racing hero. Deafness, which was discovered only when his parents found him, aged four, with his ear pressed to a radio, required the small boy to teach himself to lip read. But he overcame this affliction and a minor speech impediment with the single-minded determination that has always been his trademark. Moreover, on occasions, he used the first disability to his advantage.

The jockey, whose parsimony is legendary, was once approached by a stable lad at the races. 'Lester, can I have the pound you owe me for that winner you rode me?' said the diminutive boy. 'Sorry, can't hear you at all. It's the wind, you know,' replied the jockey in his oft-imitated clipped tones, and ambled away. Later, the lad saw Piggott engaged in animated conversation with a trainer. So the enterprising boy thought that he would have another go for his present. 'Can I have the two pounds you owe me for that winner you rode me?' said the lad. 'You said a pound last time!' said Piggott, as

he opened his wallet and gave the boy a single note.

Piggott's height was another handicap for a Flat race jockey. At five foot eight inches, he was forced to live a life of deprivation to keep his tall frame at around the eight and a half stone mark. One small non-fattening daily meal, endless cups of black coffee and plenty of large cigars, supplemented by the odd gin and tonic, glass of champagne or piece of chocolate were all that passed through those thin pale lips during a riding career that spanned nearly fifty years.

Piggott has always been a man of few words, but when he consents to speak it is often to reveal a cultivated dry wit. Many years ago, a small trainer, known for his love of the hard stuff rather than the number of his winners, was unhappy with the ride the Long Fellow had given a fancied horse. 'Piggott, you will never ever ride for me again!' shouted the incandescent handler. 'Better pack the game in then, hadn't I?' replied the jockey, who was then at the height of his powers.

It is a mistake, though, to view Piggott's life solely through rose-tinted glasses. As a young rider, his will to win, which on several occasions threatened the safety of his fellow jockeys, gained the displeasure of racing's rulers, resulting in some untimely suspensions from riding.

He has also had well-documented problems with the Inland Revenue, spending a year behind bars for tax evasion in 1987. This crime, to his great sadness, caused him to be stripped of the OBE – an award that was bestowed on him by the monarch for whom he won the 1957 Oaks on Carrozza. He fathered a child, Jamie, out of wedlock with his former PA, Anna Ludlow, in 1993 and later spent some time in intensive care in Switzerland in 2007 due to a recurring heart problem.

But racing's favourite son, who rode his first winner, aged twelve, in 1948 and thereafter became the perennial housewife's choice, has always been a survivor and, despite more than his fair share of adversity, has never lost a formidable sense of humour.

The late Jeremy Tree, the larger-than-life Old Etonian trainer, telephoned Piggott once: 'Lester, I've got to give a talk to my old school about racing. What shall I tell them?' asked Tree. 'Tell them you've got flu,' said the maestro and quietly replaced the receiver.

A marriage of minds

Now both aged 91, Bernard Dunstan and Diana Armfield met at the Slade during the war. Her studio is at the front of their house, his at the back and they paint every day. By *Huon Mallalieu*

I t was a tonic to visit Bernard Dunstan and Diana Armfield on the first sunny day of spring. Mimosa was out by the front door, and on the porch of their inter-war house in Kew was a bowl of tadpoles. One might expect that two artists would find it difficult to preserve the equanimity of their more than sixty-year marriage when working so closely to one another. It soon transpires that it has been no problem for them. 'We've worked the relationship out so we don't clash,' they say.

The front room – south facing but with the blinds down against the sun – is Diana's studio, while Bernard has a slightly larger, more cluttered room at the back. He celebrated his 91st birthday in January, and she reaches hers this month – by which time their contributions to this year's Summer Exhibition will be hanging in the Royal Academy. Although now officially retired, he is the senior RA, having been elected to full membership in 1968; she joined him in 1981.

The Academy has been central to their lives for still longer. They first met at the Slade during the war. 'I had liked the look of him since I first saw him in a drawing class,' Diana remembers, and luckily, although they had largely lost touch, she

kept his address. So, when she liked a painting of his in the 1947 Summer Show, she sent him a postcard, which brought him straight up to London from Bristol, where he was teaching. They married in 1949, and most mornings since then have begun with Bernard doing a quick nude drawing of Diana 'to keep my mind active'.

Although his eyesight was not good enough for the RAF during the war, it was no bar to service in the Royal Observer Corps. Recently it has troubled him again, and during the long wait for a cataract operation he has relied on Diana to tell him when his colours were out of true. Nowadays he tends to draw and paint

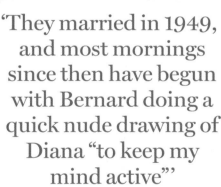

'They married in 1949, and most mornings since then have begun with Bernard doing a quick nude drawing of Diana "to keep my mind active"'

Opposite, 'Woman Dressing' (Bernard Dunstan), Roland, Browse & Delbanco Collection, London

Above, 'Nasturtiums with the Last of the Phlox'; left, 'Sheep in the Back, Llwynhir' (Diana Armfield), Browse & Darby Gallery, London

later in the day, and though, he says, he is easily distracted by tidying and organising the studio, the work still emerges. Despite an early flirtation with the drawing style of Wyndham Lewis – 'a good training, but not for me' – his paintings continue in the tradition of his great heroes, Degas and Sickert, and like the latter he often paints moody, enigmatic interiors.

Landscapes are a sideline for him: 'I am devoted to the wild mountains and the valleys of North Wales, where we spend a good deal of our time. They are threatened by wind farms, as are so many other fine landscapes. People are coming more and more to realise that wind power is not efficient – I wish politicians understood this too,' he noted in 2006.

Diana Armfield – an uncle was the artist Maxwell Armfield – is a member of the Royal Watercolour Society as well as the Royal Academy, and her credo as an artist is straightforward: 'I work from observation and experience; draw and paint what I can admire, enjoy or love; to share with others what I discover and reflect on. I hope to reveal and confirm that the things and experiences I paint are of lasting importance and enormously worth cherishing. To translate into paint is always a challenge and something of a mystery.'

Both these artists are generous champions of contemporaries whom they feel to be undervalued, among them Gilbert Spencer and John Nash (the younger brothers of Stanley Spencer and Paul Nash), Harold Gilman, Richard Eurich, Henry Lamb and Peter Greenham. Their walls are covered in drawings, paintings and prints, both theirs and by admired friends and contemporaries. Here and there gaps show wallpapers designed by Diana. These are very much her own, but one feels that William Morris would have approved.

Although Bernard Dunstan regards himself as a largely self-taught draughtsman, I suspect that he must have been a natural when he came to teach others. In 1991 he edited a new edition of Ruskin's *The Elements of Drawing*, and Ruskin supplies him with an apt motto: 'Paint what you love and love what you paint'.

OLDEN LIFE

Who was ... Lady Docker?

'Mink – it's too hot to sit on,' explained Lady (Norah) Docker, when asked why the seats of her gold-plated Daimler had zebra-skin upholstery. The car also had an ivory dashboard containing a vanity set and cigarette and lighter compartment, cut crystal decanters in the cocktail cabinet, and a Cartier picnic set in the boot, as well as an aluminium body under the gold leaf, 167 horsepower, and indirect lighting. That car, and her lavish lifestyle, kept my parents in tongue-clicking material for years.

She was born over a butcher's shop in Derby, grew up in Birmingham, and left home at eighteen for London, hoping to become an actress. Ten years later, when she was a dancing instructor and partner at the Café de Paris, she met and married Clement Callingham, chairman of Henekey's, ten years older and a millionaire. She had a son by him and during the war, according to the *Times*, 'served with a dash as a volunteer driver taking supplies to bombed towns'.

Clement obligingly died in 1945, leaving her wealthy. A year later she married Sir William Collins, president of Fortnum & Mason and chairman of Cerebos salt. He died a year later, leaving her a millionairess. Two years later she married her third and last millionaire, Sir Bernard Docker. And she became our first celebrity, famous for being famous.

'I'm not driving, sir. I'm just here to give you your opinion on topical issues'

Lady Muck? Lady Docker with Sir Bernard at one of her parties, 1955

The owner of a 880-ton ocean-going yacht and a devoted husband, Sir Bernard was chairman of Daimler and Birmingham Small Arms, and a director of a sheaf of other companies, including Midland Bank, Anglo-Argentine Tramways and Thomas Cook.

The partying began. They were the first hosts to invite the television cameras into their home, and her dresses, furs and smart parties kept the gossip columnists busy. She invited striking miners to a party on the yacht and danced a hornpipe for them. She played marbles with shop-floor workers in her husband's factories. She went to parties given by notorious criminals. She said, 'We bring glamour and happiness into drab lives. The working classes love everything I do.' In mining communities the phrase 'Lady Docker' ousted the expression 'Lady Muck'.

When she suggested that Daimler made a family model to keep the marque alive Sir Bernard decided she had a flair for business and had a drawing-board installed in their Mayfair house. Chrome was scarce and brass needed polishing, she said, so she designed it with gold from bonnet to boot. At the same time, Britain had to tighten its belt and Sir Bernard

campaigned for economy in national spending.

People travelling abroad were allowed to take only £25 with them and the Dockers were arraigned for taking a larger sum, complicatedly laundered through the crew of their yacht. Sir Bernard spent £25,000 fighting the case, which was eventually dropped. But it was too much for the Midland Bank, who expelled him from the board.

The Golden Zebra car was one of several flamboyant vehicles they had custom-built at Daimler without consulting other board members; the others were called Blue Clover, Silver Flash, Star Dust and The Gold Car. In 1955 they chartered two planes to fly Star Dust and Golden Zebra to Monaco, where they had been invited to the christening of Prince Rainier and Princess Grace's baby.

The Rainiers refused to include Norah's son, Lance, in the invitation, so the Dockers stayed away. She took Lance to a night club, where she threw a paper Monegasque flag on the floor and stamped on it: they were ordered to leave the country, and their christening gifts were returned.

This was too much for Sir Bernard's fellow directors at BSA, who voted to expel him in 1956, citing the five cars, two of which had been sold at a loss, the dresses and furs charged to the company without permission, and the losses the company had sustained since Sir Bernard took office. The company confiscated the remaining cars, while the Dockers appealed energetically but unsuccessfully.

They sold the yacht to pay their debts, bought a Bentley each to spite Daimler, and retired to tax exile in Jersey – where, said Norah, their neighbours were 'the most frightfully boring, dreadful people that have ever been born'.

Sir Bernard died in 1978 in Jersey and Norah in 1983 in a Surrey hotel; it may have been suicide. Daimler was taken over by Jaguar, but the car lives on. It has recently been lavishly restored: yours for $225,000 if you're interested.
CAROLINE RICHMOND

OLDEN LIFE

What were … restaurant trolleys?

The expression 'off your trolley', though now pejorative, was once a perfectly cordial thing to say to a restaurant waiter. 'I'd like something off your trolley, please.'

Restaurant trolleys were wagons of delight, phaetons of succulence, barouches of *bonnes bouches* – or at least they could be. At the Savile Club in Mayfair, the hors d'oeuvres trolley was a magnificent machine, but its contents were not always the freshest. It was known as the 'salmonella express'.

What a work of engineering it was, though, a six-wheeled marvel which was formed of a rotating drum with slatted compartments. These had metal covers which fell open as they rose to eye level, the drum being rotated via a Bakelite handle as large as the steering wheel of an Army four-tonner.

Inside the compartments glistened various cold collations which chef had prepared that day (or so you hoped): Greek salad, anchovies in oil, tomatoes in French dressing, stuffed vine leaves, cubes of garlicky feta, artichoke hearts, various objects smeared in salad cream decorated by cayenne pepper. Poor old cayenne pepper. That's gone too, by the by.

We also had a Savile cheese trolley, a domed affair freighted by chunks of Cheddar, Caerphilly and a full Stilton. One Friday – a candlelight evening, when girlfriends were admitted for *tables-à-deux* in the ballroom – it was piloted by an Irish waiter who had a W C Fields nose. While steering the trolley towards the ballroom from the adjacent dining-room he hit some sort of pothole in the floorboards and we heard a crash and a Hibernian oath. Seconds later the Stilton came rolling into the ballroom, pursued a few moments later by the waiter, hair and uniform askew.

Restaurant trolleys brought showmanship to troughing. Crêpes Suzette were completed at the table from a chariot equipped with a burner to heat the Grand Marnier. Once steaming, it would be set

> 'At the Athenaeum I saw Revel Barker, an executive of Mirror Group newspapers, lean over and light his cigar in the flames of a Crêpes Suzette trolley'

alight. At the Athenaeum I saw Revel Barker, an executive of Mirror Group newspapers, lean over and light his cigar in the flames of a Suzette trolley. He nearly set fire to his beard.

There seems to be less fun at restaurants these days. At La Capannina, a good Italian in London's Soho, they would wheel the fish selection to your table and you could admire the skate before it was cooked in black butter. As a child I was taken to Jimmy's Greek restaurant in Soho, a downstairs hovel decorated with postcard-type views of Aegean beaches, where I recall being presented with a trolley of lurid taramasalata and olives which looked like goat

droppings. Perhaps they were.

London eating houses also used to have lots of trolleys for roasts. Up went their swivel lids, out came the aroma of broiled goodies. Simpson's-in-the-Strand still trundles these round the dining room – don't forget to tip the carver – but they have disappeared from most other places. Maybe it's a health and safety thing. The Savile's hors d'oeuvres trolley and its fizzy egg mayonnaise would certainly have given the Food Standards Agency an attack of the vapours, yet I miss the theatricality of those trolleys.

Drinks trolleys also existed – 'Ah, here come the stickies!' – exotic bottles with Gothic-script labels, wax seals and Mexican worms. In my twenties I was hypnotised by such a trolley at a Camden restaurant run by that TV chef called the Galloping Gourmet. I drank four glasses of Chartreuse and have never felt quite the same since.

In Ibiza I worked at my late uncle's restaurant, the Wild Asparagus. It had a pudding trolley which was entrusted to an eager young Catalan called Luis. His English was imperfect. We told him to try to interest the customers in a slice of 'gâteau'. He thought we meant the Spanish noun gato (which means cat). Luis wheeled his trolley from table to table, grinning manically and saying 'Pussycat? Pussycat?'
QUENTIN LETTS

In praise of failure

Fear not: despite Mrs T's robust attempts to persuade us otherwise, we doggedly remain a nation in love with the worst. *Stephen Pile*, chronicler of the abysmal, brings us up to date

In the 1980s a woman called Margaret Thatcher, whom older people may still remember, made a preposterous speech saying that Britain is now a country dedicated to success not failure. Good God, had she taken leave of her senses? Twenty-five years later the question is this: did she succeed in changing this key part of our national character?

The British have admired failure at least since 1596 when William Shakespeare wrote lovingly of the rude mechanicals and their thrilling play. He ennobled the worst and started a tradition that became deeply embedded in our national temperament.

As a nation we once had a healthy suspicion of the sleek and the successful. As late as 1988 the British rose up to acclaim Eddie 'the Eagle' Edwards, a plasterer from Cheltenham who entered the 90-metre Olympic ski jump after a couple of dry runs on a local ski slope. An immediate national hero, he came a fabulous last, flapping both arms for mid-air balance and complaining that he could not see anything because his pebble spectacles steamed up during take-off.

In my own small way I joined in with this noble tradition in 1979, writing *The Book of Heroic Failures*. Now forgotten, it sang the praises of the worst in every sphere, the worst poet, the worst golfer, the worst playwright and the worst ever vaudeville act (The Cherry Sisters: a net had to be erected across the stage to protect them from the nightly barrage of vegetables, and the law of libel was changed in 1901 so theatre critics could describe their performance without fear of litigation).

Then Margaret struck and for two decades she seemed to be changing our island character. She turned Britain from a *Dad's Army* society (where an officer was in charge and everything needed a lick of paint, but we all rubbed along) to an *X-Factor*

society (where the winner takes all, even though it is not obvious why he deserves it, and everyone else is outside in the corridor feeling seriously cheesed off).

Suddenly we lived in a culture full of schoolgirls jumping up and down with their record exam results. Our land was now awash with people who never tire of telling us that they are delivering excellence, whether they are or not. It was a country safe for Manchester City's billions, Mrs Beckham's handbags and spin doctors saying that everything is going well when it obviously isn't.

> ## 'Suddenly there was hope in the darkness. All John Sergeant had to do was start dancing and Britain rose up'

It was deeply depressing, but then the great day dawned. Suddenly there was hope in the darkness. All John Sergeant had to do was start dancing and Britain rose up. Week after week perfection-crazed judges on *Strictly Come Dancing* condemned his exquisite rumbas and called for his immediate departure. Week after week the British voted overwhelmingly to keep him on the show and send home

John Sergeant and Eddie the Eagle: don'tcha love 'em?

his drably excellent rivals. We had rediscovered our antique virtues. Bully Bottom was himself again.

This is a fragile plant admittedly, but inspired by Mr Sergeant's example, I now lob in my own small contribution to the fightback. Communism had *Das Kapital*, but all I could manage was *The Ultimate Book of Heroic Failures*, which was compiled to point out that ever since Margaret said this is a country dedicated to success not failure we have lived through a golden age and the time has come to applaud it.

Records have been shattered. Humanity has moved onward and downward. The most callouts of a life boat during a single voyage is up from four to eleven and the most attempts to murder a spouse without him noticing there is a problem is now a highly impressive seven. There is a new record for the most lines forgotten by one actor, a new worst Olympic cross-country skier (race organisers sent out a search party) and Runcorn Highfield became the new worst ever rugby league team when they played a mouth-watering 75 games without a win. (Scouring Australia for new talent, their scout came back with the only one-armed player ever to appear in the rugby league.) Association football can better that because in 2008 Northend Thistle announced that they had not won a game for sixteen years which is an all-comers' record.

Mind you, there is stiff competition from abroad. In America we now have the definitive election at which nobody voted at all, not even the people at the ballot station. It is the first time that six candidates have stood unopposed and none of them got elected.

Oh, my fellow Britons, cast off your yoke. Say 'no' to PowerPoint presentations. There is still time to live the dream.

The Ultimate Book of Heroic Failures by Stephen Pile, Faber and Faber, £12.99

In the soup

To combat empty-nest syndrome *Roger Lewis* and his wife have started going away at the weekends – but is there anywhere worth going to?

Now that the children have finally left home and I've no longer got anyone to scream at, Mrs Lewis and myself, with time on our hands, have started to go out and about at weekends, in search of – well, what exactly? Life as it may have been before we descended into the abyss of parental responsibilities? Pockets of England before it was built over and covered with disabled-access mosques?

You'll laugh at this, but the better to fulfil my mission, I have bought a foldable picnic table and bench-set thing, which goes in the boot of the vehicle. Quite apart from being too heavy for me to pick up, the bench doesn't look as if it can bear my ample buttocks in any event, and the table fits together with elastic straps that I've already broken.

Anyway, thus equipped, and with a

'My heart sinks when I enter these places that boast about having a "Wellness Centre"'

thermos of tomato soup, off we go – or rather, off we went. For years Anna has wanted to go to Westonbirt Arboretum. Oh Christ, I was bored. It's all, well, trees.

We backtracked to Tetbury, where the Prince of Wales runs a shop for his Highgrove produce. The usual stuff. Lavender toiletries. Pots of lavender. Sachets with lavender in. Lavender-flavoured chocolate. And no Camilla behind the till, either.

Another weekend – to Stratford to see a play recommended by Paul Bailey. Paul used to be an actor and was a fairy when Charles Laughton gave the public his Bottom. I'm not able to judge the

new production of *A Midsummer Night's Dream* objectively because I fled the theatre after ten minutes. Seated miles up in the gods, I had a panic attack from a combination of claustrophobia and vertigo.

Our attempts to find nice hotels have had mixed results. Hospitality experts throughout the land are in a race to rip out period features, shove harsh spotlights into the plasterwork, and create these ghastly chi-chi boutique hotels and spas. My heart sinks when I enter these places that boast about having a 'Wellness Centre' – plunge pools, steam rooms, graduates from what used to be called polytechnics who wear T-shirts and name-tags and hand out the towels.

One place, in Stamford, which must have been glorious twenty years ago, served oysters on an oblong roof tile, steaks on a wooden chopping board, and everything else on those big white dishes that resemble Don Quixote's helmet. They

were so proud of being 'contemporary' – and had banished everything I look for: proper starched tablecloths and napkins, pudding trolleys, elderly waiters and waitresses, heavy silverware that's been in use since before the war.

But all is not lost. I have located a couple of gloriously unspoilt spots, which I recommend to readers. Everywhere in Eastbourne is pretty much up my street. For that we have to thank the Devonshires and the Cavendish Estate, who own all the freeholds and have halted the Philistines. When *Brighton Rock* was filmed again recently, it was shot in Eastbourne, because it still resembles Graham Greene's world, whereas Brighton has gone to hell.

Torquay has gone to hell, too. But along the cliffs is the best place I have stayed in for ages. The Headland Hotel used to be a villa belonging to a remote Romanov archduke. The food is ample, old-fashioned, and you feel transported back to the days of Terence Rattigan or Agatha Christie. I do hope some have-a-go new manager doesn't come along with refurbishment plans, because I'd like to move in there permanently and be like the dotty Major in *Fawlty Towers*.

Cookery

Elisabeth Luard

New England biscuits

Serve these hot to eat with soup or stew instead of bread rolls. Serve leftovers toasted with jam and butter. Makes 24.

- *4 cups plain flour*
- *1 level tablespoon baking powder*
- *1 level teaspoon bicarbonate of soda (or extra baking-powder)*
- *4 oz cold butter*
- *1 ½ cups whipping cream*
- *salt*

Sift together flour, baking powder, soda and salt in a roomy bowl. Cut in the butter till it looks like fine breadcrumbs, and work enough of the cream to make a soft dough – use your fingertips and don't overwork it. Pat the dough into a rectangle about an inch thick, mark into fist-sized squares. Bake in a hot oven at 425F/220C/Gas7 for 8–10 minutes till well-puffed and brown. If more convenient, refrigerate till you're ready to cook (overnight is fine).

Poppyseed muffins

Note from a New England kitchen (Moose Mountain Guest House, whose recipe this is): 'To measure a cupful, use an ordinary half-pint coffee mug. To measure half a cup, tip the contents of mug as if pouring till you can just see the edge of the base. To measure a quarter-cup, work it out for yourself.' Makes 12.

- *4 oz butter, softened*
- *½ cup sugar*
- *2 eggs*
- *¾ cup soured cream or plain yogurt*
- *¼ cup poppyseeds*
- *½ teaspoon ground nutmeg*
- *2 cups flour*
- *½ teaspoon salt*
- *½ teaspoon baking soda*

Preheat oven to 375F/190C/Gas5 and butter 12 muffin tins. Beat the butter with the sugar. Beat in the eggs, cream or yogurt and fold in the poppy seeds, nutmeg and flour tossed with the salt and baking soda. Spoon into muffin tins and bake for 20 minutes till tops are brown. Serve hot with butter and honey.

Crispy kale

You'll find this Chinese seaweed look-alike on sale in US supermarkets. Children will eat it by the handful. To prepare, slice a large handful of greens stripped from their thicker stalks – use curly kale or the chewy dark leaves sold as cavolo nero. Toss with a little olive oil and sea salt, spread on a preheated baking sheet and bake in a hot oven till dehydrated and crisp. Shove a trayful in the oven while you're baking something else. For superior oven chips, dice potatoes and roast in the same way. Brilliant and cheap: rural and rustic rules.

Austerity rules. Forget fancy and foamed, roll out rustic and regional. In Paris the word du jour is urban-aubergiste. In Barcelona, home of Ferran Adrià, poshest chef on the planet, the Catalan government decrees that no provider of public accommodation, however lavishly appointed, has the right to call itself five-star unless it offers pa amb tomàquet, a thick slab of grilled country bread rubbed with garlic, olive oil and the gluey juice of a rubbing-tomato. In New York, the hot ticket is Momofuku, creative Korean with a side-order of kimchee (fermented salted cabbage with added chilli). At Noma in Copenhagen, bullrush-stalk and reindeer-moss is menu of the moment, and you don't get more regionally rustic than that.

In New England, however, they don't do fancy, they don't do foam and they certainly don't do bullrush. What New Englanders really like to do is no-nonsense baking of the kind you might be offered if you dropped in, say, on a Democrat – or even a Republican – in this election year for a frank exchange of views.

New England naming can be a little confusing. You need to know that a New England biscuit is an English scone, a scone is really a rock-cake and anything served with coffee is a coffee-cake and not a coffee-flavoured cake.

My tenant's name? J R Hartley

BLOG BY VALERIE GROVE, 2017

I am thinking of getting a blue plaque for our house, inscribed, 'Here, in 1983, J R Hartley searched in the Yellow Pages for a copy of *Fly Fishing* by J R Hartley.' Last weekend, when the BBC's six o'clock news bulletin announced that Yellow Pages will soon be no more, they mentioned the J R Hartley ad.

I am sitting now in J R Hartley's chair. I still live in that house, which a location man from an ad agency happened to drive past in the summer of 1983.

I was standing on the front steps when he stopped. 'A TV commercial? Come in!' I cried, practically lassoing him into the hall. Into that hall, poor old J R Hartley would stagger, exhausted from walking round bookshops, so his daughter would say, 'Dad, why not try the Yellow Pages?' A neat little saga, just 30 seconds long, firmly wedged in the last century.

I loved the whole adventure: meeting the famous director Bob Brooks and the actor Norman Lumsden playing JRH, and having the house transformed with Victorian whatnots – and wall-mounted glass cases containing prize trout.

The producer, John Cigarini, strolled in at midday in shades and T-shirt, ignoring me and placing his trainers on the kitchen table, seizing our phone and dictating a long *Sunday Times* classified ad: '1969 Mercedes convertible for sale' etc. The cheek! Later he sent me a snapshot of himself riding a pushbike: 'This explains why I had to sell my car: I was being done for drunk driving.'

To everyone's surprise, J R Hartley was the hit commercial of the decade, spawning many comic sketches, and turning Norman Lumsden into a minor celebrity. And in December 1991 a spoof book called *Fly Fishing* by J R Hartley – actually by Michael Russell – topped the *Sunday Times* bestseller list.

Savile row

Why did the BBC drop a Newsnight report investigating allegations of sexual abuse made against its long-serving employee Jimmy Savile? *Miles Goslett* investigates

When Sir Jimmy Savile died last October he was given a generally rapturous send-off in the press, with fulsome tributes to his charitable work. Savile's old employer the BBC joined in the celebration with two tribute programmes on TV and one on radio, all broadcast over Christmas. No mention was made of the unsavoury rumours about Savile's private life which had persisted throughout his career.

Before the BBC's tributes were aired, however, journalists on the BBC2 programme *Newsnight* had been investigating the dark side of the apparently saintly entertainer. Their enquiries centred around Savile's regular visits during the 1970s to Duncroft, an approved local authority school for emotionally disturbed girls aged between 13 and 18 in Staines, Surrey, which closed in 1980. It emerged that in 2007 Surrey Police and the Crown Prosecution Service had investigated a historic complaint that Savile had abused girls at the school but that no action had been taken.

Newsnight tracked down several ex-Duncroft pupils, now middle-aged women, who confirmed that Savile had molested them when they were aged fourteen or fifteen. At least one woman gave an on-camera, on-the-record interview to *Newsnight* about the abuse she had suffered.

By any standards this was a scoop which would have attracted a considerable amount of attention. However, at a late stage the *Newsnight* report, due to be shown in mid-December, was dropped.

The BBC's official line has always been that the report was abandoned purely because there were not enough facts to substantiate a particular angle they were pursuing relating to the Crown Prosecution Service. Their spokesman said: 'Any suggestion that a story was dropped for anything other than editorial reasons is completely untrue.' However a

BBC News source has revealed to me that this is a smokescreen and there were unquestionably other reasons underlying the decision. First, the extreme nature of the claims about Savile meant that the *Newsnight* report was going to seriously compromise the lavish BBC tributes scheduled to run later the same month. And second, the allegations directly involved the BBC in that the woman who gave the interview said that she and others were abused by Savile on BBC premises. To be precise, she told *Newsnight* that some abuse took place in Savile's dressing-room at BBC Television Centre in West London after recordings of *Clunk-Click*, a children's programme which he presented in 1973 and 1974; she also alleged that two other celebrities, both still alive, sexually abused Duncroft girls at Television Centre.

I have contacted three women who were interviewed by the BBC concerning the allegations about Savile. They allege that he gave them rewards such as cigarettes, records, and small amounts of money in return for sexual favours. Two of the women said that they also recall being taken for a drive in Savile's car in the Surrey countryside where abuse took place on the understanding that they could be in the audience of *Clunk-Click*. A

third woman said that Savile had committed one comparatively minor indecent assault on her at Duncroft but that she was aware that other girls experienced far worse.

The BBC has serious questions to answer. The *Newsnight* investigation uncovered information of which Surrey Police was not aware, and moreover allegations were made about living people. Surely the BBC had a duty to inform the police about these disclosures? Yet there is no indication that it has done so, and the BBC has refused to answer questions about this. Furthermore, given that Savile was on the BBC's payroll for more than 25 years, and along with the other celebrities who are still alive, is alleged to have abused minors on BBC premises, shouldn't the Corporation have launched an in-house inquiry? When asked if BBC Director-General Mark Thompson knew of the *Newsnight* report, the BBC refused to comment. But a source has told me that Thompson was tackled about the axing of the report at a pre-Christmas drinks party, so he cannot claim to be ignorant of it.

The BBC should be aware that the matter is not at an end. Many of Savile's other victims – and those of other celebrities with whom he mixed in the 1960s and 1970s – are preparing to speak out.

'Someone throw him a punchline'

God

by *Melanie McDonagh*

Lucky Rowan Williams is off to be Master of Magdalene College, Cambridge, which will be a congenial rest cure after the hurly-burly of life in Canterbury. It's what God meant him for, the life of scholarship, but it's a shame his formidable intellectual gifts got such short shrift from the nation. He began his time in office declaring that he wanted to capture the public imagination for Christianity, but he never got a chance, poor man.

He was corralled into the CofE's dreary debates about sexuality and gender almost from the start, and the only other occasion he got a very public hearing was when he made an uncharacteristically ill-judged speech about sharia law in Britain – though, as he said, the fuss was as much about what he was thought to have said as what he did say. But so many of the really interesting things he said – I've just been reading an admirable sermon he gave at Westminster Cathedral about the contemporary distinction between religion and spirituality – were only heard by those present, because most journalists will only pick up on the subjects they think people are interested in rather than those that are really interesting – homosexuality, say, rather than the Incarnation. He may have been opaque in his way of putting things, but I can't think of anyone else who could have engaged in a public dialogue with Philip Pullman, the Anglican atheist children's writer, in front of an audience stuffed with aggressive unbelievers.

It's hard to think of a successor with the same grace and courtesy, but my own preference – not that I'm entitled to one, mind, given I don't actually believe Anglican orders are valid – would be for a professing Christian. You might think that this would come as standard, but you'd be wrong. I have just been reading a piece in the *Spectator* by Keith Ward, an Anglican theologian and cleric, which suggests that the fundamentals of Christian belief – the bodily Resurrection of Christ and the Virgin Birth, say, can be pretty well dispensed with in Rowan Williams's successor.

His prescription for a reformed Anglicanism under a new archbishop is that 'it would have to stop any ordained ministers from pretending they are "true" Christians and get them to accept, as a condition of ordination, that they are part of one inclusive church with many diverse interpretations of Scripture and tradition, none of them certain and unchangeable. It would have to accept that its real basis is not the acceptance of some formal creed, but a basic commitment to an objective morality and loyalty to a God believed to be revealed in and through Jesus, with many interpretations of that revelation being possible.'

Come again? What that amounts to is that you could hold a Muslim view of Jesus – viz, that he was a prophet but not divine or anything – and you would still be eligible for ordination. In happier days, even the heroically inclusive CofE was anchored in the Thirty-Nine Articles and the Apostles' Creed, plus the teaching of the first six ecumenical councils. In this new dispensation it would be anchored in what, exactly? A belief in God? Heaven knows, my instincts are sectarian, but the Church of Latimer and Ridley deserves better than this.

Magical mystery vs tourists

BLOG BY TANYA GOLD, 2018

In Penzance, in winter, on a spit of the land in the Atlantic, it rains for weeks – the kind of rain that engulfs you. The steep granite streets are empty by six, and you can't get a meal in the pub after eight, because the chef has gone home.

On Sundays, the bus runs every two hours, a damp, lonely journey to St Just, or Newlyn, or Mousehole. The remoteness feels absolute, and, now I have adequate clothing, I love it. Everything that makes me anxious is 300 miles away.

But come May, Penzance and the Penwith peninsula change. It is a more dramatic change than you would see in a normal landscape, but Penwith is not normal. The pound shops and the banks in Penzance feel incidental to me; they are not part of the real Penwith, which is granite and sea, but the toys of a transient interloper called civilisation. This is the gateway to Lyonesse, to the site of Arthur's last stand against Mordred at Boleigh, to the end of everything.

I fret that I sound like a tourist, even though I live here, talking nonsense about myth. My Cornish friends say they do not sense that their land is enchanted. It is, for them, mere humblebrag and too obvious to comment on.

The change is even more marked in St Just, a town with its own weather system, which is cloud. In winter it feels like a town under a witch's curse, then the sun comes, and every day feels like a jubilee.

In May, in Penzance, the town curls out happily. You walk down Chapel Street to the harbour and see that new gift shops, with ludicrous, overpriced goods, have opened for the tourists. Cornish people do not pay £25 for a mug, not being mugs themselves. The rug shop places a rug on the pavement, which feels jolly; tourists walk past Maria Branwell's house, wondering what Cornish and Irish magic made her children, the Brontës, dream as they did. The old pubs fill up; the strange, triangular lido opens; the Scillonian crawls across Mount's Bay like a clock twice a day. Penzance feels generous in May, and willing to share itself.

It won't stay like this. As summer goes on, people will drive immense, and shiny, vehicles down the lanes to Porthcurno and Sennen, and we will lose our patience. They will leave bins in the middle of the road. Cornish people are considerate drivers, and know where to put the bins, but the tourists bring their town manners and their bin idiocies. By August we will long for the rain, and the isolation, again.

I once met...

Larry Adler

Paul Taylor remembers the maestro of the harmonica – and blagging

'We've just been asked to do Larry Adler,' my wife, Suzie, the well-known Australian publicist, announced, putting down the phone.

'Who's Larry Adler?' chorused Christine and Kendra.

'Larry Adler knew Ingrid Bergman and Greta Garbo,' I explained. 'Possibly intimately. He played doubles tennis with Dalì and Paulette Goddard and Charlie Chaplin. Possibly in the nude. He knew all these people. Al Capone, the Duke and Duchess of Windsor, Cary Grant. Everyone. He's just recorded something with Sting and Elvis Costello. He's a friend of the Duke of Edinburgh. He talks about them all in his *Oldie* column. He's the undisputed heavyweight-champion name-dropper, he's – '

'Good,' said Suzie, 'He's coming to Melbourne. You can meet him at the airport and look after him.'

I waited for Larry to fly in from Tasmania. The dozen or so passengers on the light plane filed out through Gate 29. Not one looked remotely like Larry, an octogenarian whose googly eyes I was familiar with courtesy of *The Oldie*.

I phoned Suzie. 'He's not on it.'

'Nonsense. Go to the luggage carousel.'

I went to the carousel. Round and round it trundled until the last luggage had been picked up and I was left standing alone with the sinking feeling that somehow I had lost someone I'd never met.

Then, from behind the plastic strip curtain, an attractive young girl emerged, pushing a wheelchair in which a little eighty-year-old man sat clutching his luggage. He had googly eyes. Larry Adler! In a wheelchair! Oh, Lordie I'd have to get him and his chair in and out of the car wherever we went. At the top-rating radio station I'd have to lug him, over my shoulder, up two flights of stairs.

I greeted Larry with as much warmth

as I could muster, wheeled him to my car and stowed his luggage. Then he rose, gave the young girl an avuncular peck on the cheek and slipped into the back seat.

A miracle!

Larry was able to walk perfectly well. No doubt he could do the rumba if

Larry Adler, a former Oldie columnist, at The Oldie of the Year Awards in 1993

> 'Once, when we were running late for an on-air interview, he broke into a kind of canter and then, at my urging, a gallop. He was a pro. He was fun'

required. Once, when we were running late for an on-air interview, he broke into a kind of canter and then, at my urging, a gallop. He was a pro. He was fun. And he had endless stories about the famous. But he never told the tale of the miracle.

Three days later and it was time to say goodbye. At the airport again he got out of the car and said: 'Would you ask them for a wheelchair. Say I can't walk without pain.' In the Qantas Golden Wing lounge – I had talked our way in, following Larry's suggestion – I raised a glass to him. The last I saw of Larry he was waving farewell over his shoulder, the first passenger on the plane home.

Attended, of course, and in his customary wheelchair.

Sock it to me, quantum

He counted them all out, and he counted them all back: by tracking his socks in and out of the washing machine, *Paul Lewis* took physics into a new domestic domain

We've all done it. You put on the weekly wash, with its usual 12 dark socks, a pair for every day except Sunday (I know, I know, but let him who is without sin throw the first smelly shoe). But when the spin cycle ends and you take out the load, one of the identical socks has gone missing. You search inside the duvet cover, in the sleeves of jumpers and shirts, even inside other socks. And to be fair, one does sometimes pop back into the known universe. And when you replace your washing machine you are likely to find one dusty old sock snuggling behind the hot water pipe, lonely but dry. But over the years, every month or so a genuinely odd number emerges despite an even number going in. So where do they go?

It has puzzled me since I first visited the launderette as a student and persisted through washing machine renting, then ownership. Where do the odd socks go? Then suddenly it stopped.

Needing to top up my sock drawer, I grabbed a pack of twelve cotton-rich in the supermarket. They were black, of course, but each pair had a different coloured stripe around the toe and each colour spelled out a day of the week – Tuesday was a yellow stripe, Friday green, and so on. Of course, when I wore them I ignored the days – no one can say I don't still have a youthful streak of rebellion – though I was curious as to which day would begin to disappear first as they came out of the washing machine drum.

> 'It has puzzled me since I first visited the launderette as a student . . . Where do the odd socks go?'

But when I came to fold and match my washing, I had the jigsaw-completing joy of six socks of each stripe. The same thing happened the following week. And the next. In fact, in the nine months I have been using these colour-coded socks, not a single one has gone missing (I don't count the week when I thought one had, only to discover the unmatched singleton still unwashed in the bottom corner of the basket). There is only one explanation of these observations – quantum physics.

It is well said that anyone who thinks they understand quantum physics is mistaken. The famous two-slit experiment found that if you fire single photons through a pair of slits, then each single particle will go through both slits as if it were a wave, and leave a wave interference pattern where it strikes the wall behind. But if you set up a way of measuring which slit they go through, they will form two distinct clumps, as if each photon had gone through one or the other.

So measuring what they do – or rather setting up a mechanism to measure it – changes the nature of particles 'on the quantum scale' – a scientist's way of saying 'no, we don't know how it works either'. Normally, quantum effects apply only to very tiny particles like photons or electrons. But my sock phenomenon is clearly a quantum event. If the socks are all identical you cannot watch each pair in and watch each pair out. All you can do is count them afterwards. But if they have a different coloured stripe on the toe, they can be watched in, pair by pair, and then counted out, pair by pair. It doesn't matter whether you actually watch them or not. The fact that you have set up the measuring device – the coloured stripes – causes the collapse of the wave function into a singularity.

Until now the largest particle that has been shown to exhibit quantum effects is a complex carbon molecule. My washed socks take the quantum universe into a new domestic domain.

Still with us

Cliff Michelmore

TV presenters of yesteryear invariably put today's crop to shame – none more so than Cliff Michelmore, still with us at 92. Interview by *Edward Mirzoeff*

Cliff Michelmore was a favourite uncle when the BBC was still Auntie. In the Fifties and Sixties few personalities were better known, none was better liked. He was the 'anchor-man' of the popular BBC *Tonight* programme. Each weekday evening eight million or more viewers welcomed Michelmore into their living rooms as a cheerful, enthusiastic and unpatronising guest. Producers appreciated his relaxed calm. In unpredictable live studios, before such comforts as teleprompters or pre-recorded videotape, they relied on breezy unflappable Cliff to get them through. And he always did.

Today Michelmore is 92. When I visited him at his converted barn in unspoiled country on the Hampshire-Sussex border, he seemed very much as he has always been – benign, charming, avuncular. His voice is unchanged, his figure, in blue pullover and grey flannel trousers, is upright, though walking is a little more difficult than it used to be.

The house is rich in memories of his wife Jean Metcalfe – her accomplished watercolours on the walls, her favourite yellow roses newly cut. They first 'met' over the airwaves: from London she presented *Two-Way Family Favourites,* a popular radio request programme that linked the forces in Germany with their families at home; in Hamburg the new announcer was Squadron Leader Cliff Michelmore. It was love at first hearing. They finally met face to face at Broadcasting House ('You must be Jean...'), wed in March 1950, and enjoyed an idyllically happy marriage. She died just weeks short of their Golden Wedding.

Today he lives alone, though his two children, composer Guy and actress Jenny, are not far away.

Michelmore, an Isle of Wight boy, joined the RAF at the age of fifteen as

an Aircraft Apprentice. His father had died of TB years before, and it was a way of getting a good education. By 1940 he was in France with 12 Squadron: 'We were the very last people out, miles after Dunkirk...' He became an Engineering Officer and served in Bomber Command headquarters. In Germany, after the war, he helped out with sports commentaries, played Little John in a radio *Robin Hood* and drifted into broadcasting for the British Forces Network. When he and Jean decided to marry he returned to England, and the new world of television.

A stint on children's TV led to his taking over as presenter of the stylish, inquisitive and unstuffy *Tonight*. Everyone interesting came to talk to him – Gene Kelly, Queen Frederica, seventeen-year-old David Bowie (then David Jones, appearing in his capacity as founder of the Society for the Prevention of Cruelty to Long-Haired Men), Ionides (the handler of the world's most poisonous snakes). Multimillionaire Nubar Gulbenkian brought his new gold-plated London taxi into the studio. Why a taxi? 'They tell me that it can turn on a sixpence – whatever that is.'

Cliff's role was not only to interview, but also to anchor the show. 'You're the one we always come back to – you're the one the audience trusts,' they said. He was on the air when the phone rang, with the news that the plane carrying the Manchester United team had crashed in Munich. 'I had to say something, but I have no memory what it was. It was the worst moment.'

He recalls another. He was playing golf with Eric Sykes, Harry Secombe and Max Bygraves when a message came to travel immediately to Wales. A landslide of coal tippings and mud had buried over a hundred children in Aberfan. 'Men coming up out of shifts, straight up to the school... the worst situation I've ever had to face. One man, he was the Methodist minister, talked about how dreadful it was, what could he do, and so on. It was only after he'd gone that somebody told me he'd lost two sons. It was the most shattering experience.'

Later Michelmore handled the *Holiday* programme and many others. He became Mr BBC, presenting the great events – Apollo space broadcasts, general elections, the Prince of Wales's Investiture. There is, deliberately, no such figure today, he points out, which may account for the lamentable Jubilee coverage. His last broadcast was four years ago, for the BBC Parliament channel. He finds most television now stereotyped. Presenters today 'perform', he says. Not then. 'You'd soon get a boot up your bum if you did that. You have to be yourself. That's the secret.'

He reaches for a quote from Lord Reith: 'The public must be offered something better than it knows it wants.' He pauses. 'It's a pity that the people in the BBC don't think of that now.'

Cliff Michelmore died in March 2016

OLDEN LIFE

What was … scrimshaw?

Whaling in the nineteenth century was big business. Before mineral oil came to be widely used, whale oil was the best and almost only source of oil for lubrication and for burning as candles and in lamps. There were also by-products: meat, fat, bone, baleen, pharmaceuticals, ambergris and ivory teeth. The teeth were cleaned, polished and decorated in a process called scrimshaw.

The whaling ships would go to sea and not return until their holds were filled with barrels of oil. Such voyages would last from two to five years, so there was much spare time to fill between bursts of excitement and danger when harpooning whales. The best oil came from the sperm whale, which has about forty teeth, all on the lower jaw, slotting into sockets above. Many teeth are four to six inches long, but some go up to a lovely eleven inches of curved white ivory.

The art etched on the tooth was drawn by ordinary sailors and was often naïve, depicting their ship, whales, harpooning incidents, sweethearts back home and other subjects. The drawings were outlined by rubbing lamp soot or ink into the scratches.

The earliest dated scrimshaw

Scrimshaw inscribed on the back with 'The ship Alexander in Dundee'

(marked 1829) was done on the ship *Susan* by Frederick Myrick – a simple and rather satisfactory way of achieving immortality.

Whaling was a dangerous trade. Once a whale was spotted, small boats were lowered from the mother ship with six men: four rowers, a steerer and a harpooner. Harpooning was done by hand by a man standing in the bow. The whale could tow the boat at speed for some distance. These boats were sometimes sunk by the flip of a whale's tail or crushed between its jaws. There are tales of ships sunk by an outright attack, with whales charging and ramming into them. The whales could be sixty feet long and weigh sixty tons.

Once killed, a flag would be posted on the carcass to denote ownership. The heavy and greasy work then began: cutting up and rendering the blubber

by boiling it and storing it in barrels. A big whale could provide seventy barrels of oil. Then there was time to kill. One sailor's journal notes, 'The sky is clear with fresh winds. We are now regularly cruising, with not enough to do to keep a man off a growl. I prefer to scrimshaw.' Another writes: 'I am unsettled in mind for want of work. Saw nothing, and all work done. An idle head is a workshop for the devil. Employed scrimshawing.'

The US whaling fleet once comprised over 700 vessels, with tens of thousands employed on board and ashore. Many other countries participated: Hull was a centre in the UK. The industry faded as stocks were depleted through overfishing, and mineral oil took over. Today the oil has been consumed, the ships and crews have gone, and all that is left of this once great global industry are the scrimshaw teeth, much treasured and collected. President Kennedy had some on his desk in the White House, and his wife had one inscribed with his seal of office. She put it into his coffin.
JOHN MACLAY

The first rule of MIME CLUB is: YOU DO NOT TALK about Mime Club!

Dr Stuttaford's surgery

Your medical queries answered by our resident doctor

When good juice goes bad...

A Norfolk reader asks if there is any justification for the recent report that grapefruit juice can combine dangerously with medication prescribed for some common forms of heart disease.

For at least twenty years it has been known that grapefruit juice could interact with some drugs. The resulting reaction could upset the metabolic pathways so that a drug that was normally relatively safe could be rendered toxic. Initially it was thought that one or two drugs reacted to grapefruit so that the drug was inadequately metabolised (broken down) and therefore accumulated in the patient's system. Until recently this problem had only been reported with 17 commonly used pills or potions, but in the last four years the number has leapt to 43, quite enough to make it worthwhile for all grapefruit aficionados to ask their doctor, each time they are given a fresh prescription, whether it mixes well with grapefruit.

An example of an unhappy union is that of grapefruit with amiodarone, a drug used in the treatment of cardiac arrhythmias. If amiodarone is taken with a traditional two-star hotel glass of grapefruit juice or the seemingly innocent but aesthetically unpleasing grapefruit with a glacé cherry in its centre, breakfast might be transformed into a pot of poison. If amiodarone accumulates in the system its effect could be so increased that it induces a potentially fatal heart rhythm. Just to add to a heart patient's troubles it could well be that they are also taking a statin. Some statins react with grapefruit so that they are inadequately metabolised and accumulate, though the levels reached only rarely cause significant trouble. Other heart drugs that are adversely affected by grapefruit include some of the beta blockers and calcium channel blockers.

The ability of grapefruit juice to interfere with a treatment regime isn't confined to those with heart problems. In one way or another grapefruit can also affect the action of anti-depressants, antipsychotics, tranquillisers, steroids and other hormones.

The effect of one or two 'lifestyle' drugs may also be altered by grapefruit. The pleasure of coffee may be enhanced with a glass of grapefruit juice at breakfast, but that combination taken in the evening could put paid to a good night's sleep, for it prolongs as well as increases the action of the caffeine. It might be suggested to the hapless and sleepless coffee drinker that adding Viagra to the mix might be a way to fill his sleepless hours with something more interesting than counting sheep. But beware, the power of Viagra may well be increased by grapefruit, but so would the likelihood of suffering from one or another of Viagra's undesirable side effects.

Drugs that interfere with doctors' treatment regimes achieve their devilment in different ways and the extent that these interactions affect someone varies from person to person. Good medicine has to be bespoke rather than off the peg. My comments about warfarin in the December *Oldie* annoyed at least one person as I didn't define which of the confounding factors listed enhanced the anticoagulant effect of warfarin and which reduced it. I probably should have done, but what really matters is that whenever the effect of warfarin is either increased or decreased, the treatment regime is destabilised.

Mouth organs

A Surrey reader says that in the 1930s doctors always looked at a patient's

K.J. Lamb

'If anyone calls, I'm in the bath'

tongue. It was an essential part of any visit to the surgery. Does it no longer matter as a diagnostic guide? The reader also wonders why so many children with tongue-tie never have the frenulum that ties it down snipped. Should doctors still look at tongues?

Yes. Tongues are as important a diagnostic guide as they were 75 years ago, although now doctors have many other ways of determining what is wrong with their patients. The doctor looks to see if the tongue is moist and the patient well hydrated, or if it is dry and coated. If coated brown there could be kidney trouble, if black it's usually a benign fungus. If white, is the coating of uniform consistency? If patchy with plaques, thrush is a possibility.

If the tongue is a healthy pink, all well and good, but if slightly bluish, suspect heart or lung disease. A shiny, smooth, bright red tongue may indicate anaemia or vitamin deficiency. A dark red tongue, textured like the surface of a strawberry with a few white patches, may suggest streptococcal infection. A red tongue with large irregular white patches, just as if a map had been drawn on it, has no single cause.

The tongue is a muscular organ with an excellent nerve supply. When a patient puts out their tongue, the doctor notices if it comes out straight as a die or if it deviates to one side. A deviating tongue raises suspicions of a stroke. A tremulous tongue may be evidence of Parkinson's disease, an overactive thyroid or simple anxiety. There is much, much more that can be learned from a tongue, but the story is too long to fit the page!

Tongues are still snipped, but caution is called for as an artery may be lurking in the frenulum.

Dr Stuttaford died in June 2018

I once met...

The Rector of Stiffkey

Richard Whittington-Egan recalls his childhood encounter with the 'Prostitutes' Padre'

It was the blazing blue summer of 1934. He lay in a glass coffin packed in ice. Such was the curious circumstance in which, as an eleven-year-old schoolboy on holiday in Blackpool, I made the acquaintance of the Reverend Harold Davidson, the notorious Rector of Stiffkey (locally pronounced 'Stewkey').

He lay there, the Prostitutes' Padre, wrapped in an invisible robe of martyrdom. He was exhibiting himself thus in a sideshow on Blackpool's Golden Mile in an endeavour to raise funds to fight the verdict which had been brought in against him and led to his being unfrocked.

The accusation levelled was that of immorality, and he was said to have neglected his parish, deep in rural Norfolk, where he and his wife had lived for twenty-six years and brought up five children.

It was alleged that no sooner on a Sunday had he stepped down from the Stiffkey pulpit than he stepped onto the London train and headed for his chosen West End parish of gamey Soho. There, proudly bearing his self-bestowed title of the Prostitutes' Padre, he set zealously about his Gladstonian mission of rescue and reform of fourteen- to twenty-year-old apprentice girls of the streets, before catching the last Saturday night train back to Stiffkey, and his foursquare flint and brick rectory.

It is likely that the prostitutes used him as a channel of grace rather than that he used them as conduits of disgrace.

Sadly, with not untypical lack of Christian charity, the Church authorities would not hear of the possibility of his innocence. At the end of a twenty-five-day hearing in the Great Hall of Church House, Westminster, the Reverend

Harold Francis Davidson was pronounced guilty and, in October 1932, was unfrocked at a bell, book and candle ceremony in Norwich Cathedral. The wagging tongues of gossip had won the day.

I can still hear the Rector's voice. His

> 'He set zealously about his Gladstonian mission of rescue and reform of fourteen- to twenty-year-old girls of the streets'

was the most beautiful that I have ever heard; a mellifluous amalgam of the Oxford accent and ecclesiastical tone. Clergymen and barristers are often actors. Both are declamatory. His first love had been the stage, a passion which he shared with his schoolfellow, Maundy Gregory, the honours and titles tout.

I went back to see him in his glass coffin every day. We talked of fossils, the stories of Edgar Allan Poe, the mystery of Jack the Ripper. I told him that I did not like school. His reply, steadfast and unblinking, befitted the Royal Naval chaplain he had been from 1916 to 1920: 'Always stick to your guns. Tell the truth and fear no man.'

The fortnight's holiday came to an end. I returned to school. It was one July day three years later that I heard again of my Blackpool holiday friend. Striving still to raise the wherewithal to re-open his case, he betook himself, like Daniel, into the lion's den. The particular den he chose was at Skegness Amusement Park. The crowd paid their silver sixpences to see him in the cage with Freddie the lion and Toto the lioness, and listen to his well-rehearsed denials and claims of innocence.

This time he made a small but fatal mistake. He somehow managed to trip over Toto's tail. Freddie, misinterpreting the accident as an attack on Toto, sprang up to Davidson, fatally mauling him with tooth and claw. The Old Testament Daniel was rescued by an Angel of the Lord. It was sixteen-year-old Irene Somner, the sideshow's girl lion-tamer, who dragged the blood-drenched Rector out of the cage.

He was rushed to Skegness Cottage Hospital. Two days later, on 30th July 1937, he died. They buried him in the graveyard of his old church at Stiffkey.

Blazing saddles

Southwest Spain is a horse-lover's paradise. Prepare to be dazzled, says *Elinor Goodman*

The Jerez Feria del Caballo

According to the artist Snaffles there was no better view in Europe than that seen through the ears of a horse. He was referring to the sight of hounds in full cry as seen by a rider. Until I went to the Jerez horse fair in Spain I would have agreed with him – but now I think that there is no better view in Europe than the fairground seen through the ears of a pair of Andalucian carriage horses and the liveried shoulders of two coachmen.

All around the fairground are carriages, each drawn by up to five horses immaculately turned out with bells and tassels. The passengers – as many as ten per carriage – are waving and drinking sherry. Between the carriages parade women in spectacular flamenco dresses. This is the Jerez equivalent of Ladies' Day at Ascot, and women start planning their outfits for it as soon as one fair is over. Flamenco music is everywhere. Groups of women start dancing. In some of the restaurants lining the parade ground there are private flamenco parties hosted by famous names in the sherry industry. In others, anyone can join in.

Jerez is a wonderful base for touring southwest Spain, the region of sherry, bulls and horses. The area's richest landowners were, traditionally, the big sherry producers like Domecq and Osborne. They also kept bulls for meat and for the bullring, and to control them they needed powerful, fearless horses. The *vaqueros* (livestock herders) still ride these horses, most of them Andalucian stallions, and compete in *la doma vaquera*, a specialised form of dressage. By the standards of British dressage, the horses are over-bent, their powerful necks arched, and their heads tucked into their chests. They wear severe bits in their mouths, and inside their nosebands there are studs, or even spikes, to get them to tuck their heads in. But the result is beautiful. The best almost dance, and skid to a stop from a gallop with their front feet braced together. The riders sit bolt upright with one hand on the reins, the other carried at hip height as if holding a glass of sherry (which some do), or a whip.

During the fair the *vaqueros* compete in the stud opposite, where the horses are also prepared for the parade of carriages. But you can see displays at other times of the year at the ranches of some of the great sherry producers, and the Carthusian monks have a stud, the Hierro del Bocado, in their grounds near Jerez.

Spain claims to be the only country to have made horses a national monument, and in the south they remain an important part of life. El Rocío, about an hour from Seville in the Doñana National Park, calls itself the 'international village of the horse'. A tiny town of white houses with verandas and hitching posts at the front and stables at the back, its bars are designed so riders can have can have a sherry without dismounting. Quiet out of season, in May over a million people, many on horseback or in horsedrawn carriages, make a pilgrimage there. There are horses everywhere, grazing on the common land that surrounds the town, and mules are still used for pulling the heavier carts on the pilgrimage.

You can hire horses a few miles away in Matalascañas and there are several ranches which provide riding holidays, including some run by English expats, enthralled by the Spanish passion for horses. May is the best month to catch the horse fairs, but there are horse events most of the year, including, in August, a race along the beach at Sanlúcar de Barrameda, a lovely white-walled town famous for its manzanilla wine.

But this area has more to offer than horses and sherry. The marshland is full of migratory birds and the Costa de la Luz, between Algeciras and Cadiz, has some of the best beaches I have ever seen in Europe – if you don't mind the wind. It is beginning to be developed but it maintains a wonderfully wild, Moorish feel.

RANT

Where I live in north Norfolk, the speed of BT's broadband service is dismal – for those who understand these matters mine was 0.2 Mb/s, which meant that attempts to use BBC iPlayer or to watch films were futile. Hundreds of thousands of people living in rural areas suffer a similar experience, although they pay the same amount for BT's broadband as those living in its broadband hotspots.

So I read with fury the news that BT is spending £738 million to televise Premiership football for the next three seasons and still more for rights to the FA Cup and Scottish and European matches. Why can't it devote that sort of sum to its core business, telecommunications, providing all its customers with a broadband service fit for the 21st century?

My answer has been to switch to a more enterprising, rapidly expanding local service based in Norwich, which has given me a broadband speed of 6.4 Mb/s at a competitive price and transformed my life.

I rang BT to cancel my broadband deal (not the landline) and the result, a few weeks later, was that our telephone was cut off. We discovered this when friends who would normally ring resorted to having to communicate by letter. I tried to contact BT. To get through I had to tap in my telephone number, but of course that had now become invalid. I had to resort to Skype.

A few days later contact with the outside world was restored. But without even warning us BT had given us a new telephone number, meaning that we would have to spend further time and expense informing all our contacts. BT had also discontinued the 1571 answering service.

Eventually BT relented and agreed to restore our old telephone number. 'That should be £50, but I'll let you off,' said the lady at the end of the BT line.

BRIAN MACARTHUR

illustration by TOM PLANT

RIP the genius who designed jumpers for Elton, Diana – and me
BLOG GYLES BRANDRETH, 2018

My friend George Hostler has died. He was a lovely man and the designer who, in the 1980s, created an amazing array of fabulous fun jumpers worn by the likes of the Princess of Wales, Elton John – and me. Diana and Elton only had a couple of George's jumpers. I had hundreds.

I last wore one of George's jumpers in public in about 1990, but even now, nearly thirty years later, barely a day goes by when somebody doesn't ask me about them. If I'm known as 'the fellow in the woolly jumpers' (and, like it or not, if I'm known at all it's probably as that), it's thanks to George Hostler.

George was a bit of a genius. He graduated from Durham University with a BA (Hons) in Fine Art and became a sculptor – exhibiting his work in the UK, across Europe and in Australia. In the 1970s he turned from sculpture to fashion, formed his own design house and began creating knitwear for, among others, Zandra Rhodes and Stirling Cooper.

'Diana and Elton only had a couple of George's jumpers. I had hundreds'

His jumpers began to sell worldwide – at Harrods in London, at Bloomingdales in New York, in upmarket outlets in Germany, France, and Japan. In the early 1980s, walking through Kensington, I saw one of his jumpers in a shop window, went into the shop, bought the jumper and decided to find the man behind the label.

I found that he was based in Leicester, as head of the Design Foundation Department at Leicester Polytechnic, now De Montfort University. I got in touch; we met; we became friends; and over the next few years – when I was appearing regularly on TV-am, on Countdown, on game shows like Give Us A Clue, Blankety-Blank and The Railway Carriage Game – George created appropriate jumpers for me to wear for each appearance.

Because he was based in Leicester and I was in London, I'd call him to discuss an idea, or send a doodle of a design to him on a postcard; he'd then create the jumper, parcel it up and send it up to London by train. I'd be at the parcels office at St Pancras station several days a week picking up packages from George.

I'll post another blog later about my life with jumpers. This is just to salute the memory of George Hostler (1939-2018) – a completely delightful person, self-deprecating, humorous, kind-hearted, creative. I was lucky to know him. In a way, he changed my life. He certainly enhanced it. Knowing the gifted and lovely person who was George Hostler was nothing but a joy. May he rest in peace.

Teesdale treasure

Laura Gascoigne on the Bowes Museum – whose founders had an astonishingly good eye for a bargain...

Barnard Castle in County Durham has the unusual distinction, for an English market town, of boasting two French castles, one built as a fortress by the 12th-century Anglo-Picard baron Bernard de Balliol, the other as a museum by the 19th-century coal baron John Bowes and his French wife and former actress Benôite-Joséphine Coffin-Chevallier.

Joséphine was a better painter than she was an actress, and ten years into a childless marriage the couple hatched a plan to found a museum of fine and decorative arts for the 'Barney Cassel people',

funded by the sale of Joséphine's chateau. For fifteen years their agents – three in Paris, one in Ghent – combed the markets for affordable paintings, ceramics, furniture, metalwork and textiles under £10 to fill a gallery designed by French architect Jules Pellechet (Mr Pleshy to the locals) on the neo-Renaissance chateau model favoured by Napoleon.

It took a bit from the Tuileries and a bit from the Hôtel de Ville in Le Havre, which the couple got to know rather too well while confined to port by Mrs B's pathological fear of rough seas. (The captains of the Channel steamers were placated every Christmas with presents of game.)

'Squally Weather: Sketch near Boulogne' – 'a portrait of your enemy', joked her friends – was shown at the Salon and

Clockwise from top left: the mechanical silver swan; Joséphine Bowes, resplendent in Worth and diamonds – possibly a self-portrait; Joséphine Bowes's 'Squally Weather: Sketch near Boulogne'

now hangs with other landscapes by Joséphine in the company of historic masterpieces picked up for a song. These include Sassetta's 'A Miracle of the Eucharist' (£6.50), El Greco's 'The Tears of St Peter' and Goya's 'An Interior of a Prison' (£8 each) – the last two, cheap but insufficiently cheerful for the couple's tastes, were acquired reluctantly on the advice of their agent. He didn't convert them to Impressionism, unfortunately – they bought Boudin but stopped short of Monet. Courbet's 'View at Ornans' probably slipped by on the strength of its resemblance to 'Teasdale [sic] magnified'.

The museum has other glittering attractions, most famously the mechanical Silver Swan – a big-ticket item for John Bowes at £200 – which from the size of the audience for its 32-second performance on the day I went is still repaying the investment.

Joséphine had a soft spot for automata (her father had been a clockmaker), diamonds, Worth dresses and reproduction Louis XV furniture. A report by the 'Parisian Correspondent' of the *Darlington and Stockton Times* that in Paris the Bowes moved in Bonapartist circles is borne out by a parade of portraits of Napoleon's extended family, from Boney himself in full coronation fig to his old mum.

The tragedy of the Bowes Museum was that neither of its founders lived to see it open. Joséphine died aged just 48 in 1874, two weeks after the roof-raising, and John followed in 1885.

Open daily 10am to 5pm. Closed 25 and 26 December and 1 January. Annual pass £14 (concessions and passes available). www.thebowesmuseum.org.uk

I once met...

Sir Robert Mayer

Donald Trelford was astonished by the great age of the musician, businessman and philanthropist

Just over thirty years ago, I received a surprise invitation to a dinner at the Athenaeum. The surprise was that I hadn't met my host before. He was Sir Robert Mayer, a tiny figure then aged 99, who had been a great patron of music, having started Concerts for Children before the Second World War and Youth and Music after it. I never knew why he invited me, except that I had recently become Editor of the *Observer*. His other guest was Robert Armstrong, later Sir and now a lord, who became Cabinet Secretary in the Thatcher years.

The dinner was given by a secret Fleet Street club whose proceedings, by convention, were never reported and therefore attracted guest speakers of an unusually high calibre, presumably because they felt safe from the dreaded media. The speaker that night was Prince Philip, who made some remarks about the dangers of uncontrolled immigration which struck me as uncontentious, but would doubtless be regarded these days as politically incorrect.

To make conversation, I asked Sir Robert: 'You know so much about music you must be able to say who was the greatest composer – one of the three great Bs or the great M?' He replied: 'Well I'd have to say Brahms, wouldn't I?' I was surprised and asked him why. His reply was disconcerting: 'Because he was the only one I ever met.' He explained: 'I was studying music at the Mannheim Conservatoire. The winner of the student piano competition played for Brahms and the runner-up sat next to him. I didn't win,' he said defensively, 'because I was so short my feet couldn't reach the pedals,

'I used to have lunch with him occasionally at his flat, where I noticed that the first entry in his visitors' book was Béla Bartók, dated 1922'

but I did sit next to him.' Later I checked the dates: Brahms died in 1897, when Mayer would have been 18.

Rather dazed by this, I turned to the topic of the evening: immigration. 'You must have been an immigrant yourself, Sir Robert. When did you first come to this country?' '1899,' he said, which silenced me for a while until I countered with a slightly jokey follow-up: 'So which side did you fight on in the First World War – Germany or Britain?' 'First World War, old boy?' he replied in a puzzled tone. 'Much too old to fight in the First World War.'

There I was, sitting in a London club, talking to a man who went back a century. I said to him: 'You must have been remarkably fit all your life, to be still running around and dining out at your age.' 'Oh no,' he said, 'I've never been well. I had two heart attacks in my sixties. That was my crisis. Everybody has a crisis at some time in their life: if you conquer it, they seem to forget about you. Have you had your crisis yet?'

The following year he sent me an auto-biographical pamphlet entitled *My First Hundred Years*. I used to have lunch with him occasionally after that at his luxurious flat near Portland Place, where I noticed that the first entry in his visitors' book was Béla Bartók, dated 1922. Because of his great age and apparent frailty, I didn't like to stay long at these lunches, assuming he needed a nap in the afternoons. I needn't have worried. Once I stood waiting at the lift and heard him bustling up behind me, on his way to the Metal Exchange in the City, where he had made his fortune and tried to visit every day. He married again at the age of 101 and lived to be 105.

House Husbandry

with *Giles Wood*

In which Mr Wood views the natural world through the prism of socio-economic theory

BRITISH BULLFINCH (⅓)

According to breed notes our Tibetan spaniel may live up to fifteen years. For me that represents a further three years of canine servitude because Mary, in a moment of madness, took the decision to up the dog-sitting rate paid to the village urchin from a just-manageable five pounds per day to an unsustainable ten.

This own goal has had severe knock-on effects. Mary may want me to join her in London, but faced with the stark choice of seeing £70 per week go into the pocket of another villager or performing the dog-sitting chore myself, I will have to leave Mary to gallivant alone.

Luckily I have a well-stocked library, fresh supplies of windfall logs, and game from the village sportsman on a somewhat onerous 'pluck one get one free' basis to sustain me through these periods of economic house arrest.

Nor is life dull when the modest parcel of rough land attached to my hovel can be used as an open-air laboratory for the study of the laws of nature.

An early experiment to force an ash tree to grow horizontally by attaching 'Charles Atlas' dumbbells to the leading shoot proved an exercise in futility, and the following spring I saw the tree had outwitted me by sprouting multiple vertical shoots.

Meanwhile years of recycling the contents of Hoover bags into the compost heap illustrate the law of unintended consequences since, ten years after the children stopped playing with them, I continue to find Lego blocks in the vegetable garden. For these and other reasons I have a new mission statement with regard to both rough land and garden – 'relinquish control'.

In this I have been partly inspired by Natural Gardening guru Peter Harper. His advice to stop mowing has already delivered results in the form of rock-hard dock seeds, only crackable by the thick-necked bullfinch with its hook-shaped beak. Resembling miniature pink parrots, a flock of them feast on the seeds near the kitchen window.

> '**No sparrow will go back to berries and grubs once it has tasted Swoop, just as I will not go back to Maxwell House instant now I have tasted Arabica beans**'

Other laws of nature which have intrigued me include the perennial garden mystery of why some plants, like teasels and burdock, are self-supporters, while others, like delphiniums, keel over. Why do my sunflowers need staking to stay upright while serried ranks of them stand unsupported over many miles of southern France? Some of my plants even seem to collapse as I approach them, as though sensing support is on its way. Is there a chilling lesson to be learnt from my 'Kiftsgate' climbing rose, which recently strangled to death its perfectly healthy apple-tree host?

The chief conclusion of my field observations has been that, like humans, plants and animals will also submit to dependency culture. If the opportunity to lean on other plants is taken, over time a type of spontaneous mutation takes place and the plant becomes unable to stand unsupported.

And since I stopped feeding the sparrows they have deserted our garden for a dwelling at the other end of the village where feeders are replenished all year round. Fortunately the wary bullfinches are too shy of such proximity to humans to join the deserters, but no sparrow will go back to berries and grubs once it has tasted Swoop, just as I will not go back to Maxwell House instant now I have tasted Arabica beans.

Sparrows boosted by artificial feeding are less lean, have a slower reaction time and are slower to take off than their unfed colleagues. It seems obvious that benefits and subsidies distort and corrupt natural bird behaviour, leaving them more vulnerable to predators like magpies, but I am unable to test this theory because I don't think free-range sparrows exist any more.

And why has the dog, perfectly capable of charging down the staircase on its own if someone knocks at the door, begun cringing at the top of it in all other circumstances, as though it can only get down if I carry it?

This is dependency culture, both inside and outside the cottage.

Eileen Atkins is the cleverest of our theatrical dames (the only one who writes plays and film scripts too) and, aged 80 this June, she is more in demand than ever. Being 'one of the long lean bony-faced tribe', she was overlooked in her twenties – Noël and Binkie (Beaumont) took one glance and cast her as the cleaning lady.

'I had a decade of total disregard. Luckily my husband kept me: I'm so grateful to Julian.' She met her first husband, Julian Glover, in rep at Butlins Skegness and told him to try the RSC because 'Michael Redgrave is going, and they'll need tall people alongside, or he'll look weird'. Glover begged the RSC 'on his knees' to take Eileen too. 'Glen Byam Shaw said, "We don't take wives. There'll be no parts" – but then Audrey in *As You Like It* was ill, and I got it.'

They say she can steal a scene with just one line, and did, in Pinter's *Mountain Language*. Readers may recall her Joan of Arc in the 1960 BBC Shakespeare series *An Age of Kings* – available on DVD, hooray. In the late Eighties she bestrode the stage as Virginia Woolf in *A Room of One's Own*, which she adapted herself. Then she wrote *Vita and Virginia*, and played Woolf again: scholars queued at her dressing-room door.

Fame, she says, means nothing but getting a good table in restaurants. Hers got us one at the fashionable Colbert, next door to the Royal Court Theatre. With her bobbed hair and a neat black jacket with epaulettes, she looks ageless. *The Oldie* made her Refusenik of the Year when she spurned a proposition from Colin Farrell at almost 70. 'Women over a certain age shouldn't talk about these things,' she said. 'But Colin still sends me messages.'

'Everything worthwhile involves work. I am so glad I chose work over children'

She is forever grateful to Mr Burton at Latymer School, Edmonton, for getting her into Shakespeare (and RP) from a Tottenham council estate. 'He fancied me, there's no doubt about that,' she says. A gypsy had told her barmaid mother, who was 47 when she was born, that she'd be a dancer, so from the age of seven she tap-

Atkins at 80

Eileen Atkins, our brainiest theatrical dame, talks to *Valerie Grove*

danced as 'Baby Eileen', sharing the bill with Anna Neagle singing 'Yankee Doodle Dandy'. Her bewildered parents then had to watch her in Chekhov; she was a cuckoo in their nest.

Today the acting profession excludes all but those with rich enough parents, and children of famous actors. Atkins doesn't resent this effortless dynastic assumption by Foxes and Redgraves: 'It's inevitable. They grow up among actors, and most actors are quite fun to have as parents. Then they've got all the contacts they need in their godparents.'

I recalled how pleased she was with herself when she belatedly learned to drive. 'Oh God I'm always pleased with myself,' she said. 'Smugness is one of my very worst virtues.' Virtues? (Gales of laughter.) 'Vices. I know I am a horrible person, but I am never less than pleased with myself. But with work, I am never satisfied. And everything worthwhile involves work: I'm so glad I chose work over children. It lasts longer.'

Her husband these 35 years is the amiable Bill Shepherd, producer, whom she met in a lift in 1978 and married two weeks later. She is the main breadwinner now and although she sometimes moans, she approvingly quotes Emma Thompson, 'Greg [Wise] is one of my little luxuries I can't do without', and enjoys the power breadwinning bestows.

With her Woolf money she built a book-lined room of her own, overlooking the Thames, with white-painted floorboards, chairs painted in Charleston style and no phone. When filming in London she insists on staying in a hotel, as work and domestic life don't mix. (Bill isn't allowed anywhere near when she's filming or rehearsing.) 'But I love my house. I love my cats, my house and my husband, in that order.'

She insists she can't remember her mobile number, and won't use email. Above all she scorns the twittersphere. 'Why would anyone want to tweet "I'm in the Colbert having peppermint tea"? Why does someone as bright as Stephen Fry want to do it?'

After her triumph this year as Ellen Terry (another solo) in the Globe's candlelit Sam Wanamaker Playhouse, there's a new Woody Allen film; then she's off to Stratford in the title role ('God help me') of *The Witch of Edmonton*, a Jacobean comedy whose impenetrable synopsis justifies her misgivings. 'I end up getting burned. Maybe it's the first really black comedy.'

She's never done a sitcom, hates frivolous entertainment. 'If you want something popular, let's bring back public hangings.' She would have loved university, 'because I love exams. I treat every play like an exam. Work is more fulfilling than idleness or going out drinking – a deadly way to pass the time.' When in a play, she no longer joins the rest of the gang in the pub after the show. 'They don't really want an old person along with them. I remember being constrained by Alec Guinness doing that, and I don't want to be constraining.'

She has been an insomniac since she was three, when she kept the household awake. 'An Indian doctor told my parents I had too much imagination to sleep. Then when I broke up with Julian my GP gave me tablets, and I've been taking them for 5o years. I went to a sleep farm in America where they put rubber things all over me and said I stayed in the Rapid Eye Movement stage all night long. But I like the night time. And I'm still cheerful most days. That's what's so smug about me.'

OLDEN LIFE

What was... Books and Bookmen?

Ask a reader today what they understand by 'books and bookmen' and they'll probably refer you to the snide column in *Private Eye*. But once upon a time that title belonged to a remarkable little magazine. I say 'little' because its circulation was known only to God, the printer and its owner, a reclusive homosexual called Philip Dossé, who started life on the old *Greyhound Express*. But it was not little in other respects, running to almost 200 pages a month at its peak in the 1970s. Mr Dossé may have been shy in person – he would pretend to be an underling if someone he didn't know turned up at the magazine and asked for him – but he was brazen about soliciting contributors. Consequently, you never knew who you might find there. In November 1976, for instance, the masthead listed Prince Charles, Terry Eagleton, Lady Diana Mosley, Melvyn Bragg, J K Galbraith, Lord Boothby, Tariq Ali and Hans Eysenck. Among other regulars were Enoch Powell, Richard Crossman, Paul Foot, A L Rowse, Cecil King, Jonathan Meades, Sir Harold Acton, Colin Wilson and Richard Ingrams.

But the jewel in *Books and Bookmen*'s crown was Auberon Waugh, who was given *carte blanche* to display his talent to abuse. I think Bron once expressed 'mild surprise' that no one had tried to bump him off. You have only to trawl through back numbers of *B&B* to see why. Who else would have dared to describe Lady Diana Cooper, the pin-up of doomed young nobs in the Great War, as a 'cock-teaser' (an epithet Bron's besotted – and unsatisfied – father would surely have endorsed). I don't think Lady Diana herself ever wrote for *B&B*, but some of Bron's other victims certainly did. I recall seeing a letter to the editor from Peter Quennell, saying he could no longer appear beside 'that bloodthirsty stoat Auberon Waugh'; but a few months later there he was, bedding down again with Bron.

It wasn't the money that attracted people like Quennell. Except for Bron, contributors were paid peanuts (and sometimes asked to sit on their cheques for a bit). But in return they could say pretty much what they liked, at whatever length they liked, a massive incentive for a dictator manqué like King or a consummate egotist like Rowse. This could have been a licence for bores to bore but Rowse, King and the rest were usually entertaining. Only occasionally was there a piece that failed what Cyril Connolly called 'the dinner party test'. It was my misfortune, in my first – and only – week as editor, to encounter one of these.

Editing *B&B* was not a job I applied for and I don't know for sure how I came to be in the frame. I'd written for them once or twice, but my editorial credentials were slim. I'd just spent a year editing *Book Addict*, an impudent little rag, available free of charge in bookshops, which subsisted on the willingness of publishers to advertise in its pages. Some did, most didn't and that, in the end, was that. But while it lasted I acquired a taste for book launches and a dangerous dependence upon review copies, which could be flogged for half their price in cash at Gaston's, the library suppliers in Chancery Lane. So although my predecessor at *B&B*, Frank Granville Barker, cautioned that my stipend would be small and my authority very limited – Mr Dossé called the shots – I accepted.

At that time *B&B* was run from one room in a large, tatty basement flat in Artillery Mansions, off Victoria Street, the other rooms being occupied by Mr Dossé himself, whom I had yet to meet, and *B&B*'s six stablemates, *Films and Filming*, *Plays and Players*, etc, etc. I had two assistants, an anonymous young man and an elderly lady called Cis Amaral, a retired civil servant, who looked like one of the witches in *Macbeth* and warbled like a dowager. I dare say she didn't think much of me, either. But even if we had got on there would have been precious little time for gossip or pleasantries. The table around which we sat was covered with raw copy and galleys, all of which had to be read and marked. Belatedly I realised that I had signed up for a treadmill.

After three or four days of drudgery my patience wore thin, so when I began reading a review that made no sense at all something snapped. It was by Thomas Balogh, a Hungarian crony of Harold Wilson, and dealt with economic theory. With what now seems like breathtaking cheek – since I knew little about economics – I did my best to make it intelligible. When Miss Amaral saw what a mess I'd made of the galley, she grabbed it and scurried off into Mr Dossé's office. Eventually I was summoned there as well; and while I have no clear picture of Dossé himself, I remember his opening salvo: 'She won't work with you!' So ended my editorship. Miss Amaral took over, the puzzle being why she had not been offered the job in the first place, since she was far better suited to the treadmill than me.

In time, Amaral made way for the young novelist Sally Emerson, who recruited new talent like Christopher Hitchens. Then in September 1980, as the 25th anniversary edition went to press, the news broke that Mr Dossé was broke, owing more than £250,000 to his printers. A day or two later, aged 56, he gassed himself in the Notting Hill flat he shared with his mother. It then transpired that much of his time had been spent writing sycophantic letters to his star contributors; Bron Waugh claimed to have received ten in the course of one week. Yet when his old pal Godfrey Winn died suddenly he was heard to say, 'I hope that review he owed us is in the post.' What was never in the post was a cheque from the Arts Council. Whatever else *B&B* may have been, it was not a charity case.
MICHAEL BARBER

Signing off with Carpaccio

In her final book, *Jan Morris* tells of her lifelong passion for the Venetian painter Vittore Carpaccio

I have been toying for years with the prospect of old age, and have repeatedly determined that my next book will be my last. Now, as I stand on the brink of my nineties, I have decided that rather than signing off ponderously, I will go out with a little work that might, in a glancing and lighthearted way, sum up a life's attitude while the going is good. That life has been one of constant travel, but steadily near the heart of it for seventy years has been the city of Venice, and so I am making of my swan song something quintessentially Venetian.

My responses to that extraordinary place have fluctuated down the years, from my earliest experience of it to reading in the paper the other day about George Clooney's ultra-Venetian wedding celebrations. Ultra, yes, because for me the fascination of this place has always been extreme – like its history. It is not one of your normal conurbations. It is one of a kind in every sense, and through life I have responded to it as I have responded to nowhere else.

When I first saw it, as a nineteen-year-old subaltern in 1945, I was bewitched by its haunting melancholy. When I went to live there and write a book about it, in 1959, it seemed to me a crystallisation of sparkling delight and good humour. I was depressed when tourism began to rob the old place of its civic reality, and when the four golden Horses of St Mark, on their grand belvedere above the Piazza San Marco, were replaced by lifeless replicas in the cause of preservation. On the other hand, when purists were horrified by the gigantic new cruise ships that came to dominate the city skylines, spilling into its streets new multitudes of tourists, I couldn't help marvelling at the spectacle of those immense maritime machines gliding tremendously by, a very summation, I preferred to think, of Venice's immemorial and profitable alliance with the sea.

Through it all I ignored the municipal corruption. I stayed clear of tidal floods. I tried not to notice the vulgarisation of things. For me, Venice has been not only, as Byron had it, 'a boast, a marvel and a

Above: a detail from the 'Return of the Ambassadors', from the St Ursula Cycle, c 1490–98, now in the Gallerie dell'Accademia in Venice. Left: 'Miracle of the Relic of the True Cross on the Rialto Bridge', 1494, also in the Gallerie dell'Accademia. Top right: detail from 'St George and the Dragon', 1502, now in Venice's Scuola di San Giorgio degli Schiavoni

show', but a kind of unknowing bene-factor, through thick and thin, to whom I would like, in a last capricious book, to say a final thank you.

Fortunately, as it happens, Venice long ago became personified in my mind with one of its artists. Not one of the very greatest, the Titians, the Tintorettos or the Giorgiones who gave Venetian Renaissance art its towering sublimity, but a lesser master of the years before them.

Vittore Carpaccio, who died in 1520, is known chiefly to those who have come across his paintings during visits to Venice, or alternatively by those millions around the world who think a carpaccio is an item of cuisine – 'an Italian hors d'oeuvre', as the OED has it. It is indeed the artist's name that is attached to beef carpaccios or octopus carpaccios at restaurants around the world, names given to such dishes in 1970 by the creative owner of Harry's Bar in Venice, and I think Vittore would have been delighted by these cheerful contributions to his immortality – the instant pleasure of tourists, the approval of gourmands everywhere.

For I think of Carpaccio as a merry, easy-going man. Like my acquaintance with Venice itself, my relationship with him is purely imaginary, and personal. Over the long years I have come to regard him as a friend, my favourite Venetian,

personifying for me everything I have so long enjoyed about his city. I don't know what he looked like – nobody does. I don't know where he was born, or where he is buried, but I do feel I know him well, and love his company; and so it is that I am calling the very last of all my books *Ciao, Carpaccio!*, and subtitling it *An Infatuation.*

It deserves no more – and no less, perhaps! It is only a handsome little book with lots of pictures. It is not the work of a scholar, still less of a connoisseur. It is certainly not a memorial. It is only a writer's grateful response to a lifetime's amused familiarity and friendship, across the Venetian centuries.

Critics have sometimes dismissed Carpaccio as a kind of enjoyable light-weight. Even John Ruskin, who was later to become his influential cham-pion, at first thought him merely 'a kind of magic mirror ... never to be thought of as a responsible person', and he is chiefly respected still as an illustrator of Venetian life in his own time. But to my mind, though he is certainly not among the supreme artistic interpreters of the human condition, his is a genius of a gentler, subtler kind.

He is a story-teller, for a start. Much of his art is built around three series of narrative pictures, rather like graphic novels or even comic strips, which tell serious religious stories, but are en-

livened by every kind of entertaining device and wildly anachronistic detail. He loves children, from urchins to the Messiah, animals and birds from storks to dragons, ships, pomp of all kinds, colours, hats, flowers and brilliantly inventive architecture. He laughs a lot, but with his subjects rather than at them. He presents his Venice as a city of fancy, brightly coloured and inimitable. In short, to my mind he is Ultra-Venezia himself, the greatest of fun and the best of companions.

But he is more than that, too. His holy pictures are profoundly holy, but holy in his own particular way. He seems to me to be the supreme artist of that simple, universal and omnipotent virtue, the quality of Kindness.

So there we are. That's my last book. I have dedicated it to Harry's Bar in Venice, chiefly because of the many happy hours I have spent there, but partly because it has made the name of Carpaccio so universally popular: and on the corner of page 111, if ever you chance to thumb your way through *Ciao, Carpaccio!*, you will find a minute neo-Venetian illustration by my grand-daughter Begw, aged three, with a big bird on a castle wall, as it might be in a fairy tale.

'Ciao, Carpaccio!' is published by Pallas Athene

Has anybody spotted Jim Chapworthy?

After fifty years' resistance, *Oliver Pritchett* has succumbed to the school reunion

The rosy-cheeked old fellow points at me mock-accusingly and, from several feet away, booms 'I remember you!' 'Good God!' I shout, and, as we shake hands with wine-spilling vigour, I slyly look sideways at the name on his lapel badge to see if I recognise it. Unfortunately, the general bonhomie of the occasion has made my glasses mist up.

'Do you remember Dougie Rayne?' he asks, pointing to the tall man next to him. (I think he has said Dougie Rayne, but he is standing on my right, talking to my less good ear.) 'Not sure,' I say. 'What vintage were you?'

'I was a couple of years after you, actually,' the tall man says. Good heavens, the man is younger than me and he looks as if he hasn't got much time left on this earth. I notice that he is a bit show-offy with his walking stick, twirling it, prodding the floor. 'Has anybody spotted Jim Chapworthy?' I ask.

Yes, I admit it. After resisting for fifty years, I have succumbed to reunions. It's one of the perils of reaching the Age of Reminiscence. I'm not sure what sets it off; maybe a funeral or a memorial service starts one thinking about the past; maybe it's idle curiosity; maybe it's seeing 'J A Chapworthy' in the death notices in the *Daily Telegraph* and wondering if it was that J Chapworthy. Never realised he lived in Welwyn Garden City. Could be a different Chapworthy. Didn't know him all that well, to be honest.

Reunions are probably a male thing. I can't imagine many women wanting to go to the trouble of getting together with a group of half-remembered people to indulge in the simple pleasure of boring each other. The female idea of a reunion is a meeting of young mothers who were in the same ante-natal class, coming together to compare infants. These reunions are usually held in places where I am trying to have a quiet cup of coffee.

There are so many varieties – gather-ings of old soldiers, probably still addressing each other by their surnames, or maybe dinners or garden parties where former university contemporaries meet. The special pleasure of a university reunion is to observe the sleek appearance and the plump wallets of the people who read law.

There are also noisy, emotional office reunions, in a pub, of the survivors of the Great Wave of Redundancies of '74 (or whenever), or people who still remember the days before the office moved to Derby. Funerals and memorial services also make a good excuse for a reunion, but when you recognise a face from the past it's best not to grin and wave too enthusiastically across the aisle.

But the school reunion is the real thing. This is the one for the addicts, for really going back a long way, for occasions which manage to combine sentiment and bewilderment.

With luck it will be held at the school itself so we can see how the place has changed since our day. We get lost, just as we did as new boys, but eventually we make it into the brand-new luxurious Counselling Suite, which also serves as the Yoga Centre and the Multi-Faith Quiet Area, and we join a cluster of old boys. 'Carpets!' we snort. 'Under-floor central heating!' There is head-shaking. 'Duvets in the dorms,' we smirk. 'Vegetarian option in the dining hall.' (Actually the dining hall is now re-named the Student Restaurant.) 'Co-ed now, of course,' we observe gravely. Sometimes a polite pupil is on hand to show us around and listen to us crying out in dismay at the changes and in delight as we recall ancient pranks. These pupils are so well brought up that they tolerate all our stories about the old days, but I suspect they are inwardly praying, 'Please God, don't let them show me where they carved their initials.'

There is no need to worry if you show up at one of these functions and are at a loss to recognise anyone at all. Pretty soon a genial chap will wander up, introduce himself and join you in a chat about the old days. It will soon turn out that he now has grandchildren at the school. His son was here, too; that's three generations of the same family going there. It turns out that he is so devoted to the place that he has allowed himself to be co-opted onto the Appeal Committee. At this point I usually interrupt and say: 'Excuse me, but I think I've just spotted dear old Jim Chapworthy over there.'

I was first struck down with the reunion bug a few years ago when I accepted an invitation to a gathering of old boys from my former prep school. It was held in the Lansdowne Club, in Mayfair, a place that seems to go in for this kind of function. As I made my way up the stairs I rehearsed the vague distracted smile that can, if necessary, be mistaken for a look of recognition. I went into the room and did a couple of hesitant circuits, guardedly studying the faces, trying to imagine them younger. No sign of Chapworthy. No sign of anyone I knew. Not surprising, really, after very nearly sixty years. Then it dawned on me: I was at the wrong reunion. The one I was supposed to be attending was on the next floor up. The thing about reunions is they are really all the same.

'My Sunday Best' by Oliver Pritchett is published by Aurum Press at £10.99.

God

by *Sister Teresa*

Most people have never met an enclosed Carmelite nun and many of them ask questions that can be unexpected. Last week a charming stranger shook hands and said, 'Do tell me: at what time do Carmelites get up in the morning? I have always longed to know.' We get up at 5.30am, but four of us are on a weekly rota to unlock the house and church, which means getting up at five. These four pass one another a postcard of Turner's 'Sun Rising Through Vapour' to indicate whose turn it is (we don't speak from 7.45pm to 6am, during what is called the Great Silence – unless there is an emergency). Every time it is mine I am so pleased not to be gutting fish on the foreshore of an unnamed reach of the Thames estuary (as shown in the bottom half of the picture) that a trip down long, cold and dark corridors simply doesn't matter, and I positively look forward to Lauds, the first of the hours of the Divine Office which we start chanting at six.

Our days are designed to ensure that two hours of quality time (one in the early morning and the other in the evening) are given to private prayer. One of the classic definitions of prayer is 'the raising of the heart and mind to God'. How this happens in practice depends entirely on the individual, and what happens has a great deal more to do with choice and perseverance than feeling. And it has everything to do with God and not with ourselves.

A sensible abbot at the beginning of the 20th century advised one of his correspondents to 'Pray as you can, and not as you can't'. No particular techniques are involved, though I envy one of the young nuns who has practised yoga for some time and can sit totally still in the lotus position for sixty minutes, looking neat, elegant and tranquil, whereas I have a tendency to fidget and my veil slips off.

What one comes to realise is that the two times of prayer differ very much in their content. In the morning, before anything has happened either to upset or to cheer, the first half of the allotted time can seem blank, like waiting for a train: neither pleasant nor unpleasant but which has to be done, and is better done without fuss.

Then gradually the mind wakes up and begins to think, and at this point one needs to be careful not to let it wander off into enjoyable but outlandish daydreams or the working out of how many eggs are needed for the coming week. The Bible and particularly the New Testament can help one focus on higher things.

The second time of prayer is at 5pm. A lot will depend on how the day has gone; on the whole it will have been tiring and it is agreeable to be able to sit and relax. We all have difficult days, and it is not unusual to start this hour fuming, with the world, with individuals, with oneself and with God. It is advisable to give this state of affairs to God, however nasty a present it may seem. By the end of the hour one is often in a far better frame of mind without knowing how this has happened.

The first Hay Festival, 1988

BLOG PETER FLORENCE, 2018

The first Hay Festival began thirty years ago, in 1988. But it all really started with Wilfred Owen when I was seventeen. The language and narrative of his poems knocked me out, and a family friend showed me the letters. My father and I fashioned the last four years of his life into a play, *The Pity of War*, to perform at school for Armistice Day in 1981.

About thirty people came. One of them was a cousin of someone in my class, and a few months later, on 1st April, this cousin invited me to perform at the City of London Festival that June. I immediately accepted. The show was picked up and reviewed in the *FT*, and went on an extended tour that lasted on and off for ten years. I played arts centres, school halls, prisons and churches in every county.

In 1993, I got a call from the British Council to ask if I'd go on a tour of the former Yugoslavia. 'Sure,' I said. 'But isn't it a bit tactless to take a play about the First World War to Sarajevo [which at the time was in a hot war zone]?'

'Well,' they said. 'It would be if you were famous but, seeing as it's you, it's fine.'

The best gigs were always the festivals, though. I loved the buzz, the celebratory atmosphere of a festival audience who had come together to immerse themselves in plays or music and dance. And I loved the camaraderie of the green room, the crazy festival schedules, the sense that every performance only made sense in the context of all the other parts of the programmes.

How could we do this at home in Hay? We didn't have a theatre or any building that could hold more than 200 people. But we did have the mountains and the bookshops and a community who like nothing better than to throw a party. My father had run an international Shakespeare season for Sam Wanamaker in a big top at Bankside in the 1970s, long before the Globe was built.

My father wanted to bring poets and novelists to tell stories. I wanted to bring people from other cultures to tell stories of the world. My mother said, 'It has to be a party.' That's how it started, and then it got out of hand…

Nettles are the perfect spring greens
BLOG ELISABETH LUARD, 2018

Nettles, our closest plant companions, are enthusiastic colonisers of compost heaps, rubbish dumps and anywhere where gentlemen empty their bladders. It's all about the alkali. Once established, *Urtica dioica* is around for ever. Archaeologists will tell you that a patch of nettles is a sign of human habitation long after the stones they're looking for have tumbled.

Nettles were valued by our ancestors as the first blood-cleansing greens of spring, popping up their furry little heads as soon as the days lengthened after the winter solstice. Not only the leaves but the stalks were useful, providing strong fibres for sewing thread and poor-man-flax for the weavers. Left unsprayed, they provide food for the caterpillars of some our most beautiful butterflies. Peacocks, red admirals and tortoiseshells all lay their eggs on the underside of the leaves.

When gathering young nettles for the pot, snip off the top four leaves with scissors so that the roots continue to sprout. Once the plant is mature enough to produce the tassel-like flowerhead, you can still use the full-grown leaves from the top. You need plenty: at least half a litre of stripped-out leaves per person if you mean to serve it as a vegetable.

To prepare: pack the leaves in a lidded pot with a little salt and the water that clings after rinsing. Drain as soon as the leaves collapse. When it's cooked, texture and flavour are much like spinach, though the colour softens. Chop and dress as you would spinach, with lashings of butter, or a splash of olive oil, or folded into a creamy white sauce, or use as a dressing for pasta as they do in Italy and throughout the Balkans. The Turks like theirs mashed into fresh white cheese as a savoury filling for filo-pastry boreki. In Russia, the leaves are stirred straight into the midday borsch. And in Britain, nettle soup with a bacon hock and barley was the traditional dish for Shrove Tuesday. Nettle pancakes, anyone?

Brief is best
Johnny Grimond praises the use of short words

This is a fine time to praise short words. They are plain and clear. They do not test our brains too much. Most are well known, and they do their job with scant fuss. That is not to say that less is more, just that it is good – and more is too much. In short, if you can, you should use short words.

Long words have their place, and from time to time they fit the bill. But as a rule – and like most rules this one may be thought too firm – they add not much to your prose but length. That may be all right if you are paid to speak by the hour or write by the inch, but for the rest of us brief is best.

Long words can be hard to grasp. Some are hard to say. They tend to have come to our tongue from lands that lie some way from our shores, quite a lot from Greece and Rome, and more from far off places half way round the world.

That's fine, yet their bulk and length may join to make them not strong but weak. Add one word to the next or put half of the last in front of the first, and you may find you have a new word that by its fused state is just a lump. The odds are with such words that they lack the force or charm of the short words

formed from the sighs, roars, grunts and gasps of the first beasts to tread, as men, the soil of this land. They made our speech, our verse, our prose.

Long words are for things that no man can touch, or weigh or hold in the hand. They are for moods, plots, themes and thoughts, a hint or hunch, food for the mind but not the mouth. They are for aches and -isms. They are, as well, for those who look down a long nose to say their piece, who like the smug sound of their own voice, whose boots are small and feet are big, whose tongues are hewn of wood and cheeks are lined with tweed. They are for the bore.

Short words, though, are right for all men and all times. Just think of God and man, and all the things that make us laugh or cry. Think of love and life, joy and pain, hope and fear, birth and death, war and peace. What they mean to us, what they do to us and what we make of them can all be told in short words.

For the nuts and bolts of life are drawn small. One, two, three. Red, blue, green. Time and space. Hot and cold. Sun, moon and earth.

Short words point us north, south, east or west. They serve us bread, meat, beer and wine – and feed the mind as well. (To be, or not to be?) They give us sleep. They make us work and let us play. The year they split in months, the months in weeks, the weeks in days, the days in hours. They build us towns in which to live, and grow us food on which to feast. And not just us. We share our lot with the birds of the air, the beasts of the field and the fish of the sea.

No need to make too long a tale of it: you get the drift. So do those who make their point in verse. And soon we may with luck say that 'The year's at the spring/ And day's at the morn.../ The lark's on the wing;/ The snail's on the thorn.../ All's right with the world!'

Give thanks then to short words. You can start now.

'You're right. I'm not the man you married. We're having an affair'

I actually met the poet Philip Larkin twice, though the second time hardly counts. I only mention it because it occurred in a crowded room in which an interesting incident, much written about subsequently, also took place. The room was in No 10, to which Margaret Thatcher had invited various poets and writers and their spouses (I was married at the time to the writer John Gross) for a party. Larkin and I greeted each other briefly and he was soon introduced to Mrs Thatcher, whom, as he had told me previously, he 'adored'. In the course of their conversation, overheard by a group of literati, she quoted a line from one of his poems, 'Deceptions' – a wonderful line: 'All the unhurried day,/ Your mind lay open like a drawer of knives'. Larkin was delighted, even though she had slightly misquoted the first few words.

This small misquotation led various anti-Thatcherites such as Alan Bennett to conclude that the philistine Prime Minister had been hastily briefed shortly before the party; clearly she had never read a word of Larkin. However, I have since learned that Mrs Thatcher was an enthusiastic reader of poetry and that she knew lots of it by heart – Kipling, T S Eliot, Longfellow and, yes, Larkin.

In late 1979, when I was working at the *Observer*, I was asked to do a long interview with Larkin. There was no particular 'peg'. In those days it was still possible to interview people on the basis of their intrinsic interest rather than as a PR exercise. Before setting off for Hull University, where he had been librarian for about 25 years, I read all Larkin's novels and poems, talked to various of his friends, studied photographs and formed a strong impression of the kind of person he would be: lugubrious, shy, polite, physically unprepossessing, depressed, unforthcoming and charming.

As soon as I entered his spacious office I realised that most of those adjectives didn't fit. He greeted me in a positively jovial manner. There wasn't a trace of gloom about him. If he had once been shy he had completely cured himself of this disability. He seemed almost extrovert. His appearance, too, confounded my expectations. He was much taller and physically much more

Philip Larkin

by *Miriam Gross*

imposing than I had imagined. And yes, charming – and funny.

Before starting the actual interview we went, at his suggestion, to a nearby pub, where he insisted on queuing for drinks and sandwiches and was only persuaded not to pay the bill when I assured him that we were eating at the *Observer*'s expense. He drank a pint of bitter rather quickly, I remember. He told me that he liked living in Hull because it was so far away from anywhere else. There was less crap in Hull than in London. He liked peace and quiet and unpretentiousness. He was very fond of his friends, but also of solitude.

When I mentioned that I had feared that he would be difficult to talk to and a bit of a miserabilist, he laughed, saying that poems were often written out of unhappiness but that didn't mean that the poet was in a continuous state of misery. When he was young he had suffered from a stammer, he told me. I asked him to repeat all this in the interview.

He did. And he said many other fascinating things. For example, that he had dreaded that the line 'They fuck you up your mum and dad' would find its way into the *Oxford Dictionary of Quotations*.

He didn't want it thought that he didn't like his parents. He did like them. Another unexpected revelation was that he read very few serious books. He liked detective stories and undemanding fiction such as Trollope, Anthony Powell and Kingsley Amis. He read almost no poetry, he said, though he later mentioned a string of poets whom he found moving. He hated being abroad, though he wouldn't mind seeing China as long as he could come back on the same day.

During the three or so hours I spent in Larkin's delightful company his good humour never flagged. Even the sentence: 'Deprivation is for me what daffodils were for Wordsworth', which has been much quoted since, was said in a light, matter-of-fact way. There was only one moment when his darker side – the voice of the poems – showed through. As I was setting up my tape recorder before the interview, he said (off the record) in a totally un-self-pitying way, that were it not for his job as a librarian, he would long ago have killed himself.

Miriam Gross is the author of 'An Almost English Life', Short Books £12.99.

From barn to Bayreuth

Martin Graham started off as a builder's mate. Now he owns and runs the exciting and ambitious Longborough Opera. *Alexander Chancellor* met him

No one who knows anything about Martin Graham could say that this country lacks social mobility. For here is a man who started life as a builder's mate but has transformed himself into a grandee in that most elitist of social worlds – country house opera. More than that, Mr Graham and his wife, Lizzie, have achieved an ambition that none of their much posher and longer-established competitors in the field have ever dared to attempt: he has put on Wagner's *Ring Cycle* in a converted chicken barn and done so, most impressively, to universal critical acclaim. To stage the *Ring* is an enterprise on such an enormous scale, demanding such huge artistic and financial commitment, that it daunts even the world's greatest metropolitan opera houses. But the only theatre in the British Isles to have staged the cycle in 2013, the bicentenary of Wagner's birth, was the little one in the garden of Mr Martin's manor house at Longborough near Stow-on-the-Wold in Gloucestershire.

Mr Martin is now a dapper, bow-tied, charming man in his early seventies who, when people first learnt of his plan to stage the *Ring*, was generally assumed to be mad. 'I'm beginning to think that the Grahams may have fallen off the edge of a Wagnerian precipice of insanity,' wrote Tom Service of the *Guardian* five years ago. 'The whole project is blissfully barmy,' wrote Richard Morrison in the *Times*. But Mr Martin wouldn't agree. He is a quintessential self-made entrepreneur, who believes that anyone can do anything if they want to. He likes to quote Rainer Maria Rilke, the Austrian poet, who wrote in his *Letters to a Young Poet*: 'That something is difficult must be one more reason for us to do it.'

When I met Martin and Lizzie Graham for tea in London's Brown's Hotel, he kept reiterating his view that if you want something enough, it hap-

Lizzie and Martin Graham

pens. 'Those who say "it can't be done" are betraying a lack of confidence and willpower,' he said; and then, 'If you want something enough, it happens.' Would that that were always true. But how did it happen in Mr Graham's case? Unlike John Christie, the millionaire Old Etonian landowner who founded the Glyndebourne Opera Festival, he started with few advantages in life. His father was a civil servant from Yorkshire who moved to Longborough when Martin was seven. Martin went to grammar school but not to university. Instead he started work as a labourer for a Gloucestershire builder. He believed from an early age that the key to success was to acquire property. He bought an orchard. He built his own little house in Longborough. And then, after forging ahead to become one of the biggest property developers in the Midlands, built the substantial manor house nearby in which he and his wife now live.

But why risk squandering everything on an opera festival? One thing that all country house opera entrepreneurs have had in common is a passion for music. This was true of the founders of Glyndebourne, Garsington and Grange Park – Britain's three main summer opera festivals. But Martin Graham developed this passion in an unusual way, from a modest man in the village of Longbor-

ough who became his mentor. This man, said Mr Graham, was an autodidact, who had taught himself to paint, to compose music, and so on, and who had made the boy Martin listen to Schubert and Beethoven on his old-fashioned gramophone. Before long, Martin was hooked and travelling on his own to concerts and operas.

There were sown the seeds of his strange ambition to turn a chicken barn into an opera house and make it Britain's Bayreuth. Without an 'old boy network' to smooth his path, he just wrote out of the blue to Sir Georg Solti, the conductor, and to Sir George Christie of Glyndebourne, John Christie's son and successor, to tell them of his grandiose plans. Solti replied that he must be mad; Christie, however, that he would help. But perhaps none of this mattered very much, for Mr Graham not only believes that if you want something enough, it's bound to happen; he says he found that 'When you say you'll do the *Ring*, everyone just pours in to help. You don't have to do anything.' The most important person to 'pour in' was the Wagnerian Anthony Negus, who conducted the triumphant *Ring* of 2013 and is this year conducting Longborough's first production of *Tristan und Isolde* with four performances.

So, having not done anything (apart, I suppose, from making a barn into an opera house, giving it a neo-classical façade, digging out an orchestra pit, buying up discarded audience seats from Covent Garden, scrabbling for funds, hiring everybody and generally organising everything down to the lavatories with the constant support of his former schoolteacher wife Lizzie), he may possibly have fulfilled his dream. If so, he will have done so without any government subsidy and in a spirit that Margaret Thatcher would have considered exemplary. It's a pity she's not still around to give him a knighthood.

Bird of the month

The golden plover

John McEwen admires its black breast and white-edged golden shawl
Illustrated by Carry Akroyd

Between 1st September and 31st January coots, moorhens and golden plover (*pluvialis apricaria*, sunlit rain) are legal quarry. Who eats coots and moorhens? And golden plover, a famous delicacy, drew a blank at Allens, renowned Mayfair butchers. The name did not even ring bells. Clearly the golden is more observed than shot these days.

Golden and green plover, so often seen together, do indeed suit golden autumn and green spring. It is when it flies in flocks out of the breeding season that the golden is most spectacular, whereas lapwings are seen at their best when the males perform solo aerobatics over the nesting grounds.

Of course the golden too has much to recommend it in spring. In April 1947 the bird artist Charles Tunnicliffe and his wife, Winifred, moved to a shore-side house on Anglesey. He soon noted the goldens: 'The most immaculate of them appeared as black birds each clothed with a white-edged golden shawl ... W. and I agreed that the Northern Golden Plover in breeding plumage is the topmost rank of well-dressed birds' (*Shorelands Summer Diary*). J A Baker described a flock feeding in a March cornfield: '...listening and stabbing forward and down, like big thrushes ... Their black chests shone in the sun below the mustard yellow of their backs, like black shoes half covered with buttercup dust' (*The Peregrine*). The male has a spring song, which 'as he ascends with rapid wheelings high above your head ... approaches nearly to the note of a thrush or blackbird' – Charles St John (*The Wild Sports & Natural History of the Highlands*, 1919).

Tunnicliffe reported a September sighting, some retaining their black summer breasts (white in winter), most in various stages of moult, the juveniles 'like newly minted coins among old and tarnished ones'. All retain the golden shawl, which makes the flash of a flying pack, hence the bird's scientific identity, one of the world's glories. Estuaries from September through to April should offer a sporting chance of seeing it.

My first glimpse was in Baker country, coastal Essex. The September fields were glazed with cobwebs but out to sea rain threatened. Against broken cloud a pack of several hundred waders sped beyond the tide line. Strung out, they poured across the sky from black on white to white on dark, a sudden twist, glinting bright as a sun-struck windscreen, revealing their golden identity.

Baker found 619 peregrine kills over ten Essex winters and only two were golden plover, a tribute perhaps to their aerial skills. But St John, fifty years earlier, wrote they were 'a favourite prey' of Perthshire peregrines, affording them 'a severe chase'. He described seeing 'a pursuit of this kind last for nearly ten minutes, the plover turning and doubling like a hare before greyhounds ... but in vain'.

Baker: 'As I passed the farm, a flock of golden plover went up like a puff of gunsmoke. The whole flock streamed low, then slowly rose, like a single golden wing.'

How Scotland discovered Christmas

'Na,' my friend Pat said. 'I dinna hang up a stocking the nicht. I dae that on Hogmanay, an' I get my presents on Ne'er Day.'

We would have been six or seven then, 1944 or 1945. Pat was the grandson of the grieve on my mother's farm. This may have been one of my first moments of awareness of social differences; for of course, like other middle-class Scottish children, I expected Santa Claus to come down the chimney on Christmas Eve, and next day we would have Christmas dinner with a roast fowl – no turkey then – and a plum pudding with threepenny bits wrapped in cloth hidden in it.

Pat's position was more usual, however. Christmas Day wasn't a public holiday in Scotland then. Shops were open as usual. So, I think, were most offices. People went to work in factories and shipyards. Banks, as I recall, observed Saturday hours; open till midday. Scotland wasn't like England; we did things differently.

It goes back to the Reformation. In England Henry VIII broke with Rome, made himself the English Pope (Supreme Head of the Church in England) and remained, in his own eyes anyway, a good Catholic boy, persecuting Lutherans and Roman loyalists alike. His daughter Elizabeth's religious settlement took the form of a comfortable compromise between old and new. This was very English, a fudge here and there, so that almost everyone could adhere to the new national Church of England.

Things were done differently in Scotland. Our Reformation came to us from Geneva, and we drank the pure water of Calvinism. Anything that smacked of Papist idolatry was banned. Anything for which there was no scriptural authority was out of order. No celebration of Christmas, after the Nativity itself, is recorded in the Bible. Therefore there should be none in Scotland. Accordingly it was forbidden, along with the other feasts of the Roman Church.

Apart from anything, Christmas encouraged jollity, and jollity was suspect,

Children in Scotland used to wait till Hogmanay for their presents, and their fathers worked on Christmas Day. Shopping and TV have changed all that, says *Allan Massie*

feasting an invitation to sin. In any case the Presbyterian Kirk then, and for a long time after, paid little heed to 'gentle Jesus, meek and mild'. Admittedly a Presbyterian divine called Andrew Melville sternly informed James VI that there were two kingdoms, and in the Kingdom of Christ James was 'nocht but God's sillie vassal'; nevertheless the Kirk much preferred the fierce and demanding Jehovah of the Old Testament. He was the Lord with whom the God-fearing Scottish People had made a Covenant. As for the Virgin Mary, what was she but a heathen goddess dressed up in Roman garb? So she was dropped, along with all the other saints to whom benighted Papists addressed their prayers.

By the mid-17th century zealous Calvinists were as hostile to images of the Virgin and the saints as any Iconoclast in 8th-century Byzantium had been, or indeed as any devout Muslim – let alone any Islamist – today. Even Easter, which is at the heart of the Faith or the Christian message, took a back seat in Scotland. This wasn't entirely illogical. Calvinism with its doctrine of Predestination might even seem to make Easter superfluous. God had already divided men at birth into the Elect and the Damned. So what was there for Christ the Redeemer to redeem?

Gradually over the centuries the Kirk, influenced by the spirit and ideas of the Enlightenment, became more liberal. Fundamentalists might break away to form the various Free Churches, but the Established Church of Scotland softened its line. Christmas, it realised, might not be such a bad idea after all. No doubt the development of the Dickensian English Christmas had something to do with this. More to the point, perhaps, liberal-minded ministers came to realise that the Nativity, with the child in the manger, and the shepherds and Wise Men who came to worship him, was one of the most attractive elements of the Christian religion, appealing even to people who had no interest in theology and who, if they attended church at all, might do so principally, or at least in part, because this was a mark of social respectability.

So, even when I was a child, it was already usual for a Christmas tree to be erected in the kirkyard, and many ministers were already imitating the clergy of the Church of England, the Episcopal Church of Scotland and even the Church of Rome by holding services on Christmas Eve. Nevertheless, even in mid-20th-century Scotland there were a great many people who never entered a church, except for funerals or perhaps weddings, and it remained the case that the great winter festival was Hogmanay and the New Year, not Christmas. So there were many children whose fathers went to work on Christmas Day, and who, like Pat, had to wait till the New Year for their presents.

Enemies of Christmas were fighting a losing battle, however. It wasn't religion that beat them. It was commerce. Already, when I was still a child, department stores throughout the land had cottoned on to the fact that Christmas was good for sales and business. A Santa Claus was installed in every large store, and only the most flinty-hearted of parents would deny their offspring a visit to Santa's grotto where they would receive some trumpery present.

Then there was entertainment. The highlight of our Christmas holidays was a visit to the pantomime in His Majesty's Theatre in Aberdeen. There was no place

for Calvinist anti-Christmas dogma there as we delighted in – or were puzzled by – cross-dressing with an improbably long-legged girl in tights playing the principal boy and a Scots comic like the great Harry Gordon or Dave Willis as the Dame. The message was clear. Christmas was a time for fun and delight, and though one may have perceived this only dimly, for the upsetting of the natural order.

And then came television. In the days – indeed the weeks – running up to Christmas neither the BBC nor ITV paid any heed to the old Anglo-Scottish border or to historic cultural differences. Television and commercialism made Christmas the Great British Festival; only x number of shopping days to Christmas. Scots obediently, indeed enthusiastically, fell into line. Christmas became in Scotland what it had long been in England: the great winter festival. Gradually even Hogmanay and the New Year took second place. I doubt if there are children now who have to wait till then for their presents, as Pat used to.

It's part of a pattern. Over the past one hundred years the social, religious and cultural differences between Scotland and England first blurred, and then gradually disappeared. In the 1880s Robert Louis Stevenson had outlined them in an essay entitled 'The Foreigner at Home'. The difference was distinct when Stevenson wrote that essay; it was still fairly distinct when Pat had to wait till Hogmanay to hang up his stocking.

Not so now. Almost all social surveys indicate that Scots and English think alike about most things.

Paradoxical as it may seem, this blurring and erosion of differences account for the rise of Scottish Nationalism as a political force. For people who want to assert our difference from England, there is now only politics left. So England votes in a Tory government, Scotland an SNP one. It's a way of insisting – or pretending? – that we are still very different. But Christmas gives the lie to this. Christmas is British and is now celebrated as enthusiastically on either side of the old – and in so many respects superfluous – border.

Sport

Cleaning up athletics

by *Jim White*

Jon Snow was at his most forensic. Interviewing Lord Coe about the firestorm of corruption breaking out around him, the brilliant Channel 4 News anchor suggested to the new head of world athletics that – given he had been a vice-president of the organisation throughout a decade-long surge of venality – he was one of two things: either complicit or incompetent. And neither suggested he was thus the man ideally qualified to lead the urgently required clean-up.

For a moment Coe gulped, frozen in the arclight of Snow's ferocity. When it came, his elusive, equivocal answer did little beyond betraying his politician past. Snow's weary head-shake in response was telling: meet the new boss, it said, same as the old was.

Watching him squirm, you had to wonder why Coe had done it. Why, at a time when sporting governing bodies have never been so low in public esteem, had he taken on the IAAF? There he was, one of the most trusted figures in the country, the architect of the triumph that was London 2012, and he could have done anything he wanted in public life. There was talk of him chairing the BBC, or he would have been favourite to become London Mayor. Instead, he headed to world athletics. And a couple of months later, he was engulfed in sleaze, with evidence emerging of wholesale corruption, of senior figures adept at monetising the turning of a blind eye to drug testing regimes. Now Coe's entire life's work is in jeopardy. If he doesn't apply a radical and abrasive broom to the Augean Stables he has inherited, he will preside not only over the death of the sport that made him, but over his own once-unimpeachable reputation.

Athletics should be the simplest of sports: whoever reaches the finish line is the best. But if we can't trust the outcomes then it has no meaning. And what is so dispiriting about the IAAF scandal is that it makes us doubt everything. Even the glories of London 2012, when for a

Mammoth task ahead: Lord Coe

moment running, jumping and throwing lifted us from the humdrum, are put in new perspective. Were those achievements we so lauded the result of pure human endeavour? Or were they purchased through the application of hard cash?

That is the issue Coe faces. He cannot be timid in his rejoinder. His first job is to ensure his own background is expunged of doubt. He took his time, but he has finally renounced his partnership with Nike. Confident in his own honesty, he may not have believed there was a conflict of interest in association with the sportswear giant. But there cannot be any hint of equivocation. Every possible avenue of buying favour must be removed.

Plus, friends, colleagues, allies within

the organisation have to be examined with equal ruthlessness. Everything has to change. It does not help that he has inherited quite the most moribund of organisations. At London 2012, he was surrounded by the brightest and best, advisers full of ideas and energy. Seventeen years of complacent, corrupt leadership by his successor, Lamine Diack, has ossified the IAAF. His principal management skill is delegation and now he finds himself on his own. His first task will be wholesale refreshment of the executive staff. He needs intelligent, energetic lieutenants. Recruiting them to a rotting corpse of an operation will not be the easiest of sells.

But of one thing we can be certain: if any man had the motivation to take on this task it is Sebastian Coe. His love of his sport is matched only by his loathing of drug cheats. If he could apply the same ruthless determination that took him past Steve Ovett to Olympic gold 35 years ago, then athletics really could be saved. Nothing less will do.

And it is a big if. 'Watch this space,' he said to Snow of his clean-up campaign, seeking to evoke a sense of a vigorous action plan already forming. We can only hope that the word's other meaning does not apply, and that Coe's space does not turn out to be an empty politician's promise.

Hit by the juggernaut

Thanks to the wonders of the satnav, a twelve-ton truck can be directed down the most unsuitable country lane – where it would still be stuck if it weren't for *Duff Hart-Davis* and his neighbours

We were having a cup of tea in the kitchen when we heard the rumble of a heavy engine in the lane. Then came an ominous scrunch, and we nipped out to find huge stones – the innards of our boundary wall – being forced downhill past the gateway by some appalling pressure. In front of us towered the side of a colossal articulated lorry, so close that it was hardly possible to squeeze between the vehicle and the part of the wall left standing.

Up front in the cab, out of our sight, the driver was frantically trying to shift his monster by revving in forward gear, then in reverse. Already his offside wheels had obliterated my nicely mown grass verge and spread mud over the road, with the result that the trailer – 40ft long and about 14ft high – kept creeping sideways towards the house until the top corner was touching the roof.

'STOP!' we yelled. 'STOP!' Praise be, he did. Edging round to the back of the lorry, I saw that it was Polish. So was the driver – a stocky fellow called Arkadius who spoke about three words of English. The one he used most frequently, and with vehemence, was four letters long, beginning with S and ending with T.

No wonder he had ignored the notice on the village green saying 'Unsuitable for Heavy Vehicles' and the one in the valley warning of a 1:4 hill. Clearly, he hadn't understood them. No wonder he'd followed his wretched satnav into this impasse. But when I asked him where he was heading, he amazed me by answering: 'Dover' – which is about 200 miles east. What he'd tried to do was to cut a cross-country corner between the M5 and the M4.

Reiterated enquiries revealed that his lorry weighed twelve tons and was loaded with six tons of washing machines, fridges and so on. I don't think he realised how deep in the ordure he had landed – until I pointed upwards and told him: 'Hill. Twenty-five per cent' – at which he clapped his hands to his head in despair.

There was nowhere a vehicle that size could turn round. It was impossible for him to go back, reversing round the tight bends and up into the village a mile away. Under its own power his great beast would never climb the hill in front. I had visions of it remaining in situ for days or weeks – even of it having to be dismembered and taken away in pieces.

I rang 101, asking the police if the fire brigade could bring out a big rescue vehicle. After a while our friendly local copper appeared, but he said the firemen weren't interested, and there was nothing he could do – except advise us not to accept the handfuls of euros which the driver was proffering in appeasement. Better, the copper said, to go after his insurance company.

I rang Simon, who manages the farm across the lane, as his property, too, was being threatened. He soon appeared, but agreed that his tractor and mine were both too small to tow the monster, even in tandem.

The only hope seemed to be to call Dan, the young man whose family have the farm at the top of the hill, and who owns seriously large machines. By then – about 7.30pm – he was at home, five miles away, having his tea, but he gallantly agreed to turn out.

As we waited for him, I suddenly remembered that an ash tree arched over the road only a hundred yards above our house. I knew the lorry would never get under that. The only solution was to fell it at once. So off we went, and Simon, wearing a head-torch and wielding his chainsaw with great dexterity, had it down in a flash. Sparks flew into the dark as the teeth hit pieces of grit in the bark, but the tree crashed across the road with a thump, and in a few minutes it was cut into sections which we could bundle up the bank, out of the way.

We waited. At last red tail lights appeared above us as Dan backed down the hill on a mighty, four-wheel-drive tractor, to hitch up with a chain that would have towed the Flying Scotsman. With a great roaring and grinding the pair of pachyderms crawled off – and to everyone's unspeakable relief, they reached the top, minus two Polish wing-mirrors

Now the lane is carpeted with mud, its banks re-sculpted at the base, with foot-wide channels gouged out of either side. Our wall is a ruin. The lowest estimate for repairs is £250. Friends keep telling me we should have a notice at the village end of the road saying 'Don't trust your satnav' – but if drivers speak only Polish or Finnish or Serbo-Croatian, how would it avail us?

'Frankie – you're not supposed to see me on our wedding day!'

A Qatari stopover

Stunning architecture, superb art collections and a space-age man-made peninsula. *William Cook* is captivated by a brave new world

Why would anyone want to go to Qatar, when all the news about it is so bad? Its lavish preparations for the 2022 World Cup have been dogged by allegations of bribery and abuse of migrant workers. It has been accused of funding Islamists (claims Qatar denies). Surely, it's the last place you'd want to visit? Well, I've been three times in the past three years, and although I've seen lots of things I didn't like, I've never been anywhere quite so intriguing. It's like visiting a futuristic colony on a newly discovered oil-rich planet.

One good reason to visit Qatar is that if you're flying to Asia or Australia, you may well be going there anyway. Qatar Airways is fast becoming one of the world's leading airlines, and many of its

long-haul flights involve a change of planes in the Qatari capital, Doha. For most passengers this merely means a few listless hours in transit, but it's easy to extend your visit. A 48-hour stopover is enough to give you a taste of Doha. So, what should you expect?

The most impressive thing about Doha is its abundance of amazing modern architecture – not just glitzy skyscrapers but buildings by some of the world's greatest architects. You'll see one of the best examples on your way into the city from the airport. Jean Nouvel's National Museum of Qatar is still a building site (it's due to open next year) but it's already a national landmark. As Qatar is evolving, it's developing its own architectural style.

A good way to get your bearings is to walk along the Corniche, a seven-kilometre promenade that runs the length of Doha Bay. You'll need to set out early, or leave it till late – even in winter the sun is strong, and there's not a lot of cover. Energetic expats go jogging at daybreak and Qatari families go for a stroll at sunset. Dusk is the ideal time to take a boat trip on a traditional wooden dhow. Afterwards, get a bite to eat at Al Mourjan, one of Doha's most atmospheric restaurants. The food is classic Lebanese, but the best part is the view. Sit outside on the terrace, and watch the dhows criss-cross the bay.

Thanks to all that oil, Qatar is now the world's richest country (per capita) but despite the flashy cars that clog the highways, conspicuous consumption isn't really what this pious kingdom is all about. The Qataris want Doha to become a cultural capital, rather than the capital of bling – and the building that sums up

its ambitions is the Museum of Islamic Art, which stands in splendid isolation on a man-made island in the bay.

Designed by I M Pei (architect of the Louvre pyramid), the Museum of Islamic Art is stunning. It contains a superb collection of paintings, porcelain, calligraphy and tapestry – gathered together at great expense from all across the Islamic world. The permanent exhibition spans a thousand years, from Spain to China, from Morocco to Indonesia. If there was nothing else to do in Doha, it would still be worth stopping off here to see it.

I had always thought the human figure was frowned on in Islamic art, but as this selection shows, that isn't always so. There are no nudes, and nothing akin to western portraiture, but there are numerous examples of the human form in secular (though not religious) contexts. These treasures are beautifully presented, but the accompanying captions are perfunctory. The facts and figures are dutifully listed, but, unsurprisingly, there's no discussion of the political or theological subtext and I searched in vain for an explanation of why Islamic Art developed so differently in different dynasties. From the Museum of Islamic Art you can catch a free shuttle bus to Mathaf, Doha's Arab Museum of Modern Art, the world's largest collection of contemporary Arab art. A lot of it is bold and striking, but there's no nudity or homosexuality, of course, and there is the same absence of frank debate.

Half a century ago, Doha was just a sleepy fishing port in a forgotten corner of the Persian Gulf. Within a few decades, the Qataris have built a

'I'll tell you the meaning of life if you tell me how to get down from here'

Reaching for the skies: the West Bay central financial district of Doha

brand-new metropolis out of nothing. One of the biggest projects is the Pearl-Qatar, an artificial peninsula that stretches right out into the Gulf. The scale of it is staggering. It's like a space-age Venice, a floating city built from scratch. There are lots of posh shops and swanky restaurants, but there's no need to spend a fortune. It's just as much fun to wander round and gawp at the immense yachts in the marina. Across the bay is Katara, Doha's 'cultural village'. A procession of plush theatres and snazzy galleries ranged along the waterfront, it looks impressive, from a distance. Up close, it feels like a film set.

Booze is of course severely restricted here. Tourists are allowed to drink, but only in western hotels at nightclub prices. Unless you're gasping for a beer, it's more fun to sip a mocktail in the places where the locals gather. The best place to do this is at Doha's covered market, Souq Waqif. It includes a gold market, a spice market, a fabric market and a falcons market (Qataris love falcons). Look out for men playing dama – an ancient board game a bit like draughts. There are loads of cheap places to eat; the cuisine is typical Middle Eastern (mezzes, shawarmas). Check out the Bedouin women selling homemade stews and pastries from makeshift roadside stalls. For a place to stay, look up one of nine Souq Waqif Boutique Hotels within the souk. They have all the usual mod cons, but unlike the chain hotels downtown, they're distinctly Arabic. Al Jasra has a Turkish spa and a

> **'Qatar is a paradox – both progressive and reactionary'**

fine Moroccan restaurant. Doubles from £150, including breakfast.

Qatar is a paradox – both progressive and reactionary, a land of enlightened despots. They're mad about modernity – art, science, education – but they're not so keen on some of the things we tend to think go with it, like free expression. They've fast-forwarded into the 21st century, leapfrogging several hundred years along the way. Men and women are expected to dress modestly, with no naked midriffs or bare shoulders on show. Skirts should be knee length. Women can wear trousers but not leggings. Kissing in public is taboo.

How will they cope with the World Cup? I've been to a couple of football matches here, and they were fairly lively, but it was hardly England versus Germany. What happens when the fans want to strip off, have a few drinks and throw a party? Who'll get the biggest culture shock in 2022 – us or them?

The hunt for the hieroglyph

Nicholas Garland has captured the essence of politicians on paper for fifty years. *Harry Mount* talks to the great caricaturist

For nearly half a century, an unconventional figure sat in on leader conferences at the *Daily Telegraph*. While Boris Johnson, W F Deedes and Charles Moore nattered away, Nick Garland sat sketching in the corner, absorbing the political gossip. The leader writers wore suits, while Garland wore open-necked shirts and sweaters. His politics, too, were different: he is a social democrat, just left of centre, as opposed to the High Tory leader writers.

Still, the contrary combination was a natural fit. Garland, who has just turned eighty, was the Leftish grit in the Conservative oyster. From 1966 until 2011 – with a five-year interlude at the *Independent* in the late 1980s – he produced a daily cartoon for the *Telegraph* that defined two political generations.

'He is the best political cartoonist in Britain since Vicky and Low,' says Charles Moore, Margaret Thatcher's official biographer and Garland's former editor at the *Telegraph*. 'He doesn't rely on stirring up moral indignation. His cartoons depict the situation. He's good at taking the political pulse. He is less strident and more intelligent.

'With Margaret Thatcher, he caught

Garland defined the Thatcher era

her manic quality, the panic behind the energy; as a slightly demented woman in a hurry. He got her character better than other cartoonists who presented her as an evil, threatening monster, which she wasn't.'

More than any other cartoonist, Garland defined the Thatcher era. By the time she became Opposition leader in 1975, Garland had been the *Telegraph* cartoonist for nearly a decade. He continued to draw her for the next 40 years, until her death in 2013.

'That scurrying, strange, authoritarian, dominant, schoolmistressy look came

later in her career,' he says in the Belsize Park house he shares with his third wife, Priscilla Roth, a psychoanalyst. 'To begin with, she had those absurd hats, wildly over-decorated with bows and bits hanging off them. Then there was the bouffant hair. She quickly turned into a hieroglyph.'

'Hieroglyph' is one of Garland's favourite words – the cartoon image that immediately captures a person's look.

'I discovered Margaret Thatcher's – and it's just like finding a box of treasure,' he says. 'The eyes are lower at the outside corners than the inside corners. The rather sharp nose. After a bit, it was easy. As she got older, I made her cheeks a lot more hollow, her face more lined, her posture more stooped.'

For fifty years, Garland has captured the hieroglyphs of thousands of politicians, from Harold Wilson to David Cameron. 'Cameron's not so difficult,' Garland says. 'He has a high forehead, those clear, rather round eyes; the tiny mouth in a rounded, almost chubby face. I found Osborne much more difficult. That famous nose is perfectly ordinary when you meet him.'

The routine for capturing a hieroglyph

barely changed over the decades. First, he found out as much as possible about a new political figure, often from *Telegraph* leader writers and editors. He next established a likeness through precise drawings – helped by three years' life drawing at the Slade in the mid-1950s. Then he leapt from the anatomically correct likeness to the caricature.

'You also look at how other cartoonists deal with politicians,' he says. 'You don't borrow – you steal! I'm not a good caricaturist. Some caricaturists can graphically mimic people. Gerald Scarfe is very good at seeing where the likeness is.'

Garland has been gripped by the search for the hieroglyph ever since he was at school in New Zealand nearly seventy years ago. At school, he obsessively studied the cartoons of his heroes, Vicky, Low and Ronald Searle.

'When I was fourteen, somebody did a caricature of a master in the school magazine – and it was brilliant,' he says. 'It was one of the great moments of my life to see this very skilful caricature.'

Garland had emigrated with his family to New Zealand in 1946 – he returned to Britain, and the Slade, in 1954. But he was born in Hampstead, into a world of artists and professionals. His mother was a sculptor, his father a doctor who had been at school with W H Auden. Auden was the first person to visit his mother in hospital after Garland was born. His brother is called Wystan after the poet.

Garland's father was a communist who left the party in 1947 but remained a socialist. 'He was also a liberal and a democrat – that was what made him leave the party. It was too undemocratic, too ideologically intolerant,' says Garland. '"Always question authority," my father said – not just of a police kind, but of a cultural kind; his own authority, too.'

That explains why Garland fitted into the *Telegraph* – where I was one of those High Tory leader writers, sitting alongside him for five years. Our politics may have differed from his. But we shared an anti-authoritarian outlook – the bit in the Venn diagram where conservative anarchism overlaps with social libertarianism. 'Colin Welch, Peter Utley and Perry Worsthorne were never stuffed shirts,' Garland says. 'They were never authoritarian. They never said, "You can't do that."'

Garlanded: the cartoonist's-eye view of Gordon Brown, David Cameron, Kenneth Clarke and Barack Obama

Colin Welch, deputy editor of the *Telegraph*, recruited Garland to the paper in 1966. 'Colin told me cartooning is not tied to reality; it's not like a documentary,' Garland says. 'Rules don't apply there. People and genders can change. Gravity can just stop.

'I'd liked representational art, I had a passion for caricature, and there was a great clash. I had to figure out that something that doesn't look like someone is unmistakably them, with exaggerations and inventions that are exactly right.'

Garland was thirty when he joined the *Telegraph*. By then, he had already had a remarkable immersion in 1950s and 1960s culture. In 1958, he joined the Royal Court Theatre as an assistant stage manager in its golden age, under Tony Richardson and Lindsay Anderson.

He then happened on another golden age, directing the cabaret at Peter Cook's Establishment Club in the early 1960s. 'Peter was enormously gifted and terribly funny,' says Garland. 'You had to ask him to stop sometimes – he was too funny.'

Garland is an extraordinary witness to 1960s Soho life. With his confidence and diffidence, though, he is immune from the urge to name-drop. I have to grill him to get the lowdown on his evenings with Lucian Freud and Francis Bacon. 'They are always touted as these heavy drinkers but they were very hard workers,' he says. 'By the time you met them in the Colony Room, they'd been up since seven in the morning. Just look at how much they produced. When do you think they did it?'

Garland was a friend, too, of Jeffrey Bernard. Just at the moment that Bernard was gassing himself over a disastrous love affair in the early 1960s, Garland happened to ring him up, and sent the police round with seconds to spare.

After further grilling, Garland reveals the details of a terrifying dinner party, right at the apex of early 1960s music, art and satire. Peter Cook had Nick Garland round, with his wife and baby daughter – as well as Barry Humphries, who had been appearing at the Establishment club, and John Lennon.

'Peter and Barry were so very good

at repartee that most people, confronted with either of them alone, would just sit back and let it happen,' says Garland. 'John Lennon was just as good.

'They began to tease each other: "Aren't you the pop singer who made those songs?" "Don't you do some television thing?" It ceased to be good-natured and the jibes were becoming very close to the bone. They stood up and they were facing each other. I was worried about the baby, if they started throwing cushions.

'John Lennon's wife suddenly stood up and said, "Shut up, John. Sit down." And it was like a grown-up had walked into the room.

'They were all competing and they were all bloody good.'

By this stage, Garland had suggested to Cook that he might write the words to a *Private Eye* comic strip Garland had devised – about Barry McKenzie, a rough Australian recently arrived in swinging London. Cook said he couldn't, but mentioned an ideal candidate – Barry Humphries. 'Barry immediately got it,' says Garland. 'He now says he invented it. But he had another character – another Australian loose in London.'

'Peter Cook, Barry Humphries and John Lennon began to tease each other'

And so Garland moved on to another 1960s institution, *Private Eye*, then edited by Richard Ingrams.

'I was always extremely fond of Ingrams,' Garland says. 'He left you alone to do what you wanted to do. He was appreciative and very full of intense dislikes for people – something I very much approve of. I can't bear people who find good in everybody.'

Barry McKenzie appeared in *Private Eye* until 1974, when Richard Ingrams decided a necrophiliac incident in the comic strip was a step too far. By then, Garland was firmly established as the *Telegraph*'s political cartoonist.

He still paints today, and does cartoons for, among others, *The Oldie*. And he still dreams of the perfect hieroglyph for today's politicians.

'Jeremy Corbyn would be a dream,' he says. 'And Trump – off the wall!'

Taking a walk

Along the coast at Dungeness
with *Adam Nicolson*

Dungeness is the one place in England that is so all-consumingly Europhiliac it doesn't know what to do with itself. It is heading for France at between two and three yards a year, hungrily longing for the connection which hasn't been there since the end of the Ice Age.

So park at the Pilot Inn (good cod and chips for when you get back) and set off south down the coast towards the two lighthouses and the nuclear power station. Most people seem to stick to the road but that is to miss the best part: make for the surf.

The wind howls and rages across the shingle ridges. You need a good hat and Arctic underlayers. Slab tankers out at sea are the only fixed points. Cormorants flogging west are immobile in the wind. Little bundles of lichen like miniature tumbleweed blow past your feet.

The Channel itself is churning at the shingle, a Farrow & Ball concoction of Mouse's Back sea and Pale Hound surf, dragging and sucking at the flints. New promontories and inlets are being made as you watch, the flint banks so poorly consolidated that they collapse underfoot. It is the most dynamic place in the south of England but almost no one comes out here. Two fishermen—a Moldovan and a Lithuanian—were disconsolately fishing for spotted dogs in the surf but otherwise this place was empty, an uninspected graveyard of what the sea and winter storms can throw at it.

A fox was lying dead on the strand line, its tail up but its lips and face picked away by the gulls. A cluster of goose barnacles, growing on a hank of rope, lay on the shingle like a bunch of bright white goose heads on black and ochre stalks. Old clothes and rags were strewn here and there among the big broken mussels. Scallop shells, giant ridged cockles, cod carcasses stripped of their meat, a seal head with its spine

attached, the breastbone of what I think was a gull, big black mermaids' purses and whelks were littered along the beach like the contents of an old salt's attic.

Jerry Oiller, skipper of the *Fair Chance*, was down at his boat but not thinking of going out in wind like this. It was gusting Force 8. He only takes charter parties out nowadays (01797 363544 for a great day on the wrecks, rough ground and sandbanks). We chatted as the kittiwakes flustered in the wind beside us. 'The Oillers and the Tarts, they are the two Dungeness families,' he explained. The house that Derek Jarman had bought, Prospect Cottage, that was an Oiller House, and Jarman had Jerry's old boat in his garden. 'He's had all sorts there, Patsy Kensit when that Gallagher boy got rid of her, Annie Lennox.'

He told me about Mrs McNunn, who used to live two down when he was a boy. 'She liked to buy sprats off my father to feed her pet guillemot.' Every morning she brought it down to the sea in a basket for a swim. 'Then it came back in, back into the basket and she'd toddle off home with it.' But there are only four boats fishing out of Dungeness now. 'It's the EU, isn't it? Regulations.'

On the way back I found, like a sad broken penguin, an oiled guillemot standing on the beach. The oil was all down one side and over its head, which it kept shaking as if to rid itself of the poison, shuddering with its wings up then picking away at the clogged feathers, one little bright eye shining in the midst of all that.

A gang of herring gulls was settled around it, waiting for the inevitable.

Dungeness: Pilot Inn to the nuclear power station and back. 3 miles or so. Map: OS Explorer 125 Romney Marsh, Rye and Winchelsea (but you scarcely need it). Dry underfoot.

Sophia Waugh: Home Truths

A provincial thrill

Those of us who live in the country are proud, sometimes aggressively proud, of our status. We love to mock the Notting Hillers who spend hundreds of pounds on country accessories which sit in pristine splendour in their hallways. Barnes dwellers who stride along by the river wearing Hunter boots and carrying ski poles make us snigger with scorn.

But let's be honest, a little bit of this is because we are worried we are missing out. We may have proper mud, big dogs and fresh air. We may be able to pick flowers from the hedges or from our own gardens rather than spend a fortune at Moyses Stevens. But do we actually have enough to talk about?

So when a cultural event looms on our horizons, my word we get excited. Just such an occasion cheered us all up in the middle of gloomy February. The local independent bookshop held a celebration of 27 years of existence. An odd number, but it was more to do with the owner's sixtieth birthday, which his wife wanted to celebrate but he wanted to keep under wraps. The great and the good of the area put on tidy clothes and gathered together to cheer on the bookshop and all it represented.

And what a motley crew we were. Pretty middle class, but still fairly motley.

Ex-headmasters, vicars, schoolteachers, writers, judo and yoga instructors, a few hippies who have found their way west, all gathered in a bookshop drinking wine and glorying in our stab at culture. Because we were something, weren't we? We were people who read, who cared about books, who had patronised the shop over the years, congratulating ourselves on walking that tiny bit further to avoid Waterstones or W H Smith. We were not the people of the land, or people who lived off the land, but we were part of something local, something fine.

It reminded me of my childhood when a theatre was built in the town, and the middle classes went crazy. Lady volunteers made quiches for interval snacks, and their student children worked in the bar. Local painters and

potters exhibited their works in the foyer. Never mind that the theatre was tiny, the quiches leathery and most of the shows amateur, there was and is something unifying about small-town culture.

And this particular bookshop keeper is a shining light of all that is marvellous about that. Not only has he run the bookshop, surviving the double blows of chain stores and Kindles, but he has created a literary festival, at which real, proper writers appear. He has launched an arts newspaper that goes from strength to strength. He has half-persuaded, half-bullied other businesses to back the festival, to host events, to hold a steady torch for the arts in this dark, rainy corner of the world. The bookshop has undergone various facelifts: first it began to include second-hand books and then it shelved second-hand and new together, so buyers felt they had the best of both worlds.

The more I think about the evening, the more I realise what a triumph it was. So much more than a sum of its parts, it gave us all an excuse to take off our (properly dirty) wellies and scrub up into a resemblance of the people we once were or thought we would become. Intelligent, interested, cultured people who also happen to live small-town life to the full. Lucky people. Even in February.

Kitchen garden
by *Simon Courtauld*

Mint

Growing mint can be a bit of a problem. Once established, the plant's roots and runners are likely to spread and interfere with whatever is growing near it. I have tried growing mint in a pot, but the roots do not like being confined; the plant may suffer in the second year and need to be divided and replanted in fresh soil. In our kitchen garden we have spearmint growing out of gravel and roaming happily between two raised vegetable beds, and apple mint running riot underneath the currant bushes.

The ancient Greeks apparently rubbed mint leaves over their bodies, and the Romans brought plants to Britain, using them not only as a deodorant but as a medicine (ears and eyes treated with a mint infusion) and a flavouring for their food. Mint has been used in Middle Eastern cooking for centuries, but the mint sauce which we make with vinegar and sugar is, I believe, unique to this country. You certainly won't be offered it with a gigot d'agneau in France where, according to Elizabeth David, it is 'considered positively barbaric'.

A supposedly new mint called Brundall, originally from a village of that name on the Norfolk Broads, has been much promoted in recent years; and I have seen more than thirty varieties of mint listed on a herb nursery website. Among the best for making mint sauce, in my experience, are spearmint, apple mint and the similarly hairy-leaved Bowles mint.

Now that the new season's mint is appearing in the garden, we shall be sprinkling the leaves over new potatoes and spooning mint sauce, made with brown sugar and not too much wine vinegar, over roast spring lamb. Of the other, scented varieties, I would recommend eau de cologne and pineapple mint as more suitable for Pimm's. So, too, is lemon balm, a member of the mint family which in our garden spreads all too easily and self-seeds, showing itself last year between two rows of beetroot.

I was an Airfix boy

Like many of his generation, *John Walsh* spent much of his childhood in his bedroom with a lot of plastic and glue going 'Nnneeeeaaaagghhh'

One detail in the *Times*'s obituary of Sir George Martin caught my eye: the fact that a whole room in his family home was filled with plastic model aircraft. Until I left home and went off to university, and my parents cleared out my bedroom, I had one too: squadrons of aircraft, fleets of ships, world-conquering armies of uniformed soldiers with their feet clamped immovably to plastic planks.

There was nothing jingoistically British about these planes and ships and armies: they came from every country and period. Heinkels and Dorniers, Ilyushins and Mitsubishi Zeros, Mosquitos and Mustangs all flew in my bedroom along with Hurricanes and Blenheims. The *Bismarck* and the *Graf Spee* sailed in factitious, time-travelling harmony alongside the *Golden Hind* and HMS *Ark Royal*; my collection of tiny soldiers suggested unlikely alliances between the Eighth Army, the Romans and the US Cavalry. I was an equal-opportunity modeller of war stuff. I was a classic Airfix boy.

I can't remember how it started (a fond uncle venturing two shillings on a birthday present?) but I know I was eight when I made my first model plane, a Spitfire, in 1961. I finished it in a haze of triumph, with polystyrene cement coating my fingers and an ache in my joints from kneeling on the carpet for four hours. You couldn't do much with the finished object, except paint it and wave it around, going 'Nnnneeee-aaaagghhh' in a weedy simulacrum of fighter-plane glory, but I loved it. An obsession was born.

I bought the little kits from a revolving carousel at Woolworths: the small ones cost 2/6 in plastic bags, the larger ones 5s in cardboard boxes with dramatic cover art, invariably by Roy Cross, of bombing raids and bullet-whizzing dogfights in always-blue skies. I learned the arcane officer-class language of instruction, like 'Study exploded view' (which meant 'Look at the whole diagram first, dummy') or 'Locate starboard flange and affix to aileron' (about which I'm still a bit hazy). I learned to spread pages of newspaper to keep the glue off my mother's shagpile, learned to keep a pin in the cement-tube nozzle to stop it seizing up when not in use, and to use rubber bands to clamp the fuselage halves tightly together.

Poems have been written and elaborate sexual metaphors deployed in praise of these sublime convergences of plastic, the male nibs and female holes. Some have even eroticised the glue. Here's Nicholson Baker in his essay 'Model Airplanes': 'When you   tweaked off the dried wastrel from an earlier session and applied a gentle pressure to the tube, a brand-new, Steuben-grade art-blob of cooling poison would silently ensphere

The De Havilland DH9a, illustrated by Roy Cross, who painted the artwork used on Airfix kits from the 1960s

itself at the machined metal tip, looking, with its sharp gnomonic surface highlights and distilled vodkal interior purity, like...'

Sadly, the results were seldom pure. I always forgot to paint the pilot before putting him in the cockpit seat, I always got glue on the plastic windows, making them opaque. But I was soon on to the next model. I rolled the names round my tongue: the Boulton Paul Defiant, the Sopwith Camel, the Fokker Dr1 triplane (how we sniggered). I marvelled at the chunky beauty of the bombers, especially the Avro Lancaster with its complex tailfin, and the spectacular American B-17 Flying Fortress, with its belly gunner and its semi-naked pin-up girl ('A Bit o'Lace') saucily recumbent on the fuselage.

It was all about the war. I was born in 1953, eight years after it ended; the first Airfix kit – the *Golden Hind* – appeared a year before me. The Airfix company and I were both post-war phenomena, but were similarly embedded in the martial paraphernalia of 1939–45. Though we'd missed any actual experience of the conflict, my schoolfriends played Commandos, with toy Sten guns and grenades. My weekly comic, *Valiant*, celebrated a psychopathic British soldier, Cap'n Hurricane, fighting Nazis, Italians and Japanese right into the 1960s world of pop, spying and miniskirts.

Airfix shrewdly strove to keep pace with the new culture, salting its vintage planes and ships with a model of an E-Type Jaguar, a Boeing 737 and a figurine-fight between James Bond and Oddjob in *Goldfinger*. A highlight of my life was making Bond's 1967 Aston Martin DB5 with a working, spring-loaded ejector seat.

They began to cram out my room. Every surface housed a plane, helicopter, ship, car, tank, fire engine, galloping cavalier or platoon of Neanderthals. My mother complained about the dust. Like thousands of young enthusiasts, I took to hanging the aeroplanes from the ceiling with cotton thread around nose and tailfin. They looked good – but didn't seem to be flying because the propeller legs were static. So I snapped them off, to give the illusion of flight.

It was a mis-step. Once I'd vandalised a model, things went downhill fast. One Guy Fawkes Night, I destroyed a Messerschmitt ME-109 by lighting the touchpaper on a banger jammed into the cockpit. Later I incinerated a Stuka. The smell of injection-moulded plastic was dreadful.

I was growing up. Plastic model aircraft and ships, even in the most exciting warlike array, were losing their appeal for me. I abused some of the tiny militia by arranging them in indecent poses. I concealed cigarettes, stolen from my father, in the hollow legs of a plastic Napoleon (you lifted up his frock-coated top half, *et voilà*). I looked askance at the new Airfix kits in Woolworths: Ford Escort, Morris Marina ... Were they kidding? They expected us to spend hours making a suburban runabout – us, who had cut our teeth on the Bristol Beaufighter and the Hawker Typhoon?

In my A-level year of 1971, I decided to finish my model-making career in style: my last-ever Airfix model would be the big, scarily complex HMS *Victory*, a classic since 1954. Quite early in the proceedings, I became enraged when the four pieces of the hull refused to slot together. From bowsprit to poop there were so many teensy bits to fiddle with. The masts were huge and the rigging had to be wound everywhere with cotton thread. Hours into the winding and snipping, I caught a glimpse of myself in the mirror. I looked like my elderly music teacher, Miss O'Connor, busy with one of

The Oldie's debt to a Getty

BLOG JAMES PEMBROKE, 2018

I went to see *All The Money In The World* this week. While marvelling at Christopher Plummer's portrayal of J Paul Getty, history's greatest miser, I remembered that *The Oldie* had greatly benefited from the Getty family's generosity.

How lucky we were to do business with J Paul Getty II rather than Getty Senior who had a payphone installed at Sutton Place for guests. The film captures his refusal to pay his grandson's ransom, ostensibly for fear it would encourage kidnappers to prey upon his other 13 grandchildren; he only relents after he receives the 16-year-old's ear in the post, and after he is advised the ransom can be allowed for tax.

We also see his son's unhappy period as a heroin addict in Tangier in the late 1960s and 1970s. While we may have every sympathy for his plight at the hands of the world's worst dad (and even worse grandfather), there's little indication that he will recover to become a great philanthropist.

His donations were multitudinous: a cricket obsessive, he rescued and revived *Wisden* purely for his own pleasure; his cricket pitch is still one of the finest in the land.

> '**Taking a leaf out of his grandfather's book, he gave me 24 hours to raise the money**'

In August 2001, J Paul Getty II was persuaded, without the pressure of any body arts in the post, to boost *The Oldie*'s coffers with £250,000 – the greatest proof that genetics is hokum. A shy man, when he was presented with an award at an Oldie of the Year lunch, he bypassed making a formal acceptance speech in favour of making unintelligible gargling and burbling noises into a closely held microphone. After 30 seconds of babbling, he sat down with a broad grin, leaving his audience to ponder the strength of 1960s marijuana.

Upon J Paul Getty II's death in 2003, his second son, Mark, who was a distinct return to form, making a fortune from the purchase of all the picture libraries, decided *The Oldie* wasn't for him and put the magazine up for sale. Despite having agreed terms with another publisher, he was willing to heed Richard Ingrams's request of giving me a chance to raise the money. Taking a leaf out of his grandfather's book, he gave me 24 hours to raise the money. To be fair, he wanted to see whether I was serious about what was not for him a very large amount of money.

Little did he know, I was living in a small Dorset cottage without an upstairs loo. So, I fell upon the munificence of the Croesus of my own family, my cousin's American hedge-funder husband. I was very clear to him that I was ringing him in New York because he was the richest man I knew and I desperately needed cash. I thought it best to hold off telling him the title of the magazine, bearing in mind American sensibilities about getting old or, rather, 'mature'.

When he insisted, I thought the game was up as I garbled '*The Oldie*'. 'Why didn't you say?' He replied. 'I love the magazine. I've got the front cover of the first issue in my bathroom here.'

The very rich are different from you and me.

My secret valley

Less than an hour from the centre of London lies a beautiful stretch of countryside along the River Darenth. *Gavin Stamp* unselfishly shares his knowledge of this largely unspoilt oasis

The desire to keep places we love secret, fearing, with reason, that they might be ruined by too many visitors, is selfish and wrong – and, in the case of the enchanting Darenth Valley in Kent, simply absurd. A railway runs along it, as does the A225, while the M25 is close by, although out of sight. And yet, despite being less than an hour from the centre of London, it remains somehow a precious survival, a beautiful and special stretch of countryside, largely unspoiled and full of wonders. For half a century it has been, for me, a precious secret. Hooray for the Green Belt!

To get there, the train from Blackfriars first trundles through uninspiring suburbs – Catford, Bellingham, Bromley, Bickley – then through some open country to Swanley, where the line branches to the south. Then through a long tunnel to emerge as if by magic into another world, halfway along the valley of the river Darenth or Darent. The first stop is Eynsford. The village itself, winner of frequent prizes for the Best Kept in Kent, lies some way to the north. It boasts the ruin of a Norman castle, and the austere parish church is largely Norman, too, enhanced with a later slim shingled spire. The handsome, painted Royal Arms are of George III: 'Fear God Honor ye King'.

The trouble with Eynsford is that it is separated from the railway station by a long ribbon of modern houses. Better, perhaps, and more romantic, immediately to take the footpath to the west towards Lullingstone, across the fields and past a farm, with hills in the distance and the prospect of the handsome red-brick railway viaduct of 1862 marching across the river and over which you have just travelled. It is a structure of Roman grandeur – and that is appropriate as the Romans were once here. Watling Street was not far to the north and, soon after

Claudius' conquest of Britannia, many villas were built along the river in this distant outpost of Empire. And the extensive foundations of one of them miraculously survive at Lullingstone.

Lullingstone Roman Villa seems to have been begun a few decades after the conquest. For a time it may possibly have been the residence of Pertinax, governor of Britannia, and, later and typically briefly, emperor. By now much enlarged and modernised, the villa was eventually abandoned in the fifth century after a fire and the withdrawal of the Legions. But what is left of it today is not just a somewhat boring archaeological site, for some fine mosaic floors survive almost intact. The peculiar importance of this villa is that plaster fragments were found of the Chi-Rho symbol, very early evidence of Christianity in Britain and suggesting that there was a Christian house-church here. What seems extraordinary is that, although its existence was suspected earlier, the remains of the villa were only discovered

St Botolph's Church, Lullingstone, part medieval, part Georgian

in 1939, and only excavated after 1949 and opened to the public in 1963.

South of the villa, the road (a dead-end) soon arrives at Lullingstone Castle – which is not really a castle at all, though a most lovely place. A weathered red-brick battlemented gatehouse of c 1500 leads to a spacious lawn (once there was an inner moat) and to a large red-brick Georgian mansion beyond, which, we are told, does in fact embrace the remains of a castle.

Two things at Lullingstone make the place very special as well as adding to its enchantment. One is St Botolph's Church, part medieval and part Georgian, standing on one side of the lawn. There is a 16th-century rood screen, some unusual stained glass, brasses and, in the chapel north of the chancel, some splendid grand monuments – one, a recumbent figure cased within an arch, to Sir John Peche, who built the Gatehouse. But the most intriguing is that to Percyvall Hart Esq, who died in 1738. Occupying the whole of one chapel wall, it extols at length the virtues of this former Member of Parliament for Kent within what John Newman, in his 'Pevsner' for this part of Kent, rightly calls 'Rococco-Gothick arcading'.

We are told of his devotion to the Church of England and to Queen Anne, and of his 'steady Attachment to the old English Constitution' and how he lost his seat soon after the Hanoverian succession. Even a dismayed Remainer like myself is moved to read of how this old Tory, 'Conscious of having always preferred the interest of Great Britain to that of any foreign state, He passed the remainder of his Life in Hospitable Retirement'. He also became the 'munificent Repairer and Beautifier of the Church', giving it splendid new enriched plaster ceilings decorated with cherubs' heads, crowns and mitres.

The other special attraction at

'The Golden Valley', 1833–34, by Samuel Palmer, who lived in Shoreham from 1828 to 1837 and produced his best work there

Lullingstone Castle is the 'World Garden', the creation of the horticulturist Tom Hart Dyke, son of Guy Hart Dyke, the present owner and custodian (and the first cousin of the actor and comedian Miranda Hart). In 2000, travelling in Panama hunting for rare orchids, he and a friend were kidnapped and held hostage by suspected FARC guerrillas. While in captivity, constantly threatened with execution, Hart Dyke dreamed of creating a new garden back home at his beloved Lullingstone which would contain plants from all over the world. And, following his eventual release, he realised that dream. The World Garden opened in the old walled garden at the castle in 2005 and thousands of different species are planted in areas vaguely resembling the continents of the globe.

Onwards south from Lullingstone, the footpath running along a large ornamental lake through which the Darenth flows. Then on to Shoreham, either by footpaths or country lanes. One September, doing this walk, we found the roadside hedges groaning with ripe blackberries: nobody was picking them as

everyone seems to drive. How foolish! Eventually, gorged, we reached Shoreham. Although it claims to have been the most bombed village in England in the Second World War – it lies under the direct Luftwaffe route from the French coast to the capital, and it has the Shoreham Aircraft Museum, full of relics from the aerial battles that took place overhead in 1940 – it still seems a charming and typical Kentish village. There are weather-boarded and plastered cottages, half-timber and tile-hung gables, and houses of mellow red brick scattered around the Darenth – and four good pubs. There is an idyllic churchyard below the squat brick Georgian west tower of the medieval parish church, together with a fine yew avenue leading to its remarkable timber south porch, a Perpendicular Gothic structure made of huge pieces of oak. Inside there is a spectacular wide rood screen and the organ from Westminster Abbey played at the Coronation of George II – for the Dean and Chapter of Westminster are the patrons of the living.

For many of us, however, Shoreham is, above all, inextricably associated with the

name of the artist Samuel Palmer. After his death, his son affirmed that, 'What Wharfedale was, as Mr Ruskin has said, to Turner, Dort to Cuyp, Albano to Claude, what North Wales was to Wilson, Ville d'Avray to Daubigny, and Barbizon to Millet, such, to Samuel Palmer, were Shoreham and Otford-on-the-Darenth.'

In his 1948 *County Book* on Kent, the poet Richard Church wrote that he knew of only one disturbance in this village 'which sleeps on as it has slept for a thousand years ... It took place in the year 1828 when, after William Blake's death, a farm-wagon carrying Samuel Palmer and other disciples of the poet-artist-mystic rumbled into Shoreham'. And here this visionary Romantic stayed, on and off, for seven years, sometimes with his fellow modernity-rejecting artist members of 'The Ancients'. In between the cottages and in the fields around, especially in the autumn, it is still possible to appreciate what inspired Palmer to produce those intense poetic depictions of landscape and nature at sunset or by moonlight which are some of the greatest glories of English painting.

Overseas Travel

Caminos by Casas Cantabricas

Independent self-drive touring in delightful small hotels

AiTO

Discover the ageless beauty of Spain & Portugal

Casas Cantabricas · 01223 328721 · www.caminos.co.uk

Home & Garden

Made to Measure · Bespoke · **SHELVEX** · Furniture · Est 1974

Study and Living Room Shelving Specialists

SHELVEX

Quotation? Questions? Please phone

01628 522476
www.shelvex.com

TURKEY - YAKAMOZ HOTEL

Yakamoz is a small, friendly, quiet hotel situated in between Fethiye & Oludeniz in SW Turkey. Offering traditional Turkish hospitality, fabulous Mediterranean cuisine and delightful gardens. Yakamoz is an Adult only Hotel, except for UK School holidays.

Tel 0090 252 616 6238
Email: info@yakamozhotel.com
Website www.yakamozhotel.com

Wanted

Old Photograph Albums. Former British Colonies Asia, Africa and Gulf up to 1960 Wanted.

Also documents manuscripts autographs letters of all periods. We can also clear books and papers of all types and are happy to travel.

Mayflyephemera@msn.com
or 07701 034472 – John Martin

Wanted

RECORDS WANTED

(LPs, EPs, 45s)
Classical, Jazz,
Rock & Pop, etc

Buyer will travel. Fine prices for rare items.

01903 209553 | info@revolutions33.co.uk
WWW.REVOLUTIONS33.CO.UK
Revolutions Records, 67 Victoria Road, Worthing, West Sussex, BN11 1UN

Gifts

Fast becoming the latest rage...

KENTCHURCH BUTLERS

A CHRISTMAS GIFT THAT WILL LAST FOREVER

Carson !

Also ideal for that birthday, wedding, anniversary or retirement present. Hand painted, these delightful wooden side-tables are fun pieces of furniture to rest your drinks etc on and light enough to move to wherever you want: hall, study or sitting room et al. Bring a smile into your house... Their sturdy trays are 25" above ground, an ideal height to place your favourite tipple when sitting on your sofa.

Guardsman

Butlers, Maids and **Waiters** stand 38" tall and come with the option of four Jacket colours: *Red, Green, Blue or Black.* **Guardsmen** stand 45" tall and can be tailored with the insignias of the Queen's Hussar, Grenadier, Coldstream, Irish, Welsh or Scots Guards. **Jockeys** can be painted in your own silks, and **Footballers & Rugby Players** in your club colours.

Order early for Christmas

From ONLY £119 + p&p*

For more models and to order from home or abroad, email: roger@kentchurchbutlers.co.uk

or tel: **01803 732 933** or go to:

www.kentchurchbutlers.co.uk

Roger T Milton-Goodhead, Kentchurch Butlers, Sunnymead, Smallwell Lane, Ashprington, Totnes, Devon, TQ9 7ED

Footballer in your club colours

Jockey in your own silks

TOR RECORDS

VINYL RECORDS WANTED

JAZZ AND BLUES RECORDS WANTED. BEST CASH PRICES PAID, ANYWHERE IN THE UK

Chris McGranaghan | 07795 548242
thoseoldrecords@btinternet.com
WWW.THOSEOLDRECORDS.CO.UK
TOR Records, Brewery St. Shopping Centre, Rugeley, Staffordshire WS15 2DY

HiFi Hangar

VINTAGE HIFI SPECIALISTS

HIFI EQUIPMENT WANTED
GOOD PRICES PAID

Family run vintage shop, collections arranged UK wide. Turntables, Speakers, Amplifiers, Reel to Reels and Radiograms

01420 472316 · 07890 517695
Call or email Steve & Sarah
hifihangar@googlemail.com

House Clearance

HOUSES / FLATS CLEARED SYMPATHETICALLY

M25 AND SURROUNDS

John 07701 034472

Food & Drink

For Smoked Salmon, Gravadlax, Smoked Trout, Hot Smoked Salmon, Smoked Eel, Kippers and Hot Smoked Mackerel, Scallops & Langoustines, Venison & Game, Prime Quality Scottish Beef.

We offer the best products we can source with the best of personal service. Delivered by FedEx and DHL.

Order by telephone or go to our website:
Dundonnell Smoked Salmon
Tel 01349 866500
ron@smokedsalmon.uk.com
www.dundonnellsmokedsalmon.co.uk

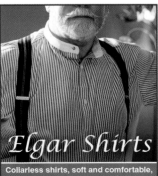